Athena's Daughters

The Television Series
Robert J. Thompson, *Series Editor*

Other titles in The Television Series

Athena's Daughters

Television's New Women Warriors

Edited by Frances Early *and* Kathleen Kennedy

With a Foreword by Rhonda V. Wilcox

SYRACUSE UNIVERSITY PRESS

First Edition 2003

03 04 05 06 07 08   6 5 4 3 2 1

We gratefully acknowledge permission from Blackwell Publisher to reprint portions
of Frances Early's essay "Staking Her Claim: Buffy the Vampire Slayer as Transgressive
Woman Warrior," *Journal of Popular Culture* 35, no. 3 (winter 2001): 11–27.

The paper used in this publication meets the minimum requirements
of American National Standard for Information Sciences—Permanence
of Paper for Printed Library Materials, ANSI Z39.48–1984.∞™

Library of Congress Cataloging-in-Publication Data

Athena's daughters : television's new women warriors / edited by Frances
Early and Kathleen Kennedy.— 1st ed.
    p. cm.—(The television series)
Includes bibliographical references and index.
ISBN 0–8156–2968–0 (cl. : alk. paper)—ISBN 0–8156–2989–3 (pbk. :
alk. paper)
1. Women heroes on television. 2. Adventure television programs. I.
Early, Frances H. II. Kennedy, Kathleen. III. Series.
PN1992.8.W65A88 2003
791.45'652042—dc21
                                                                2002153925

Contents

Foreword

Out Far or In Deep

RHONDA V. WILCOX

When I was thirteen years old, I wrote and badly illustrated a story of an all-female detective agency. The detectives had names like Hebe and Juno. My seventh-grade teacher, Mrs. Morrisette, had gotten our class to read Edith Hamilton's *Mythology*, which I had devoured as a respectable substitute for the fairy tales of my childhood, and I picked the forms of the names I wanted, mixing Greek and Roman with preacademic freedom. The head of the detective agency was, of course, my favorite: the goddess of wisdom, of defensive warfare—the shining-eyed Athena. I loved the way she misted around and tricked people with her human buddy, that appealing smart aleck Odysseus; I loved the image of her with her spear and helmet; and I loved the way she changed form. And as an automatic oddball, never-in-the-intellectual-closet smart girl, I loved the fact that she was smart and proud and strong. Through the years, she was one of the female figures I enjoyed focusing on—she and Diana Rigg as Emma Peel, Anne Francis as Honey West, Katherine Hepburn as anything, Louisa May Alcott's Polly Milton (from *An Old-Fashioned Girl*), Golda Meir, and Indira Gandhi. An odd mix, but the pickings were slim in those days.

These days my twelve-year-old nieces—one of whom looks like Xena, the warrior princess, and the other of whom looks like Buffy, the vampire slayer—have a wider array of options, as do I. *Xena, Warrior Princess* (still being rerun) and *Buffy the Vampire Slayer* (still in production) are among the most noteworthy of a proliferation of television series that highlight protagonists who might be called Athena's daughters: strong, intelligent, heroic warriors who defend the right as they see the right. A number of others might lay claim to the same general categorization: Seven of Nine on *Star Trek: Voyager*, La Femme Nikita,

ix

and, more recently, Sydney Bristow of *Alias* and Sara Pezzini of *Witchblade*. And there are a wide variety of pallid copies, such as the supernatural sisters of *Charmed*, whom I like to call Charlie's Witches. Of course, we cannot say that all women warriors are created equal, and in this volume the varying numbers of essays devoted to specific warriors reflect that fact.

One of the strengths of the best of these characters is that they are not monolithically virtuous; the series do not require absolute purity of their women heroes and do not oversimplify complex issues. Xena certainly can carry her anger too far (she drags her beloved Gabrielle behind a horse), and Buffy on occasion has given in to her dark side in terms of sex and violence (both enacted on her vampire lover Spike). In part as a result of this complexity, many viewers and scholars have questions about the warrior women's series and their portrayal of sex, gender, class, race, and violence. In particular, the correlation of female power with violence troubles many.

Violence seems very publicly present today. I live in Decatur, Georgia, a really good town with free summer concerts on the square, schools that involve parents and students, and neighborhoods where a cat can sleep in the street (that's how we chose our home). Decatur abuts Atlanta, and our town is in DeKalb County. In the year 2000, I voted (along with approximately thirty-four thousand other people) for reformer Derwin Brown for DeKalb County sheriff and was delighted to see him win the election—only to learn later that he was gunned down in his driveway three days before he was to take office. This week (July 10, 2002) the former sheriff was convicted of Derwin Brown's murder—political assassination right here in my own backyard. My town represents a combination as bizarre, in its way, as the sunny streets of Buffy's Sunnydale and its vampire-infested California underground.

In a lurching segue, I also note that my husband and I have never used any kind of corporal punishment on my well-behaved fourteen-year-old son. Put these two very disparate bits of information together—the assassination and the lack of corporal punishment—and you may see that I am a person who takes physical violence very seriously. When people question the use of violence in the women warriors' series, the question itself should be explored carefully. I confess that as a student of literature I often feel the urge to ask these same people if they have read lately the last act of *Hamlet,* in which the bodies of most of the major characters pile up on the stage. I am deeply troubled by researchers who attempt to evaluate the nature of violence by counting the number of bodies on stage or screen or by totting up the number of times a blow is struck. The effect of violence does not depend on body count, but on context. Else why are we still reading Shakespeare?

The contributors to this volume help to give us that context. When we come away from the television set (or perhaps even before we go to it), it helps to ponder larger patterns and implications not only of women and violence, but also of sex, gender, race, class, and other issues. Surely it will help if we notice the undertow of an unregenerate subtext, and it is just as important to recognize positive patterns. Why is there a cluster of women warriors now? In *Witchblade,* Sara Pezzini is supposed to have inherited her weapon from Joan of Arc, and when Buffy loses her memory in the "Tabula Rasa" episode,[1] she chooses to name herself Joan. How prevalent were figures resembling Joan of Arc and Athena in the past, how were they interpreted, and how are they now reinterpreted? Do these characters carry feminism in their subtext? What about what one contributor calls "concrete relationships among women"? Can we find strength in the friendship and love between Xena and Gabrielle or between Buffy and her best friend Willow? Should we relate to Seven of Nine's desire for a female mentor or to Nikita's sense of entrapment? Can we perhaps identify with the outsider, the other, the shadows to the warrior women, such as the violent and exiled slayer Faith? What about the quickly killed, unnamed Chinese slayer?[2] Can some viewers traditionally seen as "others," such as gay men, take pleasure in the sight of a woman whaling the patriarchal daylights out of large white males? Can fans derive meanings of their own? In these series, can we seek opportunities to dwell on the possibility for redemption and to change relations of power slowly?

I hope that the last answer is yes. Each of the series discussed in this volume has been viewed by millions of people. Each viewer comes to such a series from a different life experience and set of beliefs—as, indeed, can be seen in the diversity of views held by the writers in this volume. Each series is a text. Whether we use the term *polysemic, producerly,* or *B.Y.O. subtext* (as in *Buffy* creator Joss Whedon's "Bring Your Own Subtext" idea),[3] we acknowledge that, intentionally or not, each of us participates in the creation of meaning. In this brief foreword, I have made more personal comments than I have ever before put in print.[4] For myself, I have always focused most sharply from the angle of literary criticism and the aesthetic value of a work, but that does not mean I devalue cultural significance, for how can you tear them apart?[5] As you read this volume about these women warriors, you will be given the gift of a broad panorama of social patterns through which you may choose to see. Look at the big picture, but then remember that you live in that picture, on the other side of the screen. It matters what we see on that screen; it matters what goes on in the minds of those who watch the women warriors. Sooner or later, out far or in deep, we're all going to take it personally.

Decatur, Georgia
July 2002

Acknowledgments

We have relished the unfolding of this project on television's contemporary women warriors, marveling at how smooth and rewarding the process has been. Our contributors have shared our enthusiasm for disruptive rebel heroes, and we thank each of them for their scholarly integrity, generosity of spirit, and sense of humor. We also thank our engaging students at Western Washington University and Mount Saint Vincent University for their impressive feedback on this topic and our family members, friends, and colleagues, who seemed to enjoy serving as sounding boards and patient listeners.

We are grateful to the directors and staff at Syracuse University Press for their support for *Athena's Daughters* and for their fine professionalism and attention to detail. We are pleased that Robert Mandel, the former director of the press, suggested that we undertake this project and are appreciative that John Fruehwirth, then acting director, and Amy Farranto, acquisitions editor, have been staunchly behind us. Our anthology also has benefited from an anonymous reader's comments and suggestions. We owe a debt to Carol Way, whose expertise with computers and graciousness of manner made the task of preparing our manuscript for publication a pleasant exercise.

And we thank the Social Science and Humanities Research Council of Canada Research Grant Program, the Mount Saint Vincent University Internal Research Grant Program, and the Western Washington University Grant-in-Aid Research Program for their generous financial assistance.

June 2002   FRANCES EARLY, Halifax, Nova Scotia
                       KATHLEEN KENNEDY, Bellingham, Washington

Contributors

Helen Caudill teaches theater and directs plays at Norwich University in Northfield, Vermont. At popular culture conferences, she has given a number of presentations in gay and lesbian studies and on such topics as *Xena* fan fiction and the changing archetype of woman as hero.

Vivian Chin teaches in the ethnic studies department at Mills College in Oakland, California. Her work focuses on narrative constructions of race, the indeterminacy of origins in Asian American literature, and representations of race in mainstream U.S. movies.

Frances Early is professor of history at Mount Saint Vincent University in Halifax, Nova Scotia. Her most recent book, *A World Without War: How U.S. Feminists and Pacifists Resisted World War I* (Syracuse University Press, 1997), focuses on women and gender in relation to twentieth-century peace and civil liberties movements. This study earned her the Society for Historians of American Foreign Relations 1999 Warren Kuehl Award in International and Peace History. Early's current research interests include the contemporary Canadian women's peace movement and U.S. women's roles in war in the modern era.

Alison Futrell is associate professor of Roman history at the University of Arizona in Tucson and author of *Blood in the Arena: The Spectacle of Roman Power* (University of Texas Press, 1997). She is currently working on another monograph entitled *Barbarian Queens,* which focuses on representations of gender and power in the ancient past and in modern popular culture.

Kathleen Kennedy is associate professor of history at Western Washington University in Bellingham. She is the author of *Disloyal Mothers, Scurrilous Citizens: Gender and Subversion During World War I* (Indiana University Press,

1999) and currently is working on a study of representations of sexual violence in the antebellum United States.

Laura Ng is currently a doctoral student at Louisiana State University in Baton Rouge, where she edits the *Civil War Book Review*. Her areas of focus include twentieth-century U.S. literature, gender theory, and Renaissance poetry. She is writing her dissertation on gender and violence in hard-boiled detective fiction.

Lee Parpart is a doctoral student in social and political thought at York University in Toronto, Canada. A former journalist and film columnist, her critical work on cinema and culture has appeared in numerous Canadian publications. She has contributed to several anthologies, including *Gendering the Nation* (University of Toronto Press, 1999); *Masculinity: Bodies, Movies, Culture* (Routledge, 2001); and *North of Everything: English-Canadian Cinema After 1980* (University of Alberta Press, 2002).

Edrie Sobstyl teaches in the History of Ideas Program at the University of Texas in Dallas. Her recent work includes "All the Sisters of Shora: An Anarcho/Ecofeminist Reading of Slonczewski's *Door into Ocean*" *(Anarchist Studies* 1999), and "Cyberpunk: Liminal Space Cadets" *(Enculturation* 2000). She was a Rockefeller Fellow at the University of Oregon in Eugene in 2002.

Sue Tjardes teaches at the Pacific Lutheran University in Tacoma, Washington. She is interested in the rhetorical dimensions of humor and in the ways audiences of all kinds function as communities.

Rhonda V. Wilcox works as a professor of English at Gordon College. After writing her doctoral dissertation on Charles Dickens, she moved on to publishing on modern popular culture. With David Lavery, she is the coeditor of the collection *Fighting the Forces: What's at Stake in* Buffy the Vampire Slayer? (Rowman and Littlefield, 2002) and of the journal *Slayage: The Online International Journal of Buffy Studies* (www.slayage.tv).

Athena's Daughters

1

Introduction

Athena's Daughters

FRANCES EARLY and KATHLEEN KENNEDY

According to feminist scholar Donna Haraway, stories enable people to actualize "existing worlds" in a rational fashion.[1] Narratives tell us about the cultures in which they are produced and enable us to imagine our possibilities and to understand our limits. In Western culture, the most powerful and influential story is arguably that of the male just warrior. Told through the centuries in myth, history, and literature, and, more recently, in film and on television, the story of the male just warrior saturates our consciousness and helps to structure and define our institutions. The just warrior is the responsible citizen whose willingness to shed blood for the common good entitles him to mastery over self and others. His story is essential to masculine identity. Even those men who do not participate directly in state-sanctioned war access the warrior story or quest through such varied activities as organized sports, shared male-bonding stories of personal achievement and physical prowess, and identification with popularly created male warrior heroes.

From ancient times, Western society's just warrior narrative has been male privileged. The male "just warrior" fights and dies for the greater good, whereas the female "beautiful soul" epitomizes the maternal war-support figure in need of male protection.[2] The few women who have achieved warrior status in this hegemonic war chronicle have been portrayed as temporary transgressors and have not been permitted to form a tradition of their own. Such warrior women, with Joan of Arc providing the most well-known example, have been honored as virtuous viragos, but they also have been viewed as inherently unsettling to the patriarchal social order; their stories often have been belittled or excised from historical memory.

In the contemporary era, popular culture has promoted and sustained the gender system on which the commanding Western war narrative rests. But what happens when fierce viragos gain a foothold in popular culture? Do images of just warrior women disrupt and challenge the dominant male-centered war narrative? If so, in what ways and by what means? Or has this patriarchal hold on heroism created a closed circle? Must "women" become, in effect, "men" to achieve just warrior status?

Of late, fascinating debates have developed around these questions, with feminist scholars insisting that hidden histories of women warriors must be brought to light. Alternative storytelling that reenvisions the male-centered war saga must be embraced, some scholars insist, if women are to claim subjectivity and agency. However, modifying the dominant male story has proven difficult because the just warrior's story not only precludes women's agency, but also defines *woman* as an object of desire or as a "boundary figure"—often in the form of a monstrous mother "other"—that the male hero must overcome.[3] In this potent narrative, women serve as objects of veneration, desire, or violence and are things to be exchanged in an exclusively male political economy. Female independence inevitably threatens the male's quest and his identity as an autonomous individual.

In such a rigidly bounded system of representation, many feminist critics contend that women have little hope of changing fundamentally the twin themes of oppression and violence embedded within the just warrior's narrative. A woman's efforts to participate in this story as a just warrior are deemed dangerous because they place the liberated woman in the service of patriarchy, violence, and sadism. Female heroes cannot succeed in overturning the male-dominant image of the just warrior because, according to literary scholar Teresa de Lauretis, "The hero must be male, regardless of the text image . . . [and] the obstacle, whatever its personification, is morphologically female and indeed, simply the womb."[4] Left uncritically to do their work, female just warriors remain, in the words of art critic Marina Warner, "prisoners of the fantasy [of the male warrior hero] even in the midst of trying to turn it upside down."[5] Within these narratives, the female just warrior represents an inferior version of the male warrior and ends up reinforcing the male warrior's violent quest under the illusion that she can offer an authentic substitute story.

Nonetheless, more optimistic perspectives on the potential of alternative woman-centered just warrior narratives are gaining ground in feminist academic circles. The contributing authors to this anthology join cultural critics such as Marilyn Farwell in arguing that a female hero is capable of challenging and, to an extent, disrupting the narrative tradition of the male just warrior, notably its reliance on violence and its concomitant objectification and exploitation of women and "others." According to Farwell, the space occupied by the female hero is only "conditionally male defined [by] the result of history, tradition, symbolic connections, and reader's expectations."[6] Thus, it is possible for the female warrior to "redesign elements of the viewer's expectations of heroism, stretching [them] to accommodate female agency."[7] Feminist literary critic Sharon MacDonald's concept of "open images" reinforces Farwell's point about the power of symbols to effect alterations in the way we conceptualize female agency and subjectivity. MacDonald notes that, in contrast to closed images that can be likened to stereotypes, open images have the capacity "to be interpreted, read, and to an extent repopulated."[8] Such open images do not attempt to reflect or define what constitutes social life, but they do help, MacDonald contends, to disrupt conventional perceptions and expectations. By stressing the generative quality of specific feminist-informed symbols or "open images," Farwell, MacDonald, and other feminist critics point to the possibility of reframing cultural understandings of heroism and just warriorism.

In the past several years, television episodics have begun to reimagine the just warrior's story and the role that women play in it. Since the mid-1990s, the small screen increasingly has cast women as warriors whose capacity to fight for just causes matches or exceeds that of their male colleagues. These glamorous, larger-than-life, yet disarmingly recognizable heroes battle evil on a daily basis and, without much fanfare, repeatedly save the world from untold horror. "Western storytelling," a writer for *Psychology Today* portentously insists, "hasn't seen their ilk since the legendary female figures of the Celts."[9]

This unreflective celebration of female heroism in the popular press has had the effect of according the new woman warrior a quality of power she otherwise might not have possessed if left to the migrating time spots of syndicated television. The accolades and positive press coverage have made the new woman warrior into a North American phenomenon by crowning her a "girl-power" hero—a young, hip, and alluring portrayal of female autonomy that offers an implicit contrast to and critique of the second-wave feminist generation that came of age in the 1960s and 1970s. Whereas current stereotypical images of second-wave feminists show them as humorless, aging, and passé, media pundits admire the girl-power hero for her intelligence, mastery of martial arts, and sexual appeal. Many writers for popular audiences laud the new woman warrior as a role model for young women and men alike.[10] In general, however, girl power, so conceived, is shorn of political content, thereby ensuring that youthful, third-wave feminists' critical and public stance on numerous gender-related issues remains outside of popular consciousness.

It is important to recognize that although born in the 1990s, the new warrior woman has a family history. As Sherrie Inness demonstrates in her study *Tough Girls: Women Warriors and Wonder Women in Popular Culture,* the woman warrior hero of the 1990s did not burst forth fully formed and armed from the head of her male counterparts; unlike Athena, she has mothers.[11] Xena, Buffy, Nikita, Seven of Nine, and their many contemporary counterparts are not the first small-screen women to seize a warrior role for themselves. The new women warriors are the daughters of television heroes of the 1960s and 1970s such as Agent 99 (Barbara Feldon), Wonder Woman (Lynda Carter), Charlie's Angels (Kate Jackson, Farrah Fawcett Majors, and Jacqueline Smith), the Bionic Woman (Lindsey Wagner), and Batgirl (Yvonne Craig). These female action heroes used and controlled violence to obtain the just ends of the democratic state. Each held her own in a fight and mastered the use of weapons. Yet acceptable boundaries for female violence constrained each.[12] Moreover, this version of the woman warrior was seldom given an existence independent of a male boss or protector.[13] Only Wonder Woman came from a distinctly female lineage, the mythical Amazons, but even she had to surrender that legacy to protect and fall in love with a male just war hero. In each case, the woman warrior's heterosexuality played a fundamental role in constraining her agency and liminality.[14]

Racialist thought also influenced the depiction and range of actions of the woman warrior of the 1960s and 1970s. In addition to portraying all women heroes as white and conventionally beautiful, shows sometimes used race as a marker to define the protagonist's use of just violence. For example, the enemies whom Agent 99 faced in *Get Smart* were often exaggerations of the "evil" Asians present in spy movies.

The television woman warrior during these decades, despite her limitations, reflected efforts to come to terms with feminism and its demands that popular culture depict women as commanding and heroic. The 1980s witnessed a rupture in this pattern. As Susan Faludi noted in her shrewd polemic *Backlash: The Undeclared War Against American Women,* this decade saw the rise of "tough-guy films" and the marginalization or banishment of warrior women from the television screen. Three years after Faludi's book appeared,

James William Gibson came to a similar conclusion about the 1980s and early 1990s in his engaged study *Warrior Dreams: Paramilitary Culture in Post-Vietnam America.* His findings reinforced Faludi's observation that a "new war culture" was developing that idealized the violent and misogynous male warrior and that ignored or denigrated women or presented them as traditionally feminine in appearance and behavior.[15] Although some positive images of women's liberation survived on television, these representations were not of the woman warrior but rather of the competent and clearly defined heterosexual professional woman such as Murphy Brown or Claire Huxtable. These television women professionals of the 1980s were the quiet beneficiaries of a liberal feminist agenda, but they seldom politicized their identities or participated in political activism.

According to media critic Elyce Rae Helford, television in the 1990s represented a "careful arbitration of '70's activism and '80's backlash."[16] The woman warrior of the 1990s emerged as a reaction to the perceived limits of 1970s feminism and 1980s conservatism. She rejected the previous decade's promise of domestic safety in exchange for women's gender conformity, especially the practice of heterosexuality, and acceptance of male political leadership. Rather than depend on men to protect her, the new woman warrior mastered violence. She was not restricted in how she used her body or her weapons. She could match any man's physical prowess, command of technology, rationality, and leadership. Nor did she accept the 1980s sexual bargain. Instead, she often used her sexuality as an offensive weapon, oscillating between seducing possible foes, engaging in casual sexual encounters, and rejecting exclusive heterosexuality. Nonetheless, the new woman warrior has remained primarily white and has evinced ambivalence about the political goals of feminism. It is these two latter characteristics that most trouble feminist critics of the woman warrior.

Despite the popular press's depiction of the female just warrior as a feminist icon, the new virago appears to hold feminism in disdain. Helford has remarked on the trivializing of feminism in woman warrior shows, noting that instead of a political commitment to social change, such programs promote "girl power." According to Helford, the terrain that the new woman warrior negotiates is dominated by superficial applause for the liberal concept of tolerance combined with the liberal abhorrence of dogma, labels, or presumed restrictions on behavior. Consequently, although television images of the 1990s have produced "some of the most developed and compelling (if not contradictory and sometimes even reactionary) televisual representations of gen-

der politics and debates over (and within) feminism," at the same time they
have relegated feminism's most progressive politics to subtexts.[17] The new
woman warrior, then, presents viewers with a polysemic image that enables
both reactionary and progressive readings.

At its worst, this demotion of feminist politics to the subtexts of girl power
threatens, in the words of critic Kent Ono, "[to] redirect attention away from
the degradation and economic exploitation of women world-wide and away
from the need for vigilant social activism." Girl-power politics, Ono insists,
concerns itself solely with white middle-class individualist and ostensibly
pleasurable notions of female identity, most of them produced by commercial
enterprises largely responsible for the continuing gendered and racialized exploitation of laborers globally.[18] In other words, representing the new woman
warrior as a solution to women's oppression reproduces the tired closed image
of white middle-class heterosexuality as the desirable norm for authentic liberated women.

❧ ❧ ❧

The contributors to this anthology are both intrigued by the possibilities that
the new woman warrior offers for alternative storytelling and acutely aware of
her limitations as a model for feminism(s). Many are fans of the shows they analyze. To these contributors, the woman warrior is interesting not only because
she is a critical conundrum but also because she offers them an empowering
image of women. Vivian Chin, for example, foregrounds her personal connection to *Buffy the Vampire Slayer* by exploring how an Asian American woman
such as herself can identify with the protagonist, Buffy Summers, despite the
show's demeaning depictions of Asian culture. Frances Early's critical perspective on *Buffy* developed as she watched the show with her teenage daughter,
who delighted in the image of a resilient and powerful young woman. Laura Ng
chose to investigate the problematic relationship between female empowerment and the use of just violence in *La Femme Nikita* because of her scholarly
interest in a related topic, the representation of violence in contemporary female detective novels.

Our authors bring different disciplinary perspectives to their analyses.
Frances Early and Kathleen Kennedy are American historians whose previous
work has examined constructions of war, violence, and peace in U.S. society.
Alison Futrell is a historian of ancient Rome, and her contribution examines
how *Xena, Warrior Princess* rereads key Roman and Greek myths. Edrie

Sobstyl's training as a philosopher and feminist critic leads her to examine the investment in liberalism in *Star Trek: Voyager*. Vivian Chin, Laura Ng, and Susan Tjardes employ the techniques of critical theory to offer a "close reading" of their texts. Eight of the nine contributors to the anthology are academic critics, but Helen Caudill provides a different perspective, that of a performer who is dubious about the merits of academic approaches to criticism; she argues that such critics often privilege their own readings of art over art itself. The diverse theoretical and empirical interests of our authors offer a particular strength to this anthology, providing the reader with an opportunity to examine the new television woman warrior from a variety of viewpoints.

The individual contributions are held together by their common interest in exploring the implications—especially for alternative feminist storytelling—of the new woman warrior's appropriation of the male just warrior's exclusive claim to heroism.

Part 1 offers three essays on *Xena, Warrior Princess*. Its contributors are interested in how the show reconstructs the founding myths of Western civilization as women's stories. In chapter 2, Alison Futrell explores how *Xena, Warrior Princess* co-opts Western founding myths. Through a careful reading of two of these myths—the loss of female power in *The Eumenides* and in the Roman Empire—Futrell shows how *Xena, Warrior Princess* recasts these myths' glorification of male public achievements, offering in its stead a heroic quest that values home, family, and love.

In chapter 3, Helen Caudill explores the violent subtext of Gabrielle and Xena's relationship. In particular, she focuses on how the authors of fan fiction foreground and reinterpret the troubling connection between sex and violence in that relationship. Unlike critics who see the quest narrative as a product of Western male dominance over others, Caudill's argument points to a different historical trajectory. She reads Xena's quest, especially as retold in fan fiction, as part of an older history of ancient goddesses whose power derived from their ability to find pleasure in the dark recesses of sexuality. It is the rediscovery of this older quest narrative that, according to Caudill, distinguishes *Xena, Warrior Princess*.

Like Futrell and Caudill, Kathleen Kennedy is interested in how *Xena, Warrior Princess* rewrites patriarchal myths and in the meaning of that reinvention for the construction of Western identity. Her contribution in chapter 4 explores the tension produced by the show's attempt to face West and East simultaneously. By focusing on the divergent meanings of Xena's quest in the West and in the East, Kennedy argues that the show develops a self-reflective critique of its own investment in the Western heroic tradition, although it is a critique limited by the program's Orientalism.

Whereas *Xena, Warrior Princess* is set in the past, in the era that purportedly witnessed the origins of Western civilization, *Buffy the Vampire Slayer* takes place in the mythical embodiment of that civilization's success, the predominately white, middle-class suburbs of California. *Buffy the Vampire Slayer,* like *Xena,* self-consciously evokes myths of Western culture to examine their exclusive claim to truth. The product of a distinctly female myth—a secret lineage of female vampire slayers—Buffy Summers fights demons that embody the hell that exists under the surface of suburban life. Like the authors in part 1, contributors to part 2 examine to what degree this distinctly female myth exposes and contests the foundational myths of patriarchal Western culture.[19]

In chapter 5, Frances Early opens this part by examining the veracity of the military's exclusive claim to just violence and protection of an American way of life. Buffy's rejection of these claims as well as her own self-reflectivity challenge the hegemonic myth that state-sanctioned violence is necessary for the protection of its citizenry. Embedded within Buffy's quest, Early contends, is an important pacifist message about the use of violence and its cost to the individual and society.

In chapter 6, Susan Tjardes further develops a theme brought out in Early's contribution: the relationship between Faith, the rouge vampire slayer, and Buffy. Both authors are critical of the dichotomy the show draws between Faith as the fallen slayer and Buffy as the good slayer. But whereas Early sees a pacifist subtext in Buffy's rejection of the joy Faith expresses in the power she obtains as a slayer, Tjardes argues that Faith's punishment as a border crosser constrains Buffy's agency within traditionally female values of restraint.

Lee Parpart's contribution in chapter 7 adds a different dimension to these debates about the type of image Buffy represents. Parpart, inspired by her partner's enjoyment of *Buffy the Vampire Slayer,* examines men's interest in the show. In particular, she explores the relationships that different groups of men have with the show's feminist subtext. Through an on-line questionnaire, she discovers that for heterosexual men, Buffy's challenge to conventional gender definitions is not a significant factor in their enjoyment of the show. Instead, they expressed open hostility to suggestions that Buffy is a feminist hero. In contrast, the gay men who responded to Parpart's questionnaire were likely to identify with the show's feminist themes. Parpart concludes that her findings may well illustrate the wide range of difficulties associated with popular culture's postmodern "girl-power" approach to feminism.

The location of *Buffy the Vampire Slayer* in the predominately white suburbs of northern California enables the show to make pointed critiques of that culture but also potentially limits the program's appeal mostly to white women. In chapter 8, however, Vivian Chin argues that it is possible for an Asian American woman to identify with Buffy and with her special destiny as a just warrior. Using concepts of masquerade, Chin explores both the show's investment in Orientalism and the spaces it potentially leaves open for women of color to identify with Buffy's role as an outsider. Her examination argues for the centrality of racialist constructions in the show's myth and suggests that the show has the potential to facilitate a conversation about whiteness, masquerade, and otherness as a means of expanding the meaning of the woman just warrior in North American culture.

Whereas Buffy fights outside the U.S. military-industrial complex to protect white suburbs from internal threats, Nikita fights within its deepest recesses to protect Western culture from its external threats. As part of a covert antiterrorist organization concerned only with its ends, Nikita lives in a morally ambiguous world. In chapter 9, Laura Ng explores this ambiguity in *La Femme Nikita,* examining how the show both constructs and is constructed by Nikita's agency and subjectivity. She suggests that it is this theme of ambiguity that disrupts the show's investment in Western morality and ways of thinking. In these grey areas, she argues, Nikita emerges as a complicated woman warrior uncontrolled by patriarchal convention.

Star Trek: Voyager, like its predecessors in the *Star Trek* series, imagines a future in which a federation of different cultures and societies governs a large area of space. As representatives of the United Federation of Planets, the crew of *Voyager* is responsible for protecting the future from renegade cultures such as the Borg, who reject Federation values. Famous for its gender parity and racially diverse crews, *Voyager* is unique within the series because it is captained by a woman, Kathryn Janeway, and includes two women warriors in its main crew: engineer B'Elanna Torres and former Borg drone Seven of Nine. In chapter 10, Edrie Sobstyl argues that in spite of its liberal premise, *Star Trek: Voyager* falls short in its depiction of female agency. In particular, Sobstyl focuses on what cyborg feminists see as the promise of technology to liberate women from their bodies and circumscribed female roles. Unlike them, however, she is pessimistic about the cyborg's role in such a process, given its investment in military structures of power. Using Seven of Nine as a possible example of the feminist cyborg, Sobstyl examines how the program's continued commitment to liberalism, capitalism, militarism, and traditional gender arrangements sabotages Seven of Nine's entrance into liberal humanity. In contrast to the more optimistic interpretations of the woman warrior presented by other contributors, Sobstyl argues for a more negative reading of the new woman warrior as a product of capitalist and militarist technologies of violence. It is this pessimistic perspective, she contends, that best exposes the continued workings of patriarchy even in popular culture's most progressive efforts to tell a different story.

These diverse contributions, which analyze program runs up to the end of the 2001 television season, offer the reader several entry points into examining the sometimes contradictory meanings of the new woman warrior's appropriation of both violence and the male heroic narrative. The authors have not sought to answer the question as to whether this appropriation is helpful for feminism or for women. Rather, they have attempted to engage with that appropriation of violence in order to expose and interrogate the reactive and progressive meanings the new woman warrior obtains in television episodics, in fan fiction, among critics, and on the Internet.

It is not our intention to suggest that the new woman warrior and critics' interrogation of her story can replace feminist political organizing. At the same time, the investment that many women and men have in the new woman warrior and the popular press's adoption of her as a feminist hero invite a careful critical response that does not simply dismiss this female embodied subject and her fans as misled or dangerous. If the stories she tells enable fans to reimagine and reclaim the heroic narrative for young women, then the new woman warrior is a potential ally to the feminist project of reinventing the world. To evoke once again the words of Donna Haraway: "There is no way out of stories: but no matter what the One-eyed Father says, there are many possible structures, not to mention contents, of narration. Changing the stories, in both material and semiotic senses, is a modest intervention worth making."[20]

PART ONE

Xena, Warrior Princess

Xena, Warrior Princess chronicles Xena's quest to atone for her murderous past and to reconstruct herself as a just warrior. Set in ancient Greece, *Xena, Warrior Princess* (aired 1995–2001) draws its cast of characters from the central myths of Western culture. As Xena and her "sidekick" Gabrielle fight against and ally themselves with the heroes and antiheroes of this Western tradition, they gleefully destroy its canon and temporal boundaries. This engagement with and rereading of Western cultural myths enables the show to invent for women the heroic quest lacking in the conventional annals of Western civilization.

Blessed with superhuman fighting skills, problem-solving abilities, and healing powers, Xena travels the ancient world seeking justice for those victimized by divine and human desire for domination and lust for violence. Her struggle to find a heroic path in a world dominated by violence leads *Xena, Warrior Princess* to raise unsettling moral questions about the boundaries between good and evil, just and unjust violence, and peace and war.

2

The Baby, the Mother, and the Empire

Xena as Ancient Hero

A L I S O N   F U T R E L L

The ancients have power. Popular wisdom tells us that it is among the ancients—their symbols, standards, and traditions—that we find the fundamental institutions of Western civilization. Modern references to Greece and Rome thus have high prestige value; governmental and financial institutions, for example, frequently evoke the colonnades and white marble of classical architecture to transmit their much-desired messages of stability and permanence. Classical symbols authorize, even mandate, the use of grand, universal themes in narratives with an ancient flavor. The fall of empires, the rise of ideologies, shifting universal paradigms and root metaphors are played out on a monumental stage, in lavish costumes, the grandiosity of the classical backdrop a visual match for the timelessness of the message.[1]

Xena, Warrior Princess (hereafter *XWP*) deliberately both confronts and co-opts the defining characteristics of this idiom, skittering gleefully across the boundaries of genre and gender expectations. In a world notably devoid of colonnades and white marble, *XWP* reworks notions of heroism and history, destabilizing antiquity and our assumptions about its unchanging aspect.

At home in the ancient Mediterranean, the source of so many paradigmatic heroes' tales, Xena's path conforms in general to expectations well established in the mythological tradition for the heroic quest: gifted with special strengths and insights, Xena journeys far abroad to battle against extraordinary forces in order to heal the disruption of human community and to achieve internal transformation. Drawing also on "American" conceptualizations of the hero's task, *XWP* stresses atonement and redemption, relying on the selflessness of the hero rather more than is typical for Graeco-Roman mythology.[2]

Xena, however, is female, which distinguishes her from the vast majority of heroic figures, certainly different from those known for ancient Greece and Rome, where "heroines" exist as mothers and nursemaids of heroes and gods, fulfilling at most a supporting role in the quest.[3]

XWP creates a new definition of heroism. Like the archetypical hero, Xena is a proactive agent in the creation of a new society, her agency most typically demonstrated in the righteous use of violence to destroy "evil" and to defend the "weak." The specific targets of Xena's justice and the social and historical impact of her actions, however, separate her from the ancient heroic norm. Xena's mission tends toward the defense of domestic, female-centered institutions and goals, the home and the community—spheres where women traditionally played a prominent role. By representing the family and the home as essential to the series' concept of "good" and as jeopardized by androcentric ancient social, political, and ethical structures, *XWP* celebrates the traditional feminine sphere, giving voice to those conspicuously silenced in the ancient texts.

In this chapter, demonstration of Xena's particular heroic drive falls into three areas of focus. First, the significance of the domestic motif in the formation of Xena's character and quest is revealed by the exploration of the creation of Xena's heroic impulse: the context surrounding Xena's period as a monstrously evil warlord. Second, a more detailed analysis of a particular episode shows how Xena becomes a redefined culture hero and how the ancient understanding of domestic priorities specifically is revised, repositioning motherhood and the female as the family's ethical and emotional center. And third, a consideration of the larger context of Xena's mission not only suggests the significance of the choice of victims in need of a hero, but also demonstrates the series' use of revisionist "historiography." Xena's ancient world contrasts starkly with typical popular presentations of the Graeco-Roman past, revealing the brutality and oppression that buttressed the foundations of Western society.

Babies and Empire: Evil Xena as Roman Imperialist

Rome holds a special position in Xena's hero quest: Rome "caused" Xena. The actions of Xena's Roman nemesis, Gaius Julius Caesar, were central in the creation of the "evil Xena," the dark past for which she is driven to atone. Her years in darkness as the "Destroyer of Nations" represent an extreme version of Roman imperialism, one that focuses on acquisition of territory and power at any cost; in those years, Xena was driven to become her nemesis. Her articulation of her past actions and aims exposes the grim consequences of conquest, the brutality inherent in empire. Most often the series demonstrates this inherent brutality in the destruction of home and family as well as in the loss of human values. On the other hand, Xena's recovery, her sense of mission, is catalyzed specifically by a renewed sense of the importance of love (especially maternal love), trust, and family. To become a hero, Xena must become an anti-Rome.

Xena's and Caesar's (Rome's) paths met and were changed forever ten years previous to the main narrative, when Xena took captive the charismatic Caesar.[4] Growing bored with her current efforts to defend her homeland from external foes, she was intrigued by Caesar's explanation of "true greatness," not considering the personal cost exacted by ambitions, like Caesar's, to "rule the world." Xena offered partnership to Caesar, a partnership to be based not only on mutual desire for power but also on romantic affection. At their second meeting, she came to Caesar arrayed as a bride, with eyes shining in eager anticipation, only to be betrayed; her men were killed, and she herself was maimed and crucified. This experience of love's betrayal by Caesar caused Xena's downward spiral into evil and death, that dark period when she became the Destroyer of Nations. She launched a crusade of vengeance upon the human race as a whole, with death her only purpose in life. Her tactics, priorities, and goals during this time mimicked those of Caesar and Rome as the stereotypical evil empire.

Evil Xena exhibited a warped (albeit apparently effective) leadership style, preferring the explicit use of terror while she scorned diplomacy and alliance. Indeed, terror defined her empire quite literally: she delineated her territory with severed enemy heads in the kingdom of Chin and in Corinth boldly declared her intent to mark her conquests with a line of crucified enemies. Disregarding inconvenient rules of war, the evil Xena cut a swath of impressive destruction; she was a veritable "scourge of god," seeking riches and brutal power for the purpose of self-gratification.[5]

This Destroyer of Nations demonstrated her contempt for human values, disavowing affection and love as "soft" and inappropriate for a warlord. Her destructive mission thus undermined the ideological and social ties of human societies, destroying the "soul" of the peoples she conquered while she burned their villages and killed their loved ones. Such behavior is emphasized repeatedly as the nadir of Xena's evil past, particularly in reference to her use of chil-

dren as victims and pawns: from Callisto to Ming Tien to Otere, Xena's path
was littered with the wreckage of innocent lives. As an extremely pregnant Xena
declared at Corinth, "This baby is nothing compared to my empire!"[6] Evil Xena
was thus an antimother.

The dichotomy presented in this outburst, baby versus (evil) empire, re-
curs throughout the evil Xena arc. Xena's pregnancy and childbirth are presented as a focal time in her dark period, a point at which she hovered on the
boundary between good and evil. The child's father, Borias, saw motherhood as
an opportunity for Xena to incorporate love into her life, an option Xena rejected in favor of her role as warlord. Xena's decision to give up her child was an
acknowledgment of the "wrongness" of her lifestyle, which involved knowledge
and experiences a child should not have. She later confesses that even her brief
experience of motherhood planted a seed of change, a conviction that potential
goodness lurked even within her embittered soul. Indeed, her final shift toward
heroism and atonement was catalyzed by her rescue of a baby and the refusal to
countenance the murder of women and children; with these actions, she severed her relationship with her marauding army.

Xena's rediscovery of an emotional core confirms her strength as hero by
directing it toward a constructive goal. The difference between this model of
leadership and that of Rome is articulated in Caesar, Xena's mirror image. As
his motto, a repeated critique of Xena's heroism, Caesar emphasizes the tension
between war and human feeling: "divide a woman's emotions from her sensi-
bilities, and you have her: divide and conquer."[7] The historical Caesar's strategy
for exploiting the intertribal tensions among the Gallic peoples is here given a
gendered spin: women are perceived as more emotional than men, more apt to
be ruled by the heart. In the episode "Deliverer," Caesar expands on this perception: Xena's fatal flaw as a military leader is her tendency to empathize, to
care too much. His ideal of leadership, in contrast, excises compassion, friendship, and love, instead manipulating those emotions as weaknesses in others.
The motto, however, can be read conversely: that emotion and sense undivided
cannot be conquered, that it is only their separation that weakens the woman
warrior.

Nevertheless, Xena's dark past is a fundamental part of her identity and
strength as hero as is reiterated in a surreal reexperience of her crucifixion.
Xena "know[s] Evil, [was] Evil, and [Evil] can . . . fight Evil."[8] She has learned
to control the darkness inside her and can bring that power to bear on the dark-

ness outside. Violence has become a depersonalized tool, no longer a source of pleasure or release, no longer the defining marker of her world.

The House of Xena: Defending Mother Blood

"The Furies" episode of *XWP*, originally broadcast as the 1997–98 season opener, is a reworking of *The Eumenides*, a tragedy by the fifth-century Athenian playwright Aeschylus, usually translated into English as *The Furies*. Both the play and the television series consider concepts of justice and retribution as well as the impact of human decisions on the individual. Both particularize these issues within the context of the family. The conclusions that each version of the story reaches, however, express very different priorities: whereas the Aeschylean version is a vigorous devaluation of feminine authority in the public and the domestic sphere, the *XWP* episode catalyzes a strengthening of the mother-daughter relationship to the exclusion of the father. Indeed, the erasure of the paternal factor in Xena's family becomes proof of her status as mythic hero.

Aeschylus's *Eumenides* is the last play of his last trilogy, the *Oresteia,* which immediately achieved canonical status as a powerful articulation of the political identity of the rising Athenian Empire. Greek drama was embedded deeply in the apparatus of the Athenian state: the executive branch selected, subsidized, directed, and cast the production of these few plays chosen for performance at the state festival of Dionysus. Greek tragedies, like all forms of public discourse, were expressions of public ideology. The questions raised in Greek drama and the ways in which they were connected to concepts of family loyalties, political identity, and religious obligation established the terms for social understanding, the basis of a master narrative of lasting significance.[9]

The plot of *The Eumenides* centers on the sordid history of one of the most notorious families of Greek tragic legend, the House of Atreus. Sparking off the conflict in the *Oresteia* is the attack on Troy, led by the Atreid Agamemnon, king of Argos. In order to launch the Greek armada, Agamemnon must sacrifice his daughter, Iphigeneia; this action indicates his privileging of his political role above his familial relationship with his female child.[10] The trilogy opens ten years later, when Agamemnon returns home from defeated Troy to his wife, Clytaemnestra, who is still simmering with rage over the death of her daughter. She murders Agamemnon in retribution, thus privileging ties of blood over ties of marriage, her role as mother over her role as wife. Part two of the trilogy, *The Libation-Bearers,* focuses on their son, Orestes, whose duty it is to restore the balance, to restore justice, by avenging his father's death; to do so, of course, he must murder his mother. The matricide at the end of the second play is the catalyst for Aeschylus's discussion of justice and the family in *The Eumenides.* Orestes is obliged by natural law to seek retribution for the wrong done his kinsman, but he stands in the same parent-child relationship to both the injured party and the killer. His choice to kill his mother can be seen as a declaration of the primacy of the father. What are the consequences of his choice? Orestes' spilling of kin's blood—worse, of mother's blood—is an outrage of natural law; he is stained by his crime, and this blood pollution is demonstrated by the madness inflicted on him by vengeful Furies, who maintain that Orestes' crime can never be forgiven, that no expiatory sacrifice, no ritual purification can ever remove the guilt and horror of matricide. Apollo and Athena assert the contrary—that by following proper civic and judicial procedure, Orestes can achieve full restoration of his former status as scion of the royal household of Argos.

At a fairly basic level, the Furies understand justice as the restoration of social balance: murder must be answered by vengeance, with the victim's family responsible for exacting brutal retribution. Justice in this form is a "natural law," a law that relies on natural bonds, those of blood and family, bonds established and enforced by the oldest generation of gods. Aeschylus places Apollo and Athena in opposition to this natural law. These younger gods support human justice, one standardized, litigated, and judged by human institutions in accordance with political interests. The tensions between tradition and innovation, between natural law and human law, also are identified with the male/female dichotomy: the Furies, themselves female, support the mother-child bond as the primary human relationship, attuned to the mother blood as a force of nature. In Aeschylus, the political power of the father outvotes and dominates motherhood and nature.

The dichotomization of these viewpoints along gender lines runs throughout *The Eumenides.* Aeschylus, breaking with tradition, thoroughly demonizes the nastily feminine Furies in a number of repulsively vivid descriptions: they are dark, dank, disgusting, foul-smelling, dripping with pus; were spewed forth from the infernal abyss; and are unfit for human sight—bitches nose down on the trail of blood left by the hapless Orestes. The specific characteristics attributed to the Furies harmonize with the general negative characterization of femininity in Greek thought as chaotic, disordered, cold, moist, unbounded, and preferably invisible.[11]

Forms of human relations likewise are compared in a gendered fashion. The Furies emphasize the importance of the maternal blood tie as the closest human connection, essential to all others, to the family, the clan, the community as a whole. Apollo places the conjugal bond first, radically devaluing motherhood; the minimal importance of the mother is the basis of his argument for Orestes' acquittal. Indeed, Apollo questions the very existence of "mother blood"; he asserts that only the father is truly a parent, that the woman is merely a container for the life implanted by its sire. She is, Apollo says, *xenoi xena*, a stranger harboring a stranger; her relationship with her child is based not on the natural tie of blood but on the social bond of marriage. The child is a guest in his mother's womb, just as the wife, by Greek law, is a permanent guest in her husband's home. There is no mother. There is only the father.[12]

Weighing Clytaemnestra's crime against Orestes' retribution on these grounds doubly justifies Orestes' action. Clytaemnestra is guilty of two offenses: she killed her husband, and she killed Orestes' only parent.[13] This argument sways the verdict: Athena, caster of the deciding vote, admits that she is entirely male oriented, being mother free herself, and thus considers the death of a husband killer to be justified.[14] Orestes, vindicated, declares Athena the savior of his house, the restorer of his fatherland and of his father's heritage.

Thus, male-oriented, primarily political institutions prevail at the expense of the natural law espoused by the Furies, who lose their ancient rights and privileges and only reluctantly are reconciled by Athena to their much-diminished status as the Eumenides or "kindly ones," trusting in her gracious provision of compensation. They are now permanent guests in Athens, naturalized divine *xenai* themselves.

"The Furies" episode of *XWP* focuses on family justice as well, using the presentation of arguments before an empaneled jury as a framing device; the jury here consists of the Furies themselves.[15] In the teaser, the Furies are presented with a case, render judgment, and determine the penalty to be imposed on Xena not for matricide, but rather for not avenging the murder of her long-dead father Atreus—in other words, for making the choice Orestes did not. The penalty inflicted is expressed as "both persecution and madness," specified as a combination of human and divine power, not the competing claims to authority of the Aeschylean version.

The action is moved by Xena's increasing madness; by the end of act 1,

Xena's naked lunacy (depicted quite literally, sans clothing and under a full moon) leads to the distortion of her hero's mission: she demands "retribution in flames" from a cluster of frightened villagers, a group normally the beneficiaries of her salvific efforts. In her madness, Xena projects the role of imperialist evil-doer onto the standard victim, raving that the villagers are guilty, that they have crucified women and children. Gabrielle, Xena's companion, points out that these villagers *are* women and children, now terrorized by Xena herself.

The episode makes repeated references to Orestes, drawing direct comparisons to the "original" story laid out in Greek tragedy. The story has undergone revision: Orestes here is described as being obligated by "the code of the Furies" to kill his mother. In consultation with Xena's mother, Gabrielle seeks out Orestes himself, hoping for his insight as to how to resolve the situation without bloodshed, how to find justice without the necessity of matricide. She finds Orestes in an asylum, huddled, catatonic, mired in his own filth. He is still mad. Far from being satisfied by his fulfillment of their original directive, the Furies have only intensified their punishment of him because, it is alleged, of his greater culpability for a much worse crime. Matricide here is weighted much more heavily than duty to one's father. As Gabrielle stares in horror at what Orestes has become, the warder tells her, "It's all a lie." In the Xena narrative, this is Orestes' final fate; there is no support for the patriarchy, no zesty restoration to the fatherland, but rather a chilling demonstration of the true depth of the maternal bond. Orestes is condemned to lifelong suffering for his crime against motherhood. Xena also offers an indictment of divine justice, the "lie" referred to by the warder.

The concept of competing perspectives, different versions of the "truth" about the murder of Xena's father, underlies much of the narrative: different explanations of the murder are presented at different points, which shift responsibility for both the crime and its retribution. Implicit or explicit in each is, again, a comparison with the House of Atreus. Version one of the "truth," told by Xena's mother, Cyrene, foregrounds Xena's youth and helplessness at the time the crime was committed. Her father had come home from the sanctuary of Ares, having been ordered to sacrifice his daughter to the god of war. As with Agamemnon and Iphigeneia, fatherly ties give way to more powerful motivations: here, Xena's father is described as drunk, angry, chillingly methodical, and dedicated to the immoral war god. Met with maternal resistance, he likewise discarded his conjugal bonds, threatening to kill Xena's mother as well. Culpability in this scenario is thus fixed on the abusive father, whose psychology and its symptomatic rage and substance abuse mitigate his being murdered, in modern standards of justice, to an act of self-defense by Cyrene. Ares, god of war, offers another causal factor: it was because of "jealousy" that the father punished his wife by hurting the child. The object of this "jealousy" will be debated further in court.

The episode climaxes with a second "hearing" in the temple of the Furies. At center stage is Xena's mother, her body bound to the altar as a victim ready for sacrifice. We see thus literalized the central issue of the proceeding: maternity is placed on trial. Xena, as chief litigant, argues a different version of the crime. In this scenario, a mortal woman was raped by a god, disguised as her husband, which resulted in the birth of a hero. The mortal husband for years believed in his paternity, until divine revelation brought out the truth. The exposure of his wife's adultery and of his false paternity utterly undermined the father's domestic authority, driving him to compensatory rage and determination to murder the false child, Xena, Ares' alleged offspring. The emphasis here is on the father's "jealousy"; the explanation of this emotion likewise clarifies how different family roles are conceived. Xena claims her father was driven by a "romantic" jealousy, the destruction of marital fidelity, and the undermining of his role as husband, which led to a collapse of the family. Ares interprets the "jealousy" as narcissism, a "common phenomenon"; the unparental father resented the maternal attention given to the child, who, in turn, represented a rival focus in the family dynamics.[16]

As in *The Eumenides,* the climax of this episode centers on the mother's and the father's competing claims. Aeschylus's argument, as we saw, obliterates "mother" as a natural category. The teleplay, however, has stressed repeatedly the maternal role as positive, selfless, self-sacrificing, and divinely validated; the mere contemplation of matricide is viewed as madness. The paternal role, in contrast, is devalued in the human and the divine realm. Xena's mortal father was chaotic, in thrall to his own passions, appetites, and petty impulses; driven by superstition and suspicion, he lacked authority. Xena's divine father, Ares, embodies the chaos of war and bloodlust, thus aspectually configuring the final assessment of fatherhood. The "proof" of paternity in the courtroom is in combat: if Xena can "hold her own" against Ares, she then must be his offspring. Paternity thus is expressed most clearly in hostility: father and child are here *xenoi,* utter strangers, whose only relationship is through conflict. The proof is irrefutable; the Furies remove Xena's madness.

The final scene drives the point home in terms symbolic of natural moth-

erhood: Xena thanks her mother for her life and expresses empathy for the burden she has carried, alluding not only to the burden of an unpleasant truth but
also to the original spark of life from the mother and the burden of pregnancy.
The female family bonds have withstood, quite literally, a trial by fire and have
demonstrated their durability: "We'll be stronger than before," Xena claims.
The House of Xena is thus built on female authority; there is no father.

Imperial Families: Xena's Historiographical Mission

Xena's restored human values catalyze her recovery from darkness, demonstrated by a renewed effort to protect the "innocent" from the depredations of
casually violent warlords and politicians. The Roman Empire here is a histori-
cized monster against which Xena does battle, her efforts meant primarily to
mitigate the effects of imperialism and to defend the weak. She is presented as a
key shaper of events during a particularly dynamic period in Roman history:
the fall of the republic and the rise of the imperial monarchy. Just as Xena
"writes history" through her actions, so does the series "rewrite history" in the
Roman arc, laying bare the ethical implications and human costs of empire.
Both modern and ancient scholarship tend to credit a certain moral failure
with the fall of Rome's republic.[17] The *XWP* narrative of the First Triumvirate
era reinterprets the nature of that ethical failure along lines that prioritize its
rejection of family values and female-centered institutions. The history that
emerges is thus very different from standard popular retellings of the Roman
past: we find here no Pax Romana, no spread of civilization to benighted bar-
barism. Rather, the *XWP* narrative emphasizes the consequences of imperialism, the suffering it causes its predominantly domestic and female victims,
presenting a persistent subaltern perspective on the Roman Empire.

Resistance to Rome is often given a nationalist slant in the series: bands of
British freedom fighters declare their people "will never give in" to the oppression of Rome. A Gallic leader of the resistance to Rome declares that the nation
will survive forever, the nation's survival being identified with that of the family. At times, Rome seems bent on projects of "ethnic cleansing," a final pacification that resonates powerfully for a contemporary audience.[18]

The fate of Marcus Licinius Crassus points to Rome's loss of human values
in still more domestic terms. Instead of dying while fighting an aggressive war
against the Parthians, Crassus is rescued from the East by Xena, who intends to
use him as a hostage for an exchange of war prisoners, Vercinix in particular.

Vercinix's capture by the Romans has been presented as self-sacrificing: he fights against overwhelming odds to delay and distract the Roman forces in order to allow his family to escape. Vercinix's wife has summoned Xena to rescue the husband and father and to restore the home wrecked by Rome. Crassus has been selected deliberately for this exchange, a choice that expresses again the dichotomy between the Roman agenda and the domestic values Xena champions. Crassus, as a triumvir, has political value to Caesar and Rome and is thus a useful bargaining chip. To Xena, however, his expendability or his lack of value makes him an appropriate tool. Crassus is described as a war criminal, his "notorious" mass crucifixion of submissive women and children placing him beyond human consideration. He is a "cold-blooded murderer" who has "stopped being a man." He justifies his actions by claiming that "there are no innocents on a battlefield." Because, in the *XWP* construct, the entire world is Rome's battlefield, the statement indirectly expresses Roman disinterest in drawing boundaries around the socially sacred (the "innocent").[19]

The death of the historical Gnaeus Pompeius Strabo (commonly called Pompey Magnus) followed shortly on his failure to lead the senatorial troops to victory over the Caesarian forces at Pharsalus in 48 B.C.E. "A Good Day," the *XWP* presentation of Pharsalus, depicts the battle as a "filthy civil war" spreading its pollution into Greece and poisoning one Greek family in particular.[20] Here, Phlanacus, a Greek mercenary, has been driven to fight with the legions out of economic necessity, leaving his family for years at a time only because of the hope of being able to provide for them in the future. Once home, in order to guarantee a peaceful life for his child, he vows never again to speak of Rome and its monstrous war machine. Caesar articulates the Roman approach, his determination to achieve an advantage over Pompey, even if he has "to destroy Pompey's army and their country piece by piece." Caesar's reiteration of the homonym *piece* contrasts sharply with the preceding scene's discussion of *peace*. The clear implication is that the Roman leadership perceives humanity as merely a backdrop for personal squabbles, as a resource to be exploited.

In yet another case, the plight of the Amazons, who are teetering on the edge of oblivion, combines different categories of Rome's victims—simultaneously national, feminine, and familial, the latter constructed through the bond of "sisterhood" emphasized in the *XWP* narrative. The death of the triumvir Pompey at Xena's hands is connected directly to his genocidal exploitation of the Amazon nation. Pompey's greed for power grotesquely narrows his ethical focus to the point that the nation of women is reduced to a commodity, profits from which will fund the remaining triumvirs' naked ambition. Exchange in women and the elimination of female national agency are thus incidental costs of Roman politics. Yet Pompey's final dialogue with Xena goes so far as to assert that the civil war actually benefits Rome's subjects and that as long as Pompey and Caesar focus their hostility on each other, they will not be destroying the world. Driven by the outrageously warped perspective behind this statement and by Rome's delusion that the havoc it creates is a "balance of power," Xena kills Pompey.[21]

The period following the assassination of Caesar, marked historically by the domination of the Second Triumvirate, is encapsulated in the *XWP* episode "Antony and Cleopatra." Indeed, the role played by the Egyptian queen in this period has dominated popular visions of the Roman past for centuries.[22] The historical focus on Cleopatra, however, is itself a gendered construct, the result of the deliberate effort made in antiquity to shape popular opinion. By concentrating on the "romance" between Antony and Cleopatra, by emphasizing the conflict between Antony's life of pleasure and his own public espousal of old-fashioned Roman virtue, Octavian gains political advantage. He can use the situation to convince his Roman constituents that his goals, in contrast to Antony's, are traditional, conservative, identifiably Roman, and dedicated to the support of the patriarchal hierarchy. The Cleopatra legend is, therefore, at heart a political "spin," a deliberately warped representation of the career of the last of the Ptolemaic dynasty of Egypt. The *XWP* version reinverts this inverted history in some interesting ways, rebuilding a picture of validated, feminine authority, a kingdom in which the ruler prioritizes the subaltern and in which male leadership is accepted or rejected on particular moral grounds.

Although the setting of the episode retains the languid, feminine overtones of the legend, Cleopatra's own political agenda, independent of the Roman in-fighting, is foregrounded from the outset: her role is to protect Egypt, her people, and herself, in that order of priorities. Indeed, her devotion to Egypt exacts a high personal cost; Xena asserts that Cleopatra died hoping that the Egyptian people might "for the first time choose their next great leader," implying that both peaceful self-governance and some form of democracy are the political ideals embraced by the Egyptian queen.

The playing out of the standard Cleopatra vignettes takes place as part of a masquerade; Xena's Cleopatra charade plays on the (Roman) legend, manipulating the hackneyed scenes and dialogue of exotic allure to control the political outcome of the ongoing civil war, to bring it to the conclusion safest for Egypt and for the world at large.[23] The three Roman candidates' moral qualifications are considered carefully. Brutus is tainted; he murders Cleopatra and tries to kill Xena in her Cleopatra guise. His choice to do so is based on lack of confidence in his powers of seduction (the only alternative to murder). Assassination is presented as a disease here; once Brutus murdered Caesar, he "crossed the Rubicon of blood" and now shares the Roman trait of political ruthlessness. His efforts to justify this act as action for the greater good of Rome are pointed up as facile and self-serving. How many, asks Gabrielle, have to die for the good of Rome? Antony's moral qualifications for leadership are likewise problematic. Although Antony seems genuinely devoted to Cleopatra on a romantic level, spouting Shakespearean verses at the least opportunity, his vision of the Roman world is even grimmer than Brutus's. After defeating Brutus, Antony plans to kill his opponent and all his soldiers, the price to be paid for their opposition of Antony. He shrugs off the brutality of this agenda: "Death, execution, it is the Roman way, and I am Roman." The appeal of Octavius is based in part on his alienation from traditional modes of Roman leadership.[24] Antony describes him as a boy, ill-equipped to rule Rome and thus undeserving of his Caesarian patrimony; in effect, Octavius is a "traitor." His emotionalism and nervous hesitancy is certainly distinctive among the Roman "warlords," as is his worldview. He also identifies "his people" broadly, not just as Romans per se but as all those under the protection of Rome and therefore equally deserving of Roman peace. Octavius views the provision of these benefits as his destiny, in contrast to Caesar's destiny, which is the exploitation of the world to serve his own ambition. Octavius is hailed as the bearer of the Pax Romana, an all-too-brief reconciliation between the Roman Empire and the "land in turmoil" that "cried out for a hero."

"She Was Xena"

In many ways, the conceptualization of Xena as hero reflects changes in the modern understanding of the past as a whole and in the evaluation and practice of history. Historiography traditionally focused exclusively on political and military achievements as the only categories of human effort appropriate for scholarship. Xena, as a "warrior princess," is identified by her authority in just those legitimized fields of accomplishment. But as her journey unfolds, the series asserts that a true warrior princess, an authentic hero, finds fulfillment in the service of home, family, and love, not in domination and conquest. The humble truths inherent in Xena's heroism redefine the ancient past and the hero's quest, giving new and broader meaning to the "ancient epic" as a standard feature of popular culture. *XWP* locates Greece's glory and Rome's grandeur not in power plays and war or in monuments and maps, but in the human connections basic to the strength of individual women and men.

3

Tall, Dark, and Dangerous

Xena, the Quest, and the Wielding
of Sexual Violence in *Xena* On-Line Fan Fiction

HELEN CAUDILL

The quest is humanity's most ancient archetype, the pattern for the journey of life itself. In claiming the quest as a patriarchal narrative, however, critics have ignored its ancient roots, which incorporate a long tradition of female heroes. The origins of the quest narrative are lost in time, but they predate the establishment of patriarchal structures of power and authority.[1] When female heroes have undertaken the quest, scholars have denied to them the role of the hero, choosing instead to define them as handmaidens to the male object of their quest. Perhaps the most obvious example of this inverted reading of the quest narrative is the Isis/Osiris myth. Scholars such as Sir James Frazer, Joseph Campbell, and David Adams Leeming have designated Osiris the hero even though it was Isis who underwent the quest to find Osiris's body parts and to resurrect him.[2] In September 1995, a female warrior hero took up the quest, and without hesitation or apology she claimed the quest's power, violence, and prize as her own. This new hero was Xena, the warrior princess.

In the first two seasons (1995–97) of *Xena, Warrior Princess* (hereafter *XWP*), Xena was portrayed as a strong, complex, female character with a dark past. As Sherrie Inness argues in *Tough Girls: Women Warriors and Wonder Women in Popular Culture,* Xena is a flawed hero, haunted by her past, yet still attracted to violence; she is a hero who possesses a far more complex soul than any previous superhero.[3] Seldom, if ever, had such a female hero been seen on television. Her struggle to escape the dark deeds of her past and to gain redemption presented an interesting and challenging premise for the series.

Again, as Inness notes, "emphasizing this aspect of Xena's character is one way that *Xena, Warrior Princess* shows that toughness has a more sinister side."[4] Yet, after the first two seasons, the show began to falter with character inconsistencies and with plots alternating between Greek tragedy and slapstick. The television show failed to realize that it is exactly Xena's dark side that attracts and fascinates both her companion Gabrielle and the audience. Not until the rise of on-line alternative fan fiction was the importance of Xena's darkness, her struggle with it, and the sexual allure of that darkness fully realized. By expanding the implied sexual component of the relationship between Xena and Gabrielle, alternative fan fiction was able to explain and explore the powerful attraction that the two women have for each other and the role of the tension between dark and light in that attraction.

The chemistry between the characters Xena and Gabrielle is so explosive even within the timid limits of mainstream television that an on-line world of alternative fan fiction quickly appropriated the characters and began telling their stories in many different ways, places, and times. Coming out of the tradition of the slash fan fiction of *Star Trek,* writers, some with professional credentials, offered their readers stories about Xena and Gabrielle in which the lesbian subtext of the TV show was transformed into the main text of fan fiction.[5] As Henry Jenkins argues in *Textual Poachers,* "Slash turns subtext into the dominant focus of new texts"; as fans assert their authority to appropriate characters, they "form interpretations, offer evaluation, and constitute [a] cultural canon."[6] Most of the alternative fan fiction concerns itself with the relationship between the two characters, and some writers reach a depth and consistency of characterization that would put the TV show to shame. Many works explore the dark side with which Xena struggles, the way in which her struggle colors her relationship with Gabrielle, and the potential for sexual violence offered by that dark side.

In at least three episodes, spread over four seasons (1995–99), glimpses of Xena's dark side and of the violence toward Gabrielle of which she is capable appear in the TV show. Alternative fan fiction develops this dark side more fully by using the quest narrative and the power with which this narrative endows its hero, even its dark ones. Fan-fiction writers have reclaimed the quest narrative, harkening back to its probable prepatriarchal origins. As Annis Pratt points out in *Archetypal Patterns in Women's Fiction,* in some ancient quest myths, such as those of Ishtar/Tammuz and Isis/Osiris, remarkable power is given to the woman in the myth.[7] Unlike the appointed mainstream authorities on the quest, in particular Carl Jung and Joseph Campbell, the authors of *XWP* fan fiction have no difficulty identifying female heroes and in reclaiming this ancient quest narrative for women.

The television show also seems clear as to its hero, but the show's creators have much more trouble dealing with the dark side of the character they have created. In the first two seasons of *XWP*, Xena is very protective of Gabrielle; we do gain some insight, however, into what she must have been like as a warlord. For instance, in "The Price" we have a sober treatment of Xena's dark side. In a struggle to ensure the survival of Gabrielle and an Athenian garrison against the savage horde, Xena claims leadership of the garrison and makes difficult decisions that seem heartless to Gabrielle, including her denial of food and water to the dying. As the plot progresses, we see Xena enjoying the adrenaline rush of battle and the perks of leadership as she slides further into the darkness of her former warlord self. Her ruthlessness sparks a confrontational scene between the two women in which the dangerous Xena of old reemerges. Gabrielle stands her ground, eventually proves her way is best, and leads Xena to realize the mistake she made in allowing her destructive impulses to take control. In the makeup scene, late in the episode, Xena comes very close to telling Gabrielle she loves her: "You don't know how much I love . . . that."[8] She admires Gabrielle's trust in the basic goodness of people, a trust she can never allow herself to have.

This episode is particularly important not only because it offers an intentional subtext and a glimpse of an angry and dangerous Xena, but also because it sets a pattern that evolves into the warlord/slave genre of Xena alternative fan fiction. In this pattern, Xena reverts to her dark self, faces some sort of confrontation with Gabrielle (often a sexually charged or violent encounter), and then finds herself redeemed or transformed back into her better self by Gabrielle's love.

Until season three (1997–98), Xena's penchant for violence remains focused on her enemies: there is little to indicate that Xena ever would become violent toward Gabrielle. Nothing has created a stir in *XWP* fandom like the infamous Gabdrag of "The Bitter Suite." In this episode, Ares goads Xena into seeking revenge for the murder of her son by Gabrielle's demon child, Hope. Xena, maddened by grief, charges into the Amazon village where Gabrielle, also grieving, is undergoing an Amazonian purification ritual. Xena fights her way through a group of Amazon warriors, ties a rope around Gabrielle, and drags her behind a horse. After brutally dragging her through fire, rocks, and water,

Xena attempts to throw the bruised and battered Gabrielle off a cliff, into the sea.[9] Many fans were disturbed not only by Xena's violence, but also by her choice of Gabrielle as the object of her wrath. Based on the violence of "The Bitter Suite" episode and of at least two other episodes, Elyce Rae Helford reads the dynamic of the Xena/Gabrielle relationship as that of abuser/victim. As evidence of Xena's sadism, she points to Xena's enjoyment of her anger, how she "smiles and sneers" and never hesitates as she enacts her violent revenge on Gabrielle.[10] Like Helford, at least one fan-fiction writer, Ella Quince, whose work I examine, questioned why Gabrielle would stay with a murderous thug like Xena after this incident.[11] Gabrielle stays because, on some level, she is attracted to Xena's darkness, an idea with sexual implications that fan fiction is freer to explore than is the television program.

In the fourth season (1998–99), Xena and Gabrielle, reconciled and seeking new adventures, meet a crusader, Najara, who decides that she wants what Xena has—Gabrielle. Najara and Xena duke it out. Najara knocks out Xena and takes Gabrielle, but Xena pursues with a plan. As she says, "[Najara's] a tough girl, but she's got a weakness. It's the same one I've got."[12] The subtextual language in the scene where she executes her plan gives us more than a hint of the dynamics of the relationship between Xena and Gabrielle. Xena has tied up Gabrielle and suspended her over a chasm in a cave. Najara enters to find Xena with sword drawn, and Gabrielle warns Najara that Xena has snapped. When Najara asks whether she is expected to believe that Xena would let Gabrielle drop, Xena says, "Let's just see, shall we? I just asked her to come with me right now. You know what she said? She said she'd rather stay here and reform you. Seems your zealotry is less scary than my dark side. . . . But if I can't have her, nobody's going to have her." Najara answers, "I knew you were no good for her."[13]

The subtext in the language of the television show can only hint at the complexities in the relationship between the two women; also, the show demonstrated very little will or ability to sustain any character consistency. Although the rift of season three may explain why Xena goes from being protective of Gabrielle to trying to kill her, episodes such as "Forgiven," in which Xena lets a punk beat up Gabrielle and even to bite off part of her ear, are so far out of the canon as to be incomprehensible to fans.[14] The same inconsistency applies with regard to the treatment of Xena's dark side. Although viewers understood that Xena had destructive tendencies, the scriptwriters downplayed her struggle with the dark and seldom portrayed how that struggle colored her relationship with Gabrielle. In fact, by the middle of season four and throughout season five (1999–2000), the show ceased to center on the relationship between the two women. It was as if the creators of *XWP* had forgotten the strength of the story they were trying to tell; the change sparked a war between some fans and the producers very much like the one Jenkins documents between the fans and the creators of *Beauty and the Beast*.[15] Even though the focus of the final season (2000–2001) once again was on the relationship between Xena and Gabrielle, the struggle between the creators and the fans continued as they differed on how to end the series. Ultimately, fans felt betrayed by the show's brutal ending. Although producers and commercial interests have ultimate control over television shows, fan fiction provides a medium for fans to devise additional story lines, complete with alternative interpretations and outcomes.[16]

In *XWP* alternative fan fiction, writers have always centered their stories on the relationship between the two women and have explored areas of the relationship only hinted at in the show. One such forbidden area is the nature of that relationship. As Inness reminds us, it is the show's refusal to insist on Xena's heterosexuality that is its most revolutionary aspect.[17] Much of its appeal has been its subtext—the suggestion, whether originally intentional or unintentional, that the two women are lovers. If this relationship is a given for most fans, then one question is how Xena's dark side affects this part of their relationship. One may think back to the cave scene in "The Crusader"; the action was staged, but the language was revealing. Alternative fan fiction is much less timid than the television show in speculating on the dynamics of the sexual aspect of the women's relationship. Although much of alternative fan fiction is simply idealized romance, some of the best writers take a hard look at the threat of danger that Xena's darkness brings to her relationship with Gabrielle and at the attraction that keeps the two together no matter what may occur.

The story that may best exemplify this type of fan fiction is "The Wedding Night" by Catherine M. Wilson. In this very short story, Gabrielle pushes Xena to the limits of her anger, and Xena forces herself sexually on Gabrielle in a display of raw power. Xena lets her dark side surface, and she takes what she wants, what she has always wanted. Wilson, after suffering what she called a "storm of outrage," wrote a lengthy explanation of how she came to write the story. She called this explanation "Wedding Night: The Dissertation." According to Wilson, "a large part of what people find fascinating and attractive about Xena is her dark side. She is a dangerous woman. A dark side isn't just an interesting accessory. It's real and powerful. We may be fascinated with the *idea* of her dark side, but to be confronted with the manifestation of it is quite another thing. Something that is worth trying to understand is why we find that so fascinating and why it attracts us, when the reality and the consequences of it can be horrendous." Asked by a friend if she thought Xena was capable of raping Gabrielle, Wilson said that she thought so if the right circumstances arose. She continued: "I wanted to do several things in this story. I wanted to tap into Xena's dark side. I wanted to present her with the combination of circumstances that would push her over the edge. I wanted to understand from the inside what that experience would be like for her, given she had rejected her old ways. I wanted to test how much of a synthesis she has achieved and how much she has really changed and in what ways. As usual, I learned a great deal more than that." [18]

After reading Wilson's story, I, too, began to wonder why so many found Xena's dark side attractive and the dynamics of her relationship with Gabrielle alluring. In "Wedding Night," Wilson manages to capture two people locked in a dangerous dance. Neither will admit her feeling for the other until those feelings push them both into an extreme situation where the truth in what is between them can be told only in the physical reactions of their bodies. It is a disturbing story, one in which Xena struggles with her dark side, her feelings for Gabrielle, and her sense of her own unworthiness. She loses the struggle, and her dark side wins, only to be transformed in the end by her love for Gabrielle. Refusing to gloss over Xena's dark side and the possible consequences for her and the one she loves, "Wedding Night" is one of the most chilling stories in alternative fan fiction.

"Wedding Night" also harkens back to a rare subgenre in slash fiction. Camille Bacon-Smith, in her study *Enterprising Women*, divides slash into several categories, including rape stories. She notes that only rarely does rape occur inside the dyad of the partnership. When it does occur as an "aggressive act of sexual dominance," it usually leads to a sexual relationship as the "victim leads the aggressive partner to accept a more equal and loving relationship." [19] "Wedding Night" also highlights the differences in the two women's approaches to emotionally and sexually charged situations. Pushed to the limits, Xena resorts to violence, whereas Gabrielle turns initial resistance into caring, thus transforming Xena's violence.

Helford characterizes this difference between Xena and Gabrielle as indicative of butch/femme roles. She defines Xena's behavior as butch because it is "unashamedly violent, displaying anger without hesitation, often gleefully" and yet "uncomfortable with verbal or physical displays of emotional closeness or weakness." Gabrielle, on the other hand, displays femme characteristics, comforting and nurturing Xena and doing all the "emotional work for the couple." For Helford, the violence within their relationship is especially problematic because it draws on and reinforces stereotypes of butch/femme relationships as inherently unequal and violent.[20]

Does the story illustrate the abuser/victim dynamic that Helford postulates? As both Jenkins and Bacon-Smith observe, fans write fiction to explain and expand the world created by the TV show.[21] If the fans accept both what is given on the show and what is portrayed in alternative fan fiction, then the answer to the question is no. In the episode "One Against an Army," Gabrielle clearly tells Xena that she has accepted the consequences of their life together.[22] This acknowledgment transforms Gabrielle from a potential victim to a willing participant. She has seen and knows what it is to love a warrior, someone whose stock in trade is violence. Xena's violence, however, does not necessarily translate into her dominance of Gabrielle. Several episodes, perhaps owing more to character inconsistency than to intention, portray Xena as pretty much whipped; she often says that Gabrielle can have or do anything she wants.

That said, "Wedding Night" and other similar stories are troubling because they seem to perpetuate the rape myth that women say "no" but mean "yes." Pratt argues that the rape trauma archetype is one of the most prevalent patterns in fiction written by women.[23] The disturbing factor in alternative fan fiction is that the aggressor—the rapist—is a woman. Turning to the question one last time, Is this support for Helford's assessment of an abuser/victim dynamic in the relationship between Xena and Gabrielle? This troubling suggestion seems to echo through much of the last four seasons of the show and in some alternative fan fiction, so it perhaps may contain some truth. The dynamics of the relationship, consensual or not, may be the consequences of Xena's unadulterated usurpation of the role of warrior-hero. Xena unabashedly wields the same power, violence, strength, and desire as the male warrior-hero. If one of the prizes won in the patriarchal rereading of the quest is a woman, then Xena also claims that prize.[24]

However, if Gabrielle begins as a not-so-willing participant in "Wedding Night," she is in control by the end. As Xena tells us in the last paragraph, "I let her body tell me what to do . . . that kind of touch she needed, how long to stay with her, when to stop."[25] What began as an assertion of power ends as an act of love.

We also see a similar dynamic at work in the warlord/slave genre of *XWP* alternative fiction. In these stories, something happens to transform Xena into her previous incarnation as a warlord. Sometimes she simply impersonates her former self as part of a plan; sometimes the gods, especially her former mentor Ares, plot to transform her; sometimes a plot device, such as enchanted well water, takes away her recent memories.

The latter is the case in Ella Quince's "Well of Sighs." Xena drinks the well water and loses three years of memories, enough at that point in the *XWP* time line to turn her back into her warlord persona. Besides undergoing a few personality changes—for the most part, her inclination toward violence reasserts itself—Xena also takes a sexual interest in Gabrielle, an interest that she previously had sublimated. Xena uses Gabrielle's obvious romantic interest in her to gain information, even using lovemaking as an interrogation tool. Gabrielle finds herself unable to resist the dark warlord that Xena has become, in part because she recognizes that the warlord and her Xena are the same. Xena taunts her, "So if your Xena doesn't come back, you'll settle for a murderous warlord?" Gabrielle replies, "You're not two different people, Xena. Who you are . . . who you will be . . . all that is part of you right now." [26] As Gabrielle struggles to convince Xena to take the antidote for the enchantment, Xena continues to use sex as a weapon to gain control of the situation. She torments Gabrielle with the possible consequences of regaining her memory, "Think Gabrielle. This noble Xena you want back never even kissed you, did she? . . . What truth is in here that kept her from wrapping her arms around you and pulling you to her breast? If I drink this water, I'll remember why I've never made love to you, and I may choose never to make love to you again." [27] Gabrielle's unselfish love, her ability to see Xena as a whole person and to love both the darkness and light in her enables her to convince Xena to drink the antidote. Gabrielle's love is the redemptive force for Xena both in alternative fan fiction and on the TV show, but loving Xena has its price.

The price is that Gabrielle often endures violence at Xena's hand, especially in the warlord/slave stories. In "Blood for Blood," by Pink Rabbit Productions, a plot between Ares and Callisto, the "psychobitch" from hell, transforms Xena. Callisto throws some of Ares' blood into Xena's eyes, and she reverts to her murderous warlord self. First, Xena kisses Gabrielle and then ties her to a tree: "Xena caught Gabrielle's chin between her thumb and forefinger: 'You are beautiful,' she murmured thoughtfully. 'But you need to learn manners.' She slapped Gabrielle again, snapping her head sideways with the force of the blow:

'Don't ever resist me again.' 'This isn't you,' choked Gabrielle. 'Oh, it's me. The real me,' Xena disagreed . . . Despite her fear, Gabrielle was shocked to feel the hard burn of arousal."[28] Gabrielle escapes as Xena struggles with the resurgence of darkness. As the darkness engulfs her, however, she has one goal: to retrieve what is hers, Gabrielle. Gabrielle runs as far as she can; she finds sanctuary with friends, but Xena, with a newly formed army, follows, determined to seize Gabrielle and to teach her that resistance is futile. Faced with the destruction of her friends and of their city and with Xena's own descent into darkness, Gabrielle goes to Xena determined to redeem her even if it costs her own life.

In another erotic scene, reminiscent of "Wedding Night," what begins as an act of power becomes a night of lovemaking and ends with a resurgence of violence and finally a redemption. Xena is restored to her former self, and once again the feelings between the two women are out in the open. A definite pattern emerges in these stories: the threat of sexual violence hangs in the air, as does Gabrielle's attraction to and arousal by the dark side of Xena's sensuality. This dangerous dance between them becomes the vehicle that allows their attraction, love, and sexual need for each other to be expressed openly. And, in turn, that expression transforms the threat of sexual violence into consensual lovemaking.

Another genre of *XWP* alternative fan fiction that often explores this attraction to the dark side is Über Xena. Über Xena stories appropriate the characters of Xena and Gabrielle and put them in different time lines with different names and occupations. The characters and the dynamics of their attraction and relationship remain pretty much the same. Über runs the gamut from pure romance to sadomasochistic fantasies, but a significant segment of Über deals with Xena's darkness, Gabrielle's attraction to Xena, and the consequences that ensue.

Lucifer Rising by Sharon Bowers is one of the best of the Über novels to come out of fan fiction. In this story, the Xena *über* ego, Jude Lucien, is a drug overlord with a dark past. Operating in Miami, Jude is a former Drug Enforcement Agency undercover agent turned rogue and drug dealer. Gabrielle's *über* personality is Liz Gardener, a reporter for the *Miami Herald* who is obsessed with Jude and is looking for the real story behind the image. Jude is the classic bad girl, or, as Liz puts it, "So, you live with three dogs in a magical house, drive a fast car, and own a trendy nightclub. You sound just like the kind of woman my mother warned me about."[29]

Lucifer Rising does a good job of exploring this attraction to the dark side as Liz tries to understand it for herself. She knows that Jude is a dangerous woman, yet feels herself drawn toward her by that very danger. Liz has always felt like an observer, not a participant, in life. It is Jude's love—with its hint of violence, anger, and thundering passion—that finally frees Liz to embrace life and love, just as it is Liz's light, tenderness, and joy that begin the redemption of Jude Lucien.

This dynamic of two halves forming a whole, of opposites attracting, and of darkness and light coming together is found throughout on-line *XWP* alternative fan fiction. Even the two women's coloring suggest the theme of dark and light—Xena with her black hair and ice-blue eyes, and Gabrielle with her strawberry-blond hair and soft green eyes. The TV show played off the visual pairing of the two women, and fan fiction follows suit. Many of the stories begin with the threat or actuality of sexual violence, and almost all end in Xena's redemption and if not in the conquest of darkness, then in the merging of darkness and light.

The disturbing question remains, however, why the prevalence of the threat of sexual violence in alternative fan fiction? Whatever the reason, female-to-female sexual violence as a theme is almost nonexistent in literature. Two of the authors whose fan fiction has been considered in this study have speculated on the reasons behind this rarity. Catherine Wilson points out that twenty years ago writers who wrote lesbian fiction had to form their own publishing houses to publish their works. Now the Internet provides a venue for fiction that bypasses traditional publishing. Wilson also notes that "Now writers whose ideas are well outside the mainstream, even the mainstream of lesbian fiction, have access to this new publishing medium." [30] Ella Quince agrees: "One of the delights of the Internet is that the publishing process is no longer regulated by conventional expectations and restrictions." As well as commenting on the restraints of traditional publishing, she asks, "What man would like to contemplate having the familiar and cherished territory of femme bashing wrestled out of his hands and what woman would dare to admit that she wanted to frolic in that landscape?" [31]

The beauty of on-line fan fiction is that it not only bypasses traditional publishing and the censorship of the marketplace, but also eludes the pedantic scrutiny of academic criticism that often seems so hostile to art. It can be argued, for instance, that over the past two decades art and literary critics who identify themselves as postmodernists have had a tendency to appropriate for themselves a role in the artistic process that is not theirs to assume. Devaluing the acts of creating and viewing, some critics have claimed that understanding a text requires a postmodern critical sensibility. Taken to an extreme, such a stance threatens to subvert the process of art itself, inserting an unnecessary filter between the viewer and the viewed.

On-line fan-fiction writers and readers once again are claiming the pleasure of the artistic experience without regard for those critics who in judging artistic works would use nonartistic standards more in line with social science than with aesthetics. Whereas critics such as Marilyn Farwell are trying to find a consensus between lesbian-feminist and postmodern critics on a definition of a lesbian narrative, the writers of fan fiction are busy appropriating the narrative itself.[32] The fan-fiction phenomenon illustrates what Farwell finds in Karl Kroeber's work: "the fundamental truth about stories," according to Kroeber himself, "is not structure but the fact they are told and retold. And by retelling they are changed."[33] As Farwell herself states, "Narrative is simply how stories are told, who tells them, and who acts in them."[34] Popular-culture critics, such as Helford, Jenkins, Inness, and Bacon-Smith, recognize that shows such as *XWP* allow for as many interpretations as there are viewers.[35] The fan fiction inspired by the show is an example of fans becoming, in Jenkins's words, "active participants in the construction and circulation of [the show's polysemic] textual meaning[s]."[36]

In on-line fan fiction, women are writing stories about women for women to read, as confirmed by the surveys of both writers and readers that I conducted for an earlier study.[37] In fan fiction, women writers reclaim and reinvent narrative structures such as the quest, placing women and the lesbian love between women at the center of the narrative. The inability to use strong women characters as protagonists, which Bacon-Smith found for slash writers of *Star Trek* and similar shows, has a remedy in the character of Xena. Bacon-Smith hypothesizes that fan-fiction authors' failure to use female heroes, such as Ellen Ripley in the film *Alien,* stems from their lack of "satisfying sexual relationships unless they learn to take second place in their own adventures." Furthermore, she argues that "nowhere in the movies nor certainly on TV does the writer find any model for the sexually involved homosexual couple as active co-heroes in their own story."[38] Bacon-Smith was writing in 1992; three years later *XWP* would fill that gap, and fan fiction would never be the same.[39]

Xena is not the first female warrior-hero, but she may be the most important to appear in a very long time because, as Inness argues, Xena "possess[es] the power to change how we construct and understand gender in real life.[40] Although some female quest stories exist, they have been neglected or ignored in most scholarly literature or, to repeat Pratt, are relegated to a secondary position.[41] The story of Isis is a prime example of a female-hero quest story that critics have turned into a male-hero quest story, as has been done to quest stories that tell of Inanna's descent into the underworld to find Tammuz, of Demeter's search for Persephone, of Pele's search for a home, and of Hiiaka's journey into the underworld to find her lover.[42] These ancient tales give great power to the female deities who are the protagonists, including the ultimate power of resurrecting the dead. At its very heart, the quest is a narrative written in blood and smelling of sex, glorying in violence, and rejoicing in the power to overcome death, and it is the primary narrative of *XWP*, both over the airwaves and on the page.

As with quest characters, the possibility for violence, even sexual violence, exists within Xena's dark complexity because of her power, her past, and her anger. In fan fiction, loving Xena is analogous to a type of sympathetic magic felt by those who worshiped the dark, powerful death goddesses Kali, Anat, and the Triple Goddess of the ancient Celts. But, as in ancient lore, to love someone powerful and dangerous comes with a price—a realization that fierceness can never be tamed completely. Gabrielle can feel safe and protected lying next to Xena, but once she has witnessed the power, fury, and delight of Xena in battle, she cannot help but retain that image. The potential for violence is always there, but the exhilaration of loving power and violence in such a beautiful package outweighs the anticipation of harm. As Paulina Palmer argues in *Lesbian Gothic*, "there is always a tension between pleasure and danger in sexual relations."[43] This tension is the space at which the TV show hints and that the fan fiction inhabits and explores.

Xena and Gabrielle's attraction for each other, as portrayed in fan fiction, is ultimately an ancient dance, composed of a dichotomy of dark and light, each seeking the other within that tension of "pleasure and danger."[44] It is a powerful combination with explosive chemistry. As Sharon Bowers has Liz say at the end of *Lucifer Rising:*

> Neither woman stood alone any longer—they had found in each other the component that their souls had been lacking. Through Jude, Elizabeth had known the darkness . . . and now, through her, Jude would know the light. Simple? Perhaps . . . but she firmly believed it would be enough to carry them through the days and nights to come. It would have to be.[45]

Whether as butch and femme, abuser and victim, or equal partners, Xena and Gabrielle are soul mates, a conclusion reached both on the show and in fan fiction. They are bound together through eternity in a balance of dynamic tension of the darkness of Xena's violence and the redeeming light of Gabrielle's love.

The *XWP* on-line community has appropriated the characters from the TV show, liberated the classic quest narrative from the cultural archives, and loosened the freshly imagined characters within the multiverse of cyberspace. Like Nietzsche's communal dream of tragedy,[46] Xena alternative fan fiction is a shared dream of the on-line community. Xena and Gabrielle—inhabiting their many incarnations in classic *XWP* episodes or in warlord/slave and Über Xena stories—range freely over time, space, and alternative realities. Xena's appearance on TV and proliferation in cyberspace has signaled a significant shift in the archetype of the hero: a rediscovery of the hero's female face—Isis, Pele, Inanna, Demeter—and a reclamation of the violent heritage of goddesses drenched in blood, seeking revenge and resurrection for those they love. The goddesses who wielded sexual and creative power were as bloody as they were alluring because sex as celebrated by ancient religions was a dark and powerful force. The Christian patriarchy separated women and sex through the myth of the virgin birth, but also simultaneously separated women from the power and violence that once had been theirs to command through the worship of goddess avengers. The quest was usurped as a male prerogative, as was the power of resurrection. Xena reclaims the quest and presents the reality of women wielding violence and power and loving whom they choose—an image as powerful as those ancient goddesses, an image that is changing forever the way popular culture looks at women.

4

Love Is the Battlefield

The Making and the Unmaking of the
Just Warrior in *Xena, Warrior Princess*

KATHLEEN KENNEDY

Drawing from myth, history, and science fiction, *Xena, Warrior Princess* (here-after *XWP*) has captured the imagination of Western women, young and old alike. Xena's off-screen popularity and on-screen mastery of the warrior's fighting skills have propelled her to the head of the class of the new female warrior who has become a staple of popular culture since the mid-1990s. *XWP* blends camp with a strong moral message about violence, atonement, and the redemptive power of love. Because Xena's story is set in ancient Greece and Rome—the so-called origins of the West—and evokes most of the founding myths of Western civilization, it offers viewers and critics alike the opportunity to assess and perhaps even critique the patriarchal and imperialist history of the Western hero.

The meaning of Xena's quest, life, and death promises to become a contro-versial and compelling subject among feminist critics not because it is a feminist show, although an argument can be made that it is a popular represen-tation of liberal feminism.[1] Xena's story is interesting to feminist critics because it retains moments of hybridity, a quality that resists purity in favor of a contin-uous fusing, intermingling, and mixing of differences.[2] This mode of concep-tualizing difference enables *XWP* to explore complex and sometimes contradictory meanings of love and to challenge pivotal patriarchal, racialist, and violent legacies of the Western just warrior.

The author wishes to thank Alison Futrell, Helen Caudill, Frances Early, and Midori Takagi for their comments on an earlier draft of this essay.

By facing two seemingly opposite directions at once—east and west—this chapter explores the meaning of *XWP*'s investment in redemptive love and that investment's challenge to the violence embedded within the Western warrior tradition. Simultaneously "looking" east and west reflects the contradictory positioning of groups that both challenge their role as the colonized and at the same time participate in imperialism.[3] As *XWP* faces west, it offers a sustained critique of the male warrior story—in particular its embedded misogyny and its emphasis on the violent conquest of others. But when *XWP* faces east, its legacy is more ambivalent as it carries the burdens of Western imperialism.[4] Xena herself enters the East as the "Destroyer of Nations" and eventually dies there for her imperialist sins. Although she is able to negotiate and change her history and perhaps that of the Western heroes of violence, vengeance, and self-annihilation when she faces west, she cannot escape her imperialist history when she faces east.

Facing West

When we first meet Xena in *Hercules: the Legendary Journeys,* she is an evil warlord bent on world conquest. Her murderous reign ends, however, when Hercules "unchains her heart."[5] Xena's origins are initially in Hercules' quest. There, she serves as a conduit through which he achieves legendary status. But *XWP* rescues Xena from this fate by reinventing her origins in a multicultural tradition of warrior women such as Egypto-Celtic M'lila; Akemi, a Japanese girl who kills her father; Lao Ma, a Chinese concubine; and Cyane, an Amazon queen. From these women, Xena learns her fighting skills and uncovers her potential to love unselfishly. These qualities lay the foundation for her reemergence as a self-reflective, just warrior and hold essential knowledge about her destiny. Both M'lila and Lao Ma convey to Xena knowledge of her destiny that otherwise would be incomprehensible to her.[6] This multicultural legacy is key to the show's construction of the just warrior. Unlike the traditional Western warrior, who must reinforce boundaries between East and West, Xena must learn from and incorporate the dreams and values of women of color into her quest to achieve her full potential.[7] As I argue later in the chapter, that border crossing, although fraught with difficulties, is essential to the show's construction of redemptive love.

The final link in this legacy is Gabrielle, a peasant girl who travels with Xena to escape village life. Gabrielle's unconditional love, commitment to justice, and belief in the possibilities of nonviolence complete Xena's transformation from a killer into a just warrior. Gabrielle's gift for gab and her naïveté initially are running jokes on the show, but Gabrielle quickly matures into a sage partner for Xena. She learns fighting skills after the Amazons adopt her and develops into a reluctant warrior who is able to defeat even the most experienced of Xena's foes. Her growing self-awareness leads her to critique Xena's quest when she disagrees with the moral implications of its direction. By the end of the first season (1995–96), Xena credits Gabrielle with her salvation, and in the final season (2000–2001) she introduces Gabrielle as her "soul mate."[8]

A number of critics, some fans, and even producer Liz Friedman define Xena and Gabrielle as a butch/femme couple, a queer hybrid in which desire and love set different gender performances against each other.[9] Queer hybrids explore "the way that gender b(l)ending [*sic*] and non-normative sexualities can denaturalize and transgress" Western sex/gender systems.[10] As Joanne Morreale has argued, the use of mimicry and parody in *XWP* illustrates "the absurdity of women as spectacle" by enabling "viewers to perceive the artifice of both masculinity and femininity."[11] Without challenging Morreale's basic thesis, this essay takes a slightly different approach than queer theorists usually explore in focusing their analysis on sexuality and its relationship to gender constructions.[12] Instead, I focus on how the show queers the meaning of love and how that queering enables it to reconstruct the gender and race relationships of Western heroic narrative.

Phrased most simply, the love between Xena and Gabrielle keeps Xena on the right side and prevents her from rekindling her role as conqueror of nations. Even Ares, the Greek god of war and Gabrielle's rival for Xena's love, acknowledges the unbreakable and eternal bond between Xena and Gabrielle. Believing that they have died, he articulates his newfound awareness to Xena's lifeless form: "You are with her now. I handled you all wrong. She knew what you needed—unconditional and unselfish love. I could never give you that. But I appreciated you in ways that she never could—your rage and beauty. When you sacrificed yourself for others, you were hers; when you kicked ass, you were mine. I love you, Xena."[13]

Over time the series increasingly cast Xena and Gabrielle's relationship as embodying the love capable of overcoming violence and oppression. When Eli, the prophet of the "way of love," tells Xena and Gabrielle that "your enduring faith in one another is the greatest miracle of all," he underscores the significance of their love to the program's pacifist message.[14] But as Ares' comments also underscore, that love is not pure but is instead implicated in the evil that it fights. Despite its sentimental moments, *XWP* resists reducing love between women to a magical sign; rather, it depicts that love and its power as deriving from a complex mixture of contradictory desires.[15]

These contradictory desires are a result of the different relationship each of these women has to evil. Xena is a product of both love and hate. She cannot escape or for that matter repress her "dark side." When she does, she is impotent and unable to perform the warrior's tasks; her efforts to eliminate the darkness within thus jeopardize innocents. At the same time, Xena cannot surrender wholly to her "dark side" even when she fights for a just cause. When she gives in to that dark side, she commits horrific acts of violence not only on her enemies but also on Gabriel. Instead, she must integrate her "dark side" with "the way of love."

Gabrielle's purity initially distinguishes her from Xena. Preserving the purity of Gabrielle's faith in "the way of love" is one of the most important components of Xena's quest. The show suggests, then, that faith is the last bulwark against the warrior's ultimate triumph. Gabrielle's choice to live in Xena's world, however, makes this purity of purpose difficult to sustain. In one of the most disturbing and controversial episodes, Gabrielle loses her blood innocence when she is tricked into killing a member of a religious cult devoted to an evil god, Dahak. She then is raped by Dahak and forced to give birth to pure evil in the guise of a daughter whom she names Hope. Once Gabrielle loses her blood innocence, she is implicated in evil. That loss threatens the purity both of her belief in the way of love and of her love for Xena.

Gabrielle's inability to sustain her purity precipitates a crisis in her relationship with Xena that only her knowledge and acceptance of hybridity can resolve. Soon after her birth, Hope (who grows at an unnatural rate) allies with Xena's arch enemy, Callisto, and kills Solan, Xena's son. Blaming Gabrielle for her son's death, Xena ropes Gabrielle, ties her to the back of a horse, drags her through the countryside, and attempts to throw her off a cliff. They both tumble off the cliff and awake in the land of Illusia, where, after a number of false steps, they reject hate and reconcile. As critic Elyce Rae Helford suggests, this violence and Gabrielle's reconciliation with Xena in "The Bitter Suite" should give feminists pause. Helford reads in this reconciliation a dismissal of violence against women merely as "a product of a 'dark side' we possess."[16] But there is another plausible reading of this resolution. In the Xenaverse, love does not require the complete absence of darkness; in fact, *XWP* suggests that such purity is unsustainable in a world in which true heroes must confront evil. Instead, love derives from not allowing hate to control one's actions, relationships, and identity. The lesson Gabrielle and Xena learn in "The Bitter Suite" is how to love in a world in which purity is an illusion.

Illusia initially appears to offer Xena and Gabrielle an opportunity to return to the purity of their former selves. Here the show sets up an interesting dichotomy between the public life of the warrior and the tranquility and peaceful existence of domestic life. In Illusia, the villagers offer Gabrielle peace if she gives up her travels and returns to the domesticity of the village: "You and me love peace / with ducks and goats and geese / while the hours away baking bread, pitching hay / We love peace, peace, peace, simple joys that never cease." [17] Gabrielle's lost blood innocence, the villagers insist, is the result of a dangerous mixing of the public and masculine world of the warrior with the domestic and female world of the village. Like the New Right, the villagers promise Gabrielle security and safety in exchange for returning home, where "nothing changes but the time."

In Illusia, however, "lies may be truth and truth may be lies." The purity that the villagers offer to Gabrielle, like Ares' promise to Xena of a return to pure will, cannot be recaptured. Callisto warns Xena away from such purity when Xena first arrives in Illusia: "You've tasted how evil and good coexist / the bitter and sweet of it / all in the lips that you kissed." Further, in their relationship, Xena and Gabrielle have entered "the realm of the oxymoronic constructions" that, in the words of critic Lynda Hart, "are not intelligible from the perspective of Western heterosexual courtship rituals and romantic commitments that link permanency not with change or innovation but with constancy and statism, not with tension and resistance but with merging, not with uncertainty but with reliability." [18] Their love upsets the apple cart not simply because it is lesbian, but more significantly because it embraces the contradictions and tensions of hybridity. *XWP* sometimes portrays Xena and Gabrielle's love in romantic and sentimental terms—for example, in the episode "The Bitter Suite," when the two women are rolling in the surf and promising never to let hate destroy their love. The show ultimately rejects such sentimentality in favor of a love laden with contradictions. Moreover, such tensions, in conjunction with a lack of purity in Xena and Gabrielle's relationship, enables the show to imagine alternatives to the Western heroic narrative and its compulsory heterosexuality, patriarchy, and the violent conquest of others.

Even after "The Bitter Suite" aired, *XWP* remained ambivalent about love's hybrid or contradictory, complex nature. The show attempted to find a workable pacifism for Gabrielle in divine love. In the episodes of its final three seasons (1998–2001), *XWP* offers an escape for humans from this painful hybridity through the mysterious god of love. While in India, Gabrielle and Xena meet Eli, a messianic figure whose commitment to absolute pacifism and the "way of love" threatens the militarist traditions of Greece and Rome. Gabrielle initially understands Eli's teachings as a powerful antidote to those of the warrior and briefly adopts his ethics of absolute pacifism. Eli's way offers Gabrielle the possibility of defeating evil with pure uncorrupted love. But this is a hope that neither Gabrielle nor *XWP* can sustain.

XWP ties Xena's quest to that of the god of love through the birth of a daughter, Eve. Xena originally defends Eli and his followers, motivated by her friendship with Eli, by Gabrielle's faith in Eli's methods of nonviolence, and by her belief in justice and hatred of Rome. Eve's birth reconfigures, at least temporarily, Xena's commitment to the god of love as she must change her role from defender of Eli's followers to the defender of the faith in order to save her daughter's life. Xena's pregnancy is both a gift from Callisto to atone for her role in the death of Xena's son and an effort to ensure Xena's loyalty to Eli's cult. Callisto is Xena's monstrous "daughter." After Xena's army accidentally kills Callisto's parents, Callisto dedicates herself to vengeance, re-creating herself in the image of the evil Xena and eventually forcing the reformed heroine to destroy her. Unable to forgive herself for Callisto's lost soul, Xena saves Callisto from eternal damnation by enabling her to forget her past and to love again by becoming an agent of the god of love. Callisto repays Xena by impregnating Xena with her spirit. She later explains her decision to Xena: "I can think of no greater mother than you; [with this child] we both gave back what we once took from each other"—that is, the ability to love and to experience the love of a mother.[19] Eve's birth intimately ties Xena's past and future together because she is both the reincarnated spirit of the deadliest product of Xena's "dark side" and the new messiah who will bring about a world ruled by love rather than by warriors.

But Eve's birth also threatens to contain Xena's quest as the show comes dangerously close to placing humankind's hope for a peaceful future within the hands of a male deity similar to the Judeo-Christian God.[20] Xena's defense of her daughter makes her more vulnerable than she was earlier, and she must rely on male intervention (from Eli, Ares, and Octavius) in a manner that is unnecessary when she fights for other causes. Her role in the mysterious god of love's plan is likewise contingent on her role as Eve's mother. She receives the power to kill gods because she is "the mother of the messenger," and should her daughter die, she will lose that power. Indeed, one wonders if her pregnancy is meant specifically to ensure her loyalty and to contain her rebellion within his divine plan. With Eve's birth and Xena's destruction of the Olympian gods, *XWP* flirts with offering divine love and perfection as an antidote to the warrior tradition.

In its final season, the series rejected divine love as the salvation for humankind when Xena refuses to sacrifice her family in exchange for the god of love's promises of purity and salvation. She explicitly breaks with the god of love when his disciple, the archangel Michael, threatens her family in his effort to destroy Caligula. To bring about Caligula's downfall, Michael elicits Xena's help. When Xena does not kill Caligula immediately, Michael convinces Eve to martyr herself, expecting that Eve's sacrifice will force Xena to kill Caligula and, like Eli's martyrdom, turn the populace even further against Rome and its warrior traditions. Michael then attempts to assassinate Aphrodite, who in her insanity is giving Caligula her godhood.

Enraged by Michael's interference and callous disregard for Eve's and Aphrodite's lives, Xena foils his plans and explains to him precisely where her loyalties lie: "First you try to get Caligula to kill Eve to force my hand, and now you go after my girlfriends."[21] Michael and, by extension, the god of love disregard Xena's commitment to her family and friends when they demand that she sacrifice Aphrodite for the god's divine plan. They fail to account for the fact that Aphrodite previously had earned Xena's loyalty when she protected an injured Gabrielle during Xena's epic battle with the Olympians. During that final conflict, Aphrodite chose to save Gabrielle's life, though she knew that Xena's success would end the reign of the Greek gods. This choice integrated Aphrodite into Xena's family; and as a member of Aphrodite's "family," neither Xena nor Gabrielle will sacrifice her.

Once Xena turns against Michael, Eli takes away her power to kill gods, and both Xena and *XWP* part company with the god of love and his promise of divine perfection. Interestingly, when Aphrodite loses her godhood, all of humankind loses its ability to love, including Eli's followers. Xena restores love to the world by making Aphrodite a god once again, not by making amends with the god of love. The show's decision to remake Aphrodite as the goddess of love refashions patriarchal myths in which the feminine principle is associated with a minimized physical eroticism, whereas masculinity and male deities foster "pure" intellectual ideals of abstract love. Aphrodite earns her divinity, in spite of her continuing imperfections, because of her unselfish love for Gabrielle. Furthermore, rather than the coldly divine perfection of Eli's "way of love," the love that Aphrodite offers the world is bittersweet, containing within it desire, jealousy, and rage as well as warmth, affection, tolerance, and positive human emotion. Like the Olympian gods, the god of love falls from grace because to obtain divine perfection he demanded the sacrifice of family and the subjugation of the individual. In Xena's world, love is rooted in concrete relationships among women and in devotion to family and friends.

Facing East

When Xena leaves Greece and Rome, it is usually to repair the damage of her imperialist past. In a series of flashbacks, we learn that as the Destroyer of Nations the evil Xena had traveled east to Chin (the precursor to modern-day China) and Japan. There, she left a legacy of bloodshed, tortured souls, and political unrest. During her travels, she also fell in love with two women, Lao Ma and Akemi. At each woman's request, she returns to Chin and Japan to undo the damage of her imperialist past. In her return trips to Asia, *XWP* explores the consequences of imperialism and the possibility of a Western hero influenced and loved by powerful women of color. This love offers to Xena a new model of heroism and spiritual fulfillment that is unavailable to her in the West.

At the same time, *XWP* does not escape Orientalist thinking, an aspect of Western imperialism most prominently conceptualized by Edward Said. He defines Orientalism as the discourse by which the West dominates, restructures, and gains authority over the Orient and, by extension, over all those areas of the world viewed as non-Western. As produced within European discourses, the Orient is a reflection of and essential to the construction of Western identity and ensures the "positional superiority" of the West vis-à-vis the Orient.[22] According to feminist postcolonial critics, Western feminists participate in Orientalism by supporting imperialist projects and by producing homogenized, monolithic, and muted images of third-world women in need of rescue. Western feminists have tended to represent themselves as the sole authorities on feminism and have positioned themselves as leaders of the global women's movement, resulting in the suppression of third-world women's agency and voice. They traditionally have constructed third-world women as "other," incapable of obtaining the status of first-world women because of what are perceived to be the unusual harshness of the Orient's patriarchal structures and their lack of a feminist consciousness.[23]

Central to the project of Orientalism is the West's invention of the East as "a place of romance, exotic beings, [and] remarkable experiences."[24] Gender plays a prominent role in that invention as the West constructs the East as soft, fragrant, mysterious, seductive, and essentially female. *XWP* portrays the East as all of these things. When Xena leaves Greece and Rome, the liminality that already exists there is even more pronounced, especially in the use of magic, movement across boundaries of life and death, and transcendence of human physical limitations. Equally significant, the East serves as a possible place of spiritual rebirth for Xena. Her love for Eastern women and her mastery of their secrets enable her to transcend the limitations of her body and the impurities of her soul.

Unlike many Orientalist texts, however, *XWP* ascribes agency to Asian women, an agency that is essential to the manner in which the show constructs love as an antidote to violence of the just warrior. Lao Ma is one of the most intriguing and powerful characters in the Xenaverse. Her wisdom (identified as the Tao Te Ching) forms the foundation of Chinese thought, and she is the one person Xena cannot defeat in battle. Nor does she depend on Xena for a feminist critique of her culture's patriarchal structures. When Ming Tzu questions her loyalty for hiding Xena, Lao Ma reminds him of the sexual exchange at the heart of their relationship: "I was your courtesan, and you sold me. You expect loyalty?"[25] In spite of Chinese prohibitions against women rulers, Lao Ma has devised an ingenious plan to rule the Kingdom of Lao by keeping her evil and tyrannical husband in a coma. Her way offers to Xena an alternative model of heroism and love that she ultimately must incorporate in order to fulfill her destiny.

Long before Xena had met Gabrielle, Lao Ma had offered Xena the opportunity to "let go of all [her] hatred forever."[26] Her love for Xena and Xena's love for her duplicate the redemptive love that Gabrielle offers. Upon her return to Chin, Xena explains to Gabrielle that although she failed to take advantage of the opportunity to let go of hate, Lao Ma nonetheless saved, in Xena's words, "not just my life. She saved my soul, my spirit, my entire being."[27] Gabrielle recognizes that Lao Ma potentially might displace her, later confessing to Xena that she had sabotaged Xena's initial efforts to kill Ming T'ien because "I hated you for loving someone else."[28] By loving Xena and teaching her a way to stop hating, Lao Ma laid the foundation for Xena's redemption.

The model of heroism that Lao Ma offers Xena is fundamentally different from the model of the Western just warrior. Lao Ma explicitly rejects key components of that quest, notably individual self-actualization, and, through example, she reinforces the need for the just warrior to become one with others rather than, as in the Western tradition, to separate herself from others. For example, Lao Ma records her wisdom in her husband's name, explaining to Xena that "this wisdom comes from heaven; it doesn't matter who gets credit."[29] Similarly, Lao Ma rules the Kingdom of Lao through her husband, once again telling Xena (in the same episode) that credit is not important as long as "good is done." Lao Ma's heroism is motivated and achieved by eradicating the will to power, not by claiming that will for one side or the other, as does the Western just warrior.

As Xena later acknowledges, Lao Ma's way gave her the only chance she ever had of completely eradicating her dark side, a chance that not even Gabrielle can give her. Xena's failure to accept Lao Ma's way not only condemns her to living with her dark side but also destroys Lao Ma's plans for peace: "She [Lao Ma] had such dreams of peace for her land and for my soul," Xena explains to Gabrielle, "and I ruined them all."[30] In spite of Lao Ma's wisdom, her agency is limited by both the patriarchal traditions of Chinese society and Xena's imperialist brutality. In showing the consequences of Xena's violence, the show undergoes a self-reflective examination of Western imperialism.

Nonetheless, by reinforcing Lao Ma's dependency on Xena, the show privileges the (reformed) Western hero. Lao Ma ultimately must rely on Xena to fulfill her dreams for Chin and for her children. Lao Ma is unable to kill Ming T'ien, even as he prepares to execute her and rule Chin as an evil tyrant. Instead, she sends for Xena to "make the green dragon small."[31] On another occasion, she again must send for Xena, this time to stop her evil daughter, Pao Ssu, from using gunpowder and her wisdom to conquer the world. Xena initially defeats Pao Ssu by becoming one with Lao Ma's good daughter, K'ao Hsin in the practice of Lao Ma's wisdom. As the camera shoots Xena and K'ao Hsin from the side, they are virtually indistinguishable. In this scene, Xena has obtained a moment of hybridity; her love for Lao Ma has enabled her to become one with K'ao Hsin. Here she is neither Eastern nor Western, but instead a hybrid who disrupts rather than reinforces boundaries between the Occident and the Orient. But this moment of hybridity is short-lived. It is Xena alone who masters Lao Ma's wisdom and turns Genghis Khan's army to stone, while K'ao Hsin remains below ground bringing villagers to safety.

The Western hero's ability to master the powerful secrets held by Asian women is an essential component of Orientalist ideology. True to form, to become fully human, Xena must discover the Orient hidden behind a woman's veil; this discovery, however, confirms only her own humanity, not that of Asian women. Asian women instead fulfill their historical destiny by revealing their secrets to the Western subject.[32] In this sense, *XWP* does not seek an authoritative Asian woman's voice, but rather a confirmation of Western subjectivity, deploying, in Leela Gandhi's word, "the difference of the 'third-world woman' as grist to the mill of Western theory [or in this case, Western heroism]."[33]

Furthermore, Orientalism depicts Asian women's efforts to resist revealing their secrets (as symbolized in the veil) as a source of danger for the Western hero. Asian women's supposed duplicity is a common theme in Western popular culture.[34] Akemi represents the quintessential veiled Asian woman whose secrets threaten to undo the Western hero and whose duplicity some of Xena's fans blame for their hero's death. Through prostrations of love, Akemi twice tricks Xena into helping her destroy her evil father, and this deception does set in motion the events that lead to Xena's death. Although Akemi's love for Xena masks deadly secrets, *XWP* does not portray Akemi herself as evil or her love for Xena as disingenuous. The show instead depicts Akemi as caught in a tragic plot; she is trapped in her culture's code of honor and vengeance, from which there is no escape.

The show's Orientalism stems less from its depiction of Akemi's deceit than from its portrayal of Japanese society as hopelessly caught in this patriarchal cycle of vengeance and honor. *XWP* consistently portrays vengeance as a destructive force rather than as a restoration of social or personal balance. When Xena is faced with a similar burden in "The Furies," she is able to escape by subverting the patriarchal codes of Western civilization. Akemi has no such power, and even Xena is helpless in the face of Japanese patriarchy. However, in Japan, the only way Xena can atone for her imperialist ways is to recognize and respect that culture's value of vengeance.

Perhaps I am guilty of Orientalist thought in my expectation that the Western feminist hero and her values should be able to conquer the patriarchal traditions of the East without paying a price for her imperialist legacy. Xena's death in Japan also might be read as a commentary on the cost of imperialism. Furthermore, the show might be inviting the view that the Western hero ultimately cannot unmask the secrets of an Eastern culture and must defer to Akemi's choice to uphold those values. Xena herself must embrace Akemi's worldview. Such a reading encourages a realistic appraisal of the limits of the Western hero. Her way is neither universally applicable nor universally desirable.

But this type of relativist thinking alone does not atone for an imperialist past because it does not question the Western hero's values themselves, only whether they are universally applicable. Does *XWP* problematize these values in its critique of imperialism? To answer this question we must look at the moment of Xena's death in the opening of "Friends in Need, Part II." Faced with an unstoppable invading army, Xena touches off an explosion that obliterates a large portion of that army. During this explosion, the camera cuts to a view from space that shows a mushroom cloud and then returns to a shot on land that shows a shock wave striking Gabrielle and the enemy army. The allusion to the atomic bomb is unmistakable. For Americans who supported dropping the atomic bombs, Japan's imperialist and fascist traditions justified President Truman's order to kill thousands of civilians in Hiroshima and Nagasaki. The violence embedded in Xena's heroic quest likewise is justified by the necessity to eradicate evil in all its forms—in this case, an invading army bent on conquest and murder.

Given the show's pacifist message, however, the allusion to the atomic bomb may be a warning, a statement about where the way of the warrior will lead eventually. Furthermore, when placed within the context of Xena's own act of violence that results in the unintended death of thousands of innocents, the atomic bomb imagery also might be read as signaling the death of the Western hero's claim to just violence. The battle scene that follows the "A-bomb" is one of the series' most gruesome; Xena is pierced by arrows from thousands of assailants she cannot see and eventually is beheaded, here evoking grisly images of Vietnam, a place where Americans and many of their Western allies lost their innocence and claim to just violence. Xena's death in this battle is a conscious act of suicide, a recognition that the violence she committed in the Orient was "special." She must die in order to save the souls of those she has murdered inadvertently by touching off her own firestorm in a moment of rage and grief against those who caused her to lose Akemi's soul. This act of sacrifice and love dismantles the Western just warrior but ultimately redeems Xena as the show rejects her way in favor of that of the Eastern woman who must sacrifice her soul to challenge the patriarchal traditions of Japanese society. In her death, Xena becomes part of Akemi's quest, thereby losing the authority she once claimed over the heroic tradition of Eastern women such as Lao Ma. With her death, the Western hero "loses [her] unequivocal grip on meaning and finds [her]self open to the meaning of the other."[35]

The discovery that *XWP* posits the "way of love" over that of the warrior is not remarkable, but this chapter has attempted to demonstrate that the show's understanding of love itself is more complex and potentially more disruptive to patriarchal and imperialist traditions of the West than its overly sentimental moments alone suggest. On one level, the show draws from pacifist traditions that underscore the redemptive power of love and the destructive power of hate on the warrior.[36] But despite its efforts to ground this pacifist message in a pure and divine love, the show cannot sustain this theme. Instead, *XWP* offers a realist concept of love as the embodiment of concrete relationships between women, their friends, and their families. This vision of love, the show suggests, possesses the power to redeem us from the violence of myth and history.

PART TWO

Buffy the Vampire Slayer

Buffy *the Vampire Slayer* (first aired in 1997 and still running) like *Xena, Warrior Princess,* creates a female mythological tradition. Buffy Summers is part of a female lineage of vampire slayers who protect the world from evil by slaying vampires and other monsters. Buffy is joined in her mission by "the Scooby Gang," a group of unconventional friends anchored by Rupert Giles, Buffy's fatherly, eccentric watcher-guide.

On a day-to-day level, *Buffy* traces the journey of the slayer and her friends through high school and into young adulthood. Each new encounter with demons represents a problem faced by ordinary young people, allowing the show to explore complex social issues such as suicide, youth violence and alienation, violence against women, sexual codes and identity, moral ambiguity, and the sudden death of friends and families. Underlying the show's campy humor and violent encounters are strong moral messages about the importance of friendship and the social consequences of suburban alienation. As Buffy and her friends negotiate their unique roles and identities, they must come to grips with their social responsibilities; they also must accept that these responsibilities both set them apart from their colleagues and require that they make sacrifices for just causes.

5

The Female Just Warrior Reimagined

From Boudicca to Buffy

FRANCES EARLY

The critically acclaimed horror-adventure series *Buffy the Vampire Slayer* features witty dialog, dark campy action, ingenious plot devices and special effects, and likable characters. Critics often identify the petite, blond (white), and feisty protagonist, Buffy Summers, played adroitly by Sarah Michele Gellar, as a role model for young women: competent, responsible, assertive, and confident, albeit appealingly flawed. In this vein, Joss Whedon, the much-quoted series creator, has articulated his wish to reach boys as well as girls: "If I can make teenage boys comfortable with a girl who takes charge of a situation without their knowing that's what's happening, it's better than sitting down and selling them on feminism."[1]

Programs such as *Buffy* portend a shift in gender representation in popular culture that invites critical study. As noted in the introduction to this anthology, scholars such as Sherrie Inness in her recent study *Tough Girls: Women Warriors and Wonder Women in Popular Culture* have drawn attention to the widespread appeal of indomitable, uncompromising female heroes—often appearing in warrior roles—who challenge understandings of what it means to be a woman in contemporary times.[2] The phrase *woman warrior* resonates with culture critics and media pundits, but, to date, the treatment of the

I thank my daughter, Jasmine Figg, for introducing me to Buffy and the Slayerettes. I also am grateful for insights on *Buffy* that members of my "Women, War, and Peace" class shared with me. I owe a large debt to Jennifer Barro, my valued research assistant, for her assiduous and at times inspired help. I appreciate the critical comments Jennifer, Kathleen Kennedy, and Kathleen McConnell made on an earlier version of this essay. The Social Sciences and Humanities Research Council of Canada generously supported this project.

woman warrior as a theme in its own right in shows such as *Buffy the Vampire Slayer* has been slight.[3]

Feminist scholar Elizabeth Grosz has noted perceptively that "*any* text can be read from a feminist point of view, that is, from a point of view that brings out a text's alignment with, participation in, and subversion of patriarchal norms."[4] In this essay, I present a feminist reading of *Buffy the Vampire Slayer*, examining in particular how *Buffy* as text navigates through and around the mythic and historic image of the female just warrior. From this vantage point, I explore some of the ways the creator and writers of *Buffy* promote possibilities for disrupting dominant and deeply encoded discourses about men and women and about warmaking and peacemaking in contemporary North American society. I argue that a dynamic tension between warriorism and pacifism informs the *Buffy* narrative.

In this context, literary scholar Sharon MacDonald's concept of "open images" has been helpful in framing a reading of *Buffy* as a narrative of a disruptive female just warrior. MacDonald observes that "imagery is by no means a purely superficial phenomenon [but is rather] the means through which we articulate and define the social order and nature." She identifies "closed images" as analogous to symbols and ideals or stereotypes that appear fixed in public consciousness. Open images, in contrast, "are to be interpreted, read, and to an extent repopulated [and] the form of condensation that they employ [is] not meant to reflect or define the social life itself."[5] The fluidity of open images makes them unsettling to the way things are, and they permit their creators to focus on human agency and the potential for intentional social change.

❯ ❯ ❯

The war narrative and the male warrior hero have always held pride of place in Western mythology and history.[6] The few women who have achieved warrior status in this hegemonic war chronicle have been portrayed as exceptional "armed maidens of righteousness," as illustrated in the mythologized stories of the Celtic queen Boudicca, the Old Testament avenging Judith, and Joan of Arc. Such female heroes have not been permitted to form a tradition of their own except as temporary warrior transgressors.[7] Further, although honored as virtuous viragos, women warriors also have been viewed as inherently disruptive to the patriarchal social order; their stories often have been denigrated in or erased from the historical record. Negative images of women warriors have served concurrently as a foil to the male just warrior tradition, with the man-hating Amazon providing a case in point.[8]

Thanks to the recent and burgeoning scholarship on women's historic re-lation to war, we now possess some understanding of the woman warrior tradi-tion, especially in Western culture.[9] As historians of women bring to light this largely buried story of women warriors, feminist theorists in a wide range of fields are benefiting from their empirical findings and are attempting to gener-ate new meanings from this enlarged historical legacy. However, this project is like the effort of swimming against a strong current. Feminist political theorist Jean Elshtain states that "the woman fighter is, for us, an identity *in extremis*, not an expectation." She also identifies an uphill struggle to bring history's "Fe-rocious Few" to visibility: "Functioning as compensatory fantasy or unattain-able ideal, tales of women warriors and fighters are easily buried by standard repetitions. Framed by the dominant narrative of bellicose men/pacific women, our reflections often lack sufficient force to break out, remaining at the level of fragile intimations. As representation, the Ferocious Few are routinely eclipsed by the enormous shadow cast as the Noncombatant Many step into the light."[10]

In addition to the problem of breakthrough, problems arise even when tales of the Ferocious Few come into play. Art historian and critic Marina Warner, who has studied the image of the female form in Western culture and has authored a book about Joan of Arc, contends that women in contempo-rary society are drawn to and thereby trapped in a "phallocentric" warrior's world: "The armed maidens of righteousness and their present day dramatiz-ers . . . remain prisoners of the fantasy [of the male warrior-hero] even in the midst of trying to turn it upside down."[11] Warner's statement echoes post-modern theorist Michel Foucault's warning that marginalized people can be drawn to the power of "reverse discourse," whereby they find themselves seek-ing legitimacy "in the same vocabulary, using the same categories by which [they were] disqualified."[12]

Heeding Warner's and Foucault's observations, one might be tempted to dismiss *Buffy the Vampire Slayer* as a compensatory fantasy for young women and, by extension, Buffy herself as a protagonist whose persona reinforces rather than challenges conventional gender expectations. However, my femi-nist reading of this program presents another interpretation. I hope to demon-strate that Buffy functions effectively as an open image of an empowered transgressive female just warrior in contrast to the closed image of the iconic male just warrior. *Buffy,* as program, undermines the credibility of an abstract notion of the male soldier-hero through parody, self-deprecating humor, and ironic distancing from gender stereotypes. Further, by the manner in which it recasts just warrior material, *Buffy* offers an incipient pacifist critique of the inevitability of war and the violence it engenders.

➤ ➤ ➤

Whedon's Buffy character first appeared in the 1992 high-camp film *Buffy the Vampire Slayer* and reflected both the screenwriter's attraction to the gothic horror story and his anger at the omnipresent reality of male violence against women: "This movie was my response to all the horror movies I had ever seen where some girl walks into a dark room and gets killed. So I decided to make a movie where a blonde girl walks into a dark room and kicks butt instead." [13] Whedon is a feminist and has made a conscious effort to create a feminist character. He finds strong women interesting and has commented that "there are a lot of ways to break new ground without having original thoughts." [14]

Whedon's decision to cast Buffy, the warrior, as a small-boned, slender, stylishly feminine, white, suburban, middle-class young person points to perceived limits of what is currently acceptable for representations of young female heroes in the market-driven, consumerist, and white-privileged medium of television. The discipline of white femininity in Western culture has a hegemonic power that confounds even its most incisive critics. Nonetheless, according to feminist scholar Dorothy Smith, femininity understood as a "distinctively textual phenomenon" and as discourse can be analyzed and confronted. Texts possess a kind of permanence in the public mind, whereas discourse is constituted more broadly to include people's "actual practices and activities," which in specific settings can serve as sites of resistance to "the textual dimensions of social consciousness." [15] Smith's conceptualization of how individuals manage to contest disempowering discourses finds a complimentary resonance in feminist philosopher Elizabeth Grosz's notion of corporeality. She conceives bodies as simultaneously marked by society (inscribed bodies) and actively in tension with or in struggle against society (desiring, inscribing bodies). "Though marked by law," Grosz states, bodies "make their own inscriptions on the bodies of others, themselves, and the law in turn." [16]

Smith's and Grosz's insights help frame a way to perceive Buffy as a complex subject who is at least partially aware that she is marked by societal prescriptions of femininity as well as by the reverse discourse of the "kick-ass" tough gal. Plot structures, action, and dialog reinforce the notion that Buffy exists as a "desiring body" and takes pleasure in exploring her power (agency) in the world. Regardless of context, Buffy's body is wedded to her sense of self and is always relevant to the action at hand. Buffy's calling as a special kind of just warrior who is honor bound to protect humanity and to sacrifice for the greater cause of fighting evil exists in tension with her own desires, including erotic desires, and with her longing to enjoy a normal life.

Buffy's body has an essentialist attribute: she is stronger than others because she is the Chosen One. Yet Buffy's body-self serves as a powerful and fluid open image, too, one that often escapes the essentialist bonds of slayer status or even male-identified warriorism. Buffy fights hand to hand and is stalwart like a man, but she has an acrobatic agility and grace that cannot be easily categorized as either stereotypically masculine or feminine. Furthermore, Buffy takes joy in physical training sessions that are presented as moments of intense concentration and sensual pleasure. Her inner circle of friends, the mixed-gender "Slayerettes" and her watcher-guide, Giles, appreciate Buffy's physicality and prowess, and they exhibit in their own fashion what Grosz terms "embodied subjectivity." Willow, for instance, Buffy's most enduring female friend, first appears in the series as a brainy and physically maladroit computer nerd; by the fifth season (2000–2001), she not only occasionally "kicks demon ass," but has honed her skills as an effective Wiccan and is exploring enthusiastically a new sexual relationship with a sister witch, Tara.

To maintain her balance and perspective and to resist identifying herself solely by her special slayer status, Buffy maintains an ironic distance from her warrior role even as she embraces it: "Destructo-Girl, that's me," she deadpans. "I kill vampires; that's my job," she announces laconically in another context. Further, although Buffy struggles, at times, with her unique fate, she always knows, in contrast to male friends and lovers, who she is and what she must do. In the first double episode of the series, for example, Buffy comments on her hometown's inept police force (a kind of army), noting that they cannot handle vampires: "They'd only come in with guns." Her Slayerette friend, Xander, draws on the masculinized Western fighter-hero motif, hoping to join Buffy in battle:

XANDER: So what's the plan, we saddle up, right?

BUFFY: [No.] I'm the slayer and you're not . . . Xander, this is deeply dangerous.

XANDER: I'm inadequate. I'm less than a man.
WILLOW [to Xander]: Buffy doesn't want you getting hurt.

In another circumstance, Angel, Buffy's brooding vampire lover in seasons two and three (1997–98 and 1998–99), comments that he is "scared" to go against a particular master demon, and soon thereafter, when Buffy vanquishes the demon in question, Xander declares: "Buffy's a superhero." In an episode during season three, Angel compliments Buffy for being "a real soldier." Buffy distinguishes in her own mind between soldiering and just warriorism and is not entirely comfortable with the appellation *superhero*. In response to Angel's comment about "real" soldiering, Buffy's response is to reply sardonically, "That's me, just one of the troops." Unlike her male comrades, Buffy eschews romantic or idealized perspectives on what it means to be a soldier, preferring instead to hint at the powerlessness and entrapment that are common features in the lives of ordinary soldiers.[17]

Buffy's character as a woman warrior and hero is counterpoised not only against males but also against nonconformist females whose rebellions are located outside the bounds of just warriorism as enacted by Buffy. For instance, Faith, bad girl extraordinaire who becomes a rogue slayer, is introduced in season three to represent Buffy's darker self. Buffy is drawn for a time to Faith's self-destructive tendencies and her eroticized joy in violence. They rob a sporting goods store to procure weapons, with Faith instructing Buffy that she should work on the principle "want, take, have." Buffy tells herself that she is justified in breaking the law because she has to "save the world."[18] However, she changes her mind when Faith inadvertently kills a human being, and the following exchange takes place between the two:

BUFFY: We help people; it doesn't mean we can do whatever we want.
FAITH: You're still not seeing the big picture, B. Something made us different. We're warriors, built to kill.
BUFFY: Built to kill demons. But that does not mean we can pass judgment on people, like we're better than anyone else.
FAITH: We are better. People need us to survive. And in the balance, nobody's going to cry over some random bystander who got caught in the crossfire.
BUFFY: I AM.
FAITH: That's your loss.[19]

Over several episodes, Faith continues her downward spiral, with Giles noting that she is in denial and Angel commenting that she now "has a taste" for killing. At the end of season three, Faith lies in a coma; she reappears briefly in season four (1999–2000) but leaves Sunnydale in a shaken state after a confrontation with Buffy. In this instance, Buffy has not been tempted by her heart of darkness, but it is hinted that Faith might return, thus ensuring that the Chosen One will face another test. Life is filled with uncertainty and holds no final answers, as the following discussion between Buffy and Giles during season two makes clear:

> B U F F Y: You know, it's just, like, nothing's simple. I'm constantly trying to work it out, who to hate or love . . . who to trust. . . . It's like the more I know, the more confused I get.
> G I L E S: I believe that's called "growing up."
> B U F F Y: I'd like to stop now, then, okay?. . . . Does it ever get easy?
> G I L E S: You mean life?
> B U F F Y: Yeah. Does it get easy?
> G I L E S: What do you want me to say?
> B U F F Y: Lie to me.[20]

This conversation between slayer and watcher-father evokes the pain of growing up in the context of the show's "high school is hell" motif. But this exchange also foreshadows what will come: Buffy must expect to face new adult challenges in the near future. Life will not become easier but rather more complicated and difficult as Buffy and her friends mature.

From the program's inception, plot action has pressed forward with clever and surreal "pow, slam, bang" slayer/demon encounters.[21] At the same time, a subtle pacifist-oriented sensibility has been woven into the ongoing *Buffy* narrative; in a fairly consistent manner, the Chosen One and her surrogate family, Giles and the Slayerettes, evince a tendency to eschew killing when possible and to solve problems nonviolently. In one show, for example, Buffy and her friends decide that a human rather than a demon is responsible for a girl's death, and they work to bring the murderer before the justice system.[22] In another situation, a telepathic Buffy discovers a plot to kill high school students. She saves the day when she apprehends a lonely and confused high school student who has ascended the school tower room: "I came up here to kill myself," he explains. Buffy speaks gently to this young man, empathizing with his pain and convincing him to put down his gun. She is pleased with the outcome, remarking after the danger has passed, "It's nice to be able to help someone in a non-slaying capacity."[23]

In *Buffy*'s fourth season, nonslaying becomes a stronger theme. Plots accentuate the private-public split in Buffy's life as issues focusing on intimacy and trust in personal relationships are set against the slayer's civic responsibility to keep evil at bay in the context of ambiguous ethical situations. The shape of evil shifts, too. Demons are no longer the unproblematized enemy or "other." Spike, for instance, an extraordinarily spiteful and clever vampire who combines a Bill Sykes menace with a Billy Idol sense of style and who is well known to Buffy and her friends, has been victimized—surgically modified—by the Initiative, a special-forces government unit whose mission is to destroy demons. Other vampires have cast out Spike, and though he hovers around the Scooby Gang and even occasionally comes to their aid, he is not a Slayerette and still professes to be their sworn enemy. In season five, he develops a crush on Buffy, muddying still further the concept of enemy.

Spike's predicament accentuates the Initiative's lockstep authority structure (introduced in season four) and its overriding of civil liberties. Buffy's unique slayer role is contrasted with that of the all-male commando squad that takes orders from Maggie Walsh, the intimidating civilian leader who oversees their work and symbolizes the male-identified woman par excellence. Riley Finn, the young military head of the squad and Buffy's new love interest, is drawn gradually into the Slayerette group as he comes to realize that the military system in which he has placed his trust has betrayed his ideals. In contrast to Riley, who is a nurturing and caring New Age man as well as an efficient soldier, his commando buddies are shown to be insensitive misogynists, suggesting that such values run deep in military institutions.

An interrogation of patriarchal arrangements of power in society, including military institutions, has been a persistent preoccupation in the *Buffy* series since its inception and becomes more pronounced beginning with season three. In a crucial episode, "Helpless," Giles, Buffy's official "watcher" who takes orders from the British-based Watcher's Council, is instructed to put Buffy through a frightening rite of passage that every slayer must experience on her eighteenth birthday. Under duress, he drugs Buffy without her knowledge to effect a temporary weakening of her slayer physical prowess; in such circumstances, her demon-fighting spiritual and mental powers can be tested. After she passes the ordeal, Giles is so ashamed of his act of betrayal that he tells Buffy what he has done. This experience changes Giles; he has no regrets, telling the elderly council member who comes to check up on him, "You are waging a war; she [Buffy] is fighting it." Giles is summarily fired as watcher because, as the council representative notes, he now has "a father's love for the child." In addition to the incipient critique of warmaking, with an allusion to the Vietnam War—it is the old men who send the young out to fight under false pretenses— a gendered pacifist message has been introduced: a man can reject war and soldiering in specific contexts, and he can serve in a nurturing parental role to protect a young person from being victimized by the war system as such.[24] Although the council attempts to replace Giles with another watcher, Buffy rejects the replacement. It is soon apparent that although Giles will continue to serve as a mentor and friend, Buffy will no longer accept uncritically authoritarian patriarchal rule as symbolized by the Watcher's Council.

In season four, Buffy's questioning of male-dominant societal structures continues, and she must face squarely, again at a personal level, their destructive potential. When she begins to pry too closely into Initiative leader Maggie Walsh's mysterious project room, which holds the potential for human annihilation, Walsh tries to have her killed. In stark ironic fashion and in contrast to Giles, the humane and loving father figure, Walsh is portrayed as the fearful, monstrous ur-mother who creates Adam, a cyborg monster set to destroy all life. Adam's murder of his mother-creator in his first moments of life underlines two of the show's key themes in season four: the destructive potential of military war machines and the gender-blind corrupting power of nonlegitimized military authority.

Walsh's unsuccessful attempt to have Buffy murdered unsettles the slayer but has a graver impact on Riley, whose allegiance to the unprincipled and dangerous Initiative director has resembled a child's faith in the worthiness of a "good" father or mother. Her actions throw Riley into crisis: "I don't know which team I'm on, who the bad guys are. Maybe I'm the bad guy. Maybe I'm the one you should kill."[25] In these circumstances, Buffy helps Riley work through his misplaced loyalty to Maggie Walsh and his naïveté about the Initiative and the military as an institution. Utilizing her developing nurturing skills, Buffy, with help from the Scooby Gang, assists Riley to emerge from his Initiative-structured world:

RILEY: That's what I do, isn't it? Follow orders?

BUFFY: You don't have to.

RILEY: Don't I? All my life that's what I've been groomed to do. . . . I just don't know if it's the right job anymore.

BUFFY: I know how you feel. Giles used to be part of this council, and for years all they ever did was give me orders.

RILEY: Ever obey them?

BUFFY: Sure. The ones I was going to do anyway. The point is, I quit the council. I was scared, but it's OK now.[26]

In a reversal of the male-protector scenario, Buffy then tells Riley reassuringly: "You've been strong long enough . . . I am going to help you."

In another episode with an interesting twist, Buffy must challenge the Watcher's Council, which now resembles a Mafia of the occult. Unlike Riley, Buffy is comfortable resisting a paramilitary force (the Watcher's Council) run amok; she is confident of her ability to take a stand against evil wherever it is found. By the conclusion of season four, Buffy's subjectivity has developed well beyond that preordained for the Chosen One. She is a complex individual with strong moral authority.

❧ ❧ ❧

From its beginnings in 1997, *Buffy the Vampire Slayer* has been engaged in developing both a playful and a serious consideration of gendered relations of power in contemporary North American society. The woman warrior leitmotif has served well the aims of the program. This recognizable symbol of female agency dovetails with the current fascination with tough women in popular culture and has permitted Joss Whedon and other *Buffy* scriptwriters to explore innovatively those processes through which gendered social scripts are enacted and contested. As an open-image fantasy of female resistance to patriarchal authority, *Buffy* helps to problematize the essentialized status of gendered physical attributes, notably by representing Buffy as an embodied subject who takes pleasure in aggressive behavior. The program also endeavors to call into question aspects of just warriorism by weaving a pacifist subtext into plot structures.

Perhaps the greatest strength of *Buffy the Vampire Slayer* is its creator and writers' ability to portray relations of power, especially gender relations, both as representational systems and as social processes that can be exposed, analyzed, and changed. In this sense, the program offers a hopeful discursive space for promoting new understandings about how individuals, in particular young people, can take charge of their own lives and, if so inclined, can choose to act in purposeful ways to create a more just and less violent world.

6

"If You're Not Enjoying It, You're Doing Something Wrong"

Textual and Viewer Constructions of Faith, the Vampire Slayer

SUE TJARDES

From its debut, *Buffy the Vampire Slayer* has sparked spirited conversations among public and academic audiences alike. Some authors celebrate Buffy as a role model for teenagers, recognizing the resonance of the high-school-as-hell metaphor; *George* magazine listed Buffy as one of the "most fascinating women in politics." [1] Other critics, however, deplore the program's hegemonic subtext, whether for the actors' conventionally constructed beauty or for what cultural critic Kent Ono calls "neo-colonial power relationships." The episodic subtly advocates, he argues, "a certain kind of violent aggression deployed by white females," working toward the "subordination and eventual elimination" of others, particularly people of color. [2]

Without challenging Ono's overall thesis, it is possible to argue that Buffy's "white-girl power" in fact is restrained and, moreover, that dominant readings (Buffy the vampire slayer as warrior or "grrl" hero) and oppositional readings (*Buffy the Vampire Slayer* as heteronormative, unself-consciously white, commodified text) falsely dichotomize what is largely a polysemic, open text, available for a variety of readings by a variety of active readers. A particularly available site for this argument is the character of Faith, whose nature, motives, and fate are posited and debated by both creators and viewers. [3]

Faith arrives in season three (1998–99), the second slayer to be activated by Buffy's momentary death during season one (1996–97). Originally conceived as a minor character, Faith proved so engaging that she became a major part of the third season's narrative arc. Buffy's status as just warrior is largely accepted in academic and popular press; Faith is a more provocative object because she illustrates the still-precarious position of a warrior woman balanced on these borders between good and evil. Socially, sexually, and morally ambiguous, her presence on the show and her journey through the season offer an opportunity not only to examine the construction of two warriors but also to explore the meanings that viewers make of the narrative and characters.

Science fiction and fantasy television has long been known for having devoted viewers who engage programs sincerely and thoroughly. These viewers already recognize what critic John Fiske calls television's "producerly" status: "the work of the institutional producers of programs requires the producerly work of the viewers and has only limited control over that work. The reading relations of a producerly text are essentially democratic, not autocratic ones. The discursive power to make meanings, to produce knowledges of the world, is a power that both program producers and producerly viewers have access to."[4]

The meaning of a show or episode, then, is a process that includes both the creator and the viewer: a cocreation, negotiation, or even struggle of sense making. Fiske notes that meanings are created not only from the level of the televised text itself, but from the level of secondary texts, such as industry publicity, and from a third level: the readings that people make of television, "the talk and gossip they produce."[5] All of these levels can be read against each other, creating a web of meanings that is at once hegemonic, constrained by genre and dominant ideology, and yet resistant and individual.

Clearly, tensions can result in this web of coproduced meanings. The role of readers or viewers conventionally has been taught as being a passive, reactive one, the text as an array of meanings for their deciphering. Most viewers recognize the cultural authority of the creator and the "author centeredness" of a correct reading. This author centeredness implies an ownership of text and meaning that then may be challenged by what Michal DeCerteau calls "poaching": an active appropriation of a text by readers. Cultural studies scholar Henry Jenkins uses this term in his work on fan-authored narratives, or "fan fiction." As fans write original works using authored characters, Jenkins argues, "[they] recognize that their relationship to the text remains a tentative one, that their pleasures often exist on the margins of the original text and in the face of the producer's own efforts to regulate its meanings." Fans are "acutely and painfully aware" that the characters and narratives legally and intellectually belong to the creators despite the viewers' strong attachment. The attitude toward the creators, he posits, can be worship or antagonism, as fans attempt to balance their conceptions of characters and plots with the creators' legal and cultural authority.[6]

In addition to poaching, viewers now negotiate meaning by "posting"—that is, commenting via the Internet. The pervasiveness of the Internet has magnified the significance of Fiske's secondary and tertiary levels of intertextuality in several ways. First and most simply, fan communities emerge and persist in cyberspace, allowing viewers to explore the pleasures of sense making with others outside of their own viewing group or at the workplace water cooler.[7] Second, electronic sites also provide fan fiction with faster and further availability than earlier print media and fan conventions. And third, the Internet has enabled communication, or at least the perception of communication, between creators and viewers. Viewers can question creator Joss Whedon or story editor Doug Petrie and attain a kind of dialogue. Access to creators' perspectives is far more available than earlier, and the communication among producers and viewers is perceived as more interactive. Although poachers still preface their fictions with acknowledgment of copyright ownership, comments posted by crew serve as evidence that both creators and viewers are participating in the production of meaning. Faith is a rich object for this meaning making, as sites such as Faithrocks.com attest: the Web site declares itself for "those want to go in there and make [the show] their own, like Henry Jenkins talked about."

From her first appearance on the show, Faith, played with flair by Eliza Dushku, is marked as an outsider. In the precredit sequence of "Faith, Hope, and Trick,"[8] the camera pans slowly across the Bronze (a popular spot where Sunnydale teens gather) as Faith dances in the foreground of a medium-long shot. Cordelia draws the group's attention to Faith's "slut" attire, and the subsequent shot of Faith and her dance partner confirms her as sexually aggressive: her clothes are tight; she is gyrating seductively with a partner who is not responsive; it is she who invites the vampire outside. The gang follows, only to watch rather than rescue as Faith casually dispatches the vampire. Her fighting and flip attitude leave the group gawking as the credits begin.

The next scene places Faith as the spatial and conversational center as she tells the entranced gang tales of alligator wrestling and nude slaying. Immediately she is placed in contrast to Buffy, seated directly opposite and in a lower chair: Faith is relaxed, loud, and bawdy, her gestures broad, whereas Buffy sits tightly and still, arms in. The group is highly attentive to Faith; even the laconic

Oz inquires as to her position on werewolves. Her flouting of decorum titillates the gang and unnerves Buffy, who sinks deeper into her chair as the scene proceeds; Faith is attractive but clearly other. Her sensuality and appetite are foregrounded as she devours appetizers, licking her fingers and remarking to Buffy, "Isn't it funny how slaying just makes you hungry and horny?" This line is one of the most quoted in viewer sites; it often is used as symbolic of Faith's attitudes. Although comically at Buffy's expense in this scene, the sentiment is echoed more darkly in later episodes.

Viewers frequently cite Faith's experienced sexuality, references to dropping out of school, and revealing clothing as evidence of a lower-class background, a status that further marks her as an Other among the stylish, privileged Scooby Gang. As a member of an underclass, Faith is already outside of the constraints of "proper" actions and responsibilities; her warrior status is thus less transgressive than Buffy's. This class and sexual border crossing allows Faith a freedom not available to Buffy; it also maximizes the pleasures of meaning making because much about Faith is left to viewers. She has no last name; she has no past except as a slayer. She is spatially unrestrained, moving freely through the town, library, and school. She appears briefly in several episodes, training or patrolling with Buffy, but is otherwise uninvolved in these narratives. One viewer Web site notes that she "disappears for several episodes, long enough for you to forget she exists." She is outside the group, whether through her volition or their exclusion. Poachers posit her background and class status, building from primary textual cues and supplying Faith with a fan-fiction childhood of neglect and abuse.

At first, Faith's social and physical voraciousness and confident warrior status seem to appeal to everyone except Buffy. Whereas Buffy has always longed for a "normal life," Faith is completely identified with and driven by her life as a slayer. When it is revealed that Faith was unable to stop the murder of her watcher, Buffy accepts this incident as the reason for Faith's "rage." If so, some viewers conclude, this aspect of Faith's history further proves her superior status: she is guilty of and angry at failing in her slaying responsibilities. Later she challenges Buffy to deny the urgency she feels while slaying: "Slaying's what we're built for. If you're not enjoying it, you're doing something wrong." [9] This certainty becomes enticing to Buffy, who reacts in this conversation as she reacted earlier to nice-guy Scott Hope's invitation to dance, with a demure smile and playful, sideways glances. One Web site touts this scene as proving Faith's security in herself and her slaying ability, while placing Buffy in a more hesitant, self-conscious position.

Secondary and tertiary cues attest to Faith's border status as well. The character and actor are absent from official publicity photos and Web site, although viewer Web sites about her proliferated quickly. Critics have noted Eliza Dushku's reluctance to be a series regular because of her desire to attend college.[10] The actor, like the character, stands outside the group. Secondary texts often mention that the Faith storyline was not predetermined; Whedon cites a lack of chemistry between the intended season villains (the mayor and Mr. Trick) as impetus for Faith's role in the narrative. He stresses the importance of Dushku in "finding" the character and in creating the concomitant darkness and vulnerability in Faith. He also admits, "we wanted to explore being a slayer—the power of it, the fun it could be, how intoxicating it could be. We used Faith as a vessel."[11]

The two slayers often are framed in two-shots that emphasize their note-for-note contrasts while simultaneously presenting them as equals. Buffy's light hair and clothing mark her as softer, whereas Faith slightly taller and larger frame stamp her as more aggressive. "We're the same, girlfriend, the Chosen Two," Faith tells Buffy.[12] Later, Buffy defends Faith to Willow: "In different circumstances, that could have been me."[13] Writer and producer Marti Noxon echoes Whedon's comment: "Faith was Buffy's shadow self, the expression of the darker side of what it might mean to be empowered as a slayer."[14] It seems obvious that Faith and Buffy are framed as opposite equals.

What this framing disguises, however, is the converse function of the Buffy/Faith contrast. With the exception of a single episode ("Bad Girls"), Faith is presented not as what Buffy might be, but as what she is *not* and never will be. Faith's willingness to conflate violence and sexuality, to attempt self-reliance and autonomy, and to exist as slayer-warrior is rejected, marginalized, and ultimately disciplined within the created world of the show. The borders she crosses are marked to restrain Buffy, the just warrior, who wears her slayer-warrior status with repression and unease.

This function is perhaps easiest to observe in their contrasting sexualities. Buffy's only sexual experience during the "Faith" era has been with Angel, her soul-laden vampire boyfriend. Whether in parody of the punished sexuality in slasher films or as a supernatural Romeo and Juliet, their lovemaking turns Angel to a soulless killer. This loss of innocence results in Buffy's return to innocence, as she wishes for a nice, safe dating life with the decidedly nonsexual Scott. Faith, as discussed earlier, is highly sexualized. Her sexual aggression is presented early on as scandalous but attractive, even when associated with violence. Her first seduction of Xander is prompted by violence but played comically as she throws him out afterward, clothes bundled in his arms, with a hurried, "That was great. I gotta shower."[15] More notably, her references to the "lust" that slaying brings and her sexualized movements when discussing slaying equate violence and sexuality, both eroticizing her use of violence and emphasizing the violence of her sexuality. This equation becomes overt midseason when in a breath Faith turns from seducing Xander to strangling him, continuing to kiss him as he chokes.

Some viewers interpret Faith's sexual appetites as gay or bisexual; fan fiction often poaches her relationship with Buffy as romantic, requited or not. These viewers cite Faith's tactile and verbal cues toward Buffy: affectionate touches, sustained eye contact, and frequent comments about sex are referenced as evidence of attraction. These readings offer a resistant construction of the season's events, with Faith's actions following from her love for and loss of Buffy. Whedon, in a post that is cited widely in Web and print sources, responds to one of these readings, playfully acknowledging the cocreation of the producerly text: "I just read the piece on Buffy and Faith . . . and by God, I think she's right! I can't believe I never saw it! (Actually, despite my facetious tone, it's a pretty damn convincing argument. But then I think that's part of the attraction of the Buffyverse. It lends itself to polymorphously perverse subtext. It encourages it. I personally find romance in every relationship, with exceptions; I love all the characters, so I say Bring Your Own Subtext!)"[16]

However viewers read Faith's sexuality, most regard it as important. Presented as playfully scandalous and attractive in early episodes, her aggression becomes more predatory, and she is punished through Buffy's betrayal and Angel's rejection and ultimately by a sexually charged near-death.

According to the reasoning within the narrative and most secondary texts, Faith's "downward spiral" is the result of her accidental murder of a human during a vampire fight. The "previously on Buffy" montage that begins each episode, for example, juxtaposes a clip of the slayers' conversation, cutting between extreme close-ups of the two as Buffy accuses, "You don't seem to get it, Faith. You killed a man," to which Faith replies, "No, you don't get it. I don't care." In voiceover, Giles asserts, "she's unstable." This condensed explanation is reasserted with each episode and becomes the dominant explanatory reading.

Some viewers, though, find evidence that Faith does show remorse over the deputy mayor's death, citing her "horrified" facial expression as she realizes she has stabbed a man or her murmur that "he just came out of nowhere" as she gazes at a picture of him after the killing. The encapsulated images of the pre-credit summary also obscure other scenes of conversation, such as a conversation in which Faith acknowledges that she is sorry and argues that the slayers' repeated saving of the world has left them "in the plus column":

> FAITH: You're still not seeing the big picture, B. Something made us different. We're warriors, built to kill.
> BUFFY: Built to kill demons. But that does not mean we can pass judgment on people like we're better than everyone else.
> FAITH: We are better. People need us to survive. And in the balance, nobody's going to cry over some random bystander who got caught in the crossfire.
> BUFFY: I am.
> FAITH: That's your loss.[17]

Giles, too, seems ready to "see the big picture," reminding Buffy that "a slayer is on the front line of a nightly war. It's tragic, but accidents happen." Some viewers find echoes of posttraumatic stress disorder in Faith's reaction and in Buffy, Xander, and Angel's attempts to "connect" with her and to correct her behavior. But Faith the warrior is unwilling or unable to respond "appropriately" through feminized dialogue and emotional processing when individuals offer or force the opportunity on her. She preempts Buffy's attempt at reflective listening by asserting, "Whatever. I'm not looking to hug and cry and learn and grow."[18] It is Xander's offer of help that leads to her attack on him.

Angel's intervention is the most extensive and in some ways the most polysemic. "She killed a man," he tells Buffy, "That changes everything for her. . . . she's got a taste for it now." His subsequent monologue to Faith, who is shackled to the wall, can be read as a celebration of violence and power. This scene is the first time these motives have been articulated thoroughly, and although Angel attributes the feelings to Faith, it is he who voices them with the camera remaining on him throughout: "I know what it's like to take a life. To feel the future, all the possibilities, snuffed out by your own hands. I know the power in it, the exhilaration." Faith is shown in quick reaction shots, without expression or with an impatient retort, allowing viewers a clear opportunity to construct their own reading of her motives while simultaneously accepting Angel's explanation. These intervention scenes support the most frequent readings of the character and season: that Faith has rejected all attempts to connect to her or to help her through feminized, therapeutic talk; that Faith's jealousy of Buffy drives her insane; that Faith desires Angel and that his rejection or betrayal of her sparks her turn to the dark side; and that Faith desires Buffy and Buffy's rejection causes Faith's fall.[19]

Despite Faith's seeming rejection of the group, shot composition and dialogue allow a continued ambiguity. In the later episodes of the third season, Faith is shown increasingly in brief reaction shots. Buffy, Willow, and the mayor attribute thoughts, feelings, and motivations to her; she doesn't voice them herself. Posters and fan-fiction writers may not agree on the reasons for her actions or on the direction of her feelings, but many recognize that the complexity and attendant openness of her character arise from the lack of information directly from her. Active viewers apprehend and appreciate the open nature of the character and the polysemic potentialities of the series. Even when Faith physically and symbolically steps across the threshold of the mayor's office at the end of "Consequences," posters contemplated whether this act is a slayer scheme. Faith's position in the villain team is less ambiguous by the end of "Enemies."[20] Viewers are challenged to determine motives, sincerity, and off-scene occurrences as Faith tricks and attempts to seduce Angel; as Buffy voices jealousy over the relationship between Angel and Faith; and as the mayor hires a magician to remove Angel's soul.

Scenes that join violence and sex are compelling in "Enemies." As the action continues, Angel and Faith alternately fight and kiss as they prepare to torture the captured Buffy. Faith at last gets a monologue, explaining: "You know, I come to Sunnydale. I'm the slayer. I do my job kicking ass better than anyone. What do I hear about everywhere I go? Buffy." After Buffy provokes Faith into revealing all she knows about the mayor's plans, Angel reveals he is in league with Buffy. A slow-motion shot of Faith turning to face him emphasizes the significance of this final betrayal. Before escaping, Faith reminds Buffy and thus the viewers, "You kill me, you become me."

This final intervention scene again allows viewers to produce a variety of readings. Faith's "I-hate-Buffy" speech, as one poster terms it, is evidence that her actions result from jealousy of Buffy's role as the "good slayer" and her awareness of her own failure as just warrior. The significance of Faith's sexual excesses is found in the scene's sadomasochistic images, which are frequently referenced on sites and quoted in fan fiction; one site even provides audio files of dialogue, such as "if you're a screamer, feel free." Faith's alliance with Angel supports readings of the season as offering more a romantic triangle than a battle of warriors for good and evil.

Still, the pleasures of cocreating a text's meaning has limits. Like Faith, some viewers felt betrayed at the structure of "Enemies." Posters found the plot "full of holes" and even badly written, noting continuity problems in the time lapses and in the overall lack of information presented. Whether claiming they spotted the ruse or appreciating the pleasures of being taken in by it, most viewers did seem to ask, "What did Buffy know, and when did she know it?"[21] Viewers wondered whether Faith and Angel had the opportunity to consummate their violent lust because it would explain Buffy's later willingness to kill Faith. Other viewers read Faith as the victim, vulnerable through her class and social otherness, deceived once more by the privileged Buffy.

As defiant border crosser, Faith is marked for discipline institutionally and morally. Her murder of the deputy mayor confirms her as a criminal; more significant, her last encounters with each of the hero team—her attack on Xander, her attempted seduction of Angel, her capture of Willow—prepare her as deserving of defeat and punishment in the season's final showdown. Faith's social and sexual transgressions are disciplined, and the creators' experiment concludes with the lesson that the power of a slayer must be positioned within not just a code of warrior justice, but one of feminized responsibilities and restraint.

This contrast can be read through the oppositions constructed between Willow—the shy, kind girl—and Faith—the aggressive border crosser. Only Willow does not try an intervention. "It's way too late," she tells Faith instead, explaining that Faith could have had Buffy's friendship but gave that up and so has nothing.[22] Abandoning and being abandoned by a social support system has robbed the warrior of necessary guidance. Producer Noxon notes the importance of this socialization: it explains Faith's transformation—this fate is what happens to a warrior without a family—and it protects Buffy because she can turn to her gang for assistance.[23] Cultural critic Susan Owen also discusses the matrilineal and communal elements of the series; both elements exclude Faith.[24]

Viewers and creators often recognize the mayor as father figure for Faith; some posters are explicit in their sympathy for Faith in joining him: "He's the only grown-up who is nice to her." Somewhat surprisingly, fan fictions continue this construction of the mayor as father rather than lover, although he sets up the hypersexual Faith in an apartment, compliments her appearance, and buys her gifts. This distinction is notable because most adult characters frequently are portrayed as lovers of one or more of the teen characters.

The mayor, too, is aware of Faith's social otherness, chastising her for jumping on the bed and putting her feet on the furniture, although these moments function as part of the villain's idiosyncrasies even as they continue to mark Faith as a border figure, whom the mayor disciplines in these small ways. He, too, attributes motives and feelings to her as she listens impassively. Frequent scenes later in the season show him advising her to disregard Buffy and the gang, a low camera angle adding power to his words.

Most important, the mayor gives Faith a large combat knife that she unwraps, caresses, and even smells lovingly, concluding, "Boss, this is a thing of beauty." [25] The knife figures prominently in the remaining episodes; it also figures prominently in many fan fictions and is mentioned occasionally on posting boards as an obvious phallic symbol. Correspondingly, as film theorist Carol Clover notes, a knife allows and requires a "tactility" that is in keeping with Faith's sensualist ways; as a gift from the mayor, it is "overcoded" with personalization. [26] The knife ultimately is representative of Faith's continued ambiguity. She captures Willow with it, stroking her cheek sensuously and threateningly, but soon thereafter hurls the knife to save the heroes from a killer spider. She exits without retrieving the knife, causing some viewers to ponder if she had the prescience to leave it deliberately, enabling her own demise. It is Buffy who takes the knife, arming herself as potential transgressor, prepared to violate the social and sexual borders that have been delimited for her.

The textual cues in the season's final episodes lead many viewers to conclude that Buffy's willingness to kill is, as one poster puts it, "all about the boyfriend." The poisoning of Angel legitimizes Buffy's transgression: her willingness to transgress comes from her desire not to save the world but to save Angel by draining a slayer's blood. A montage pans from Buffy, gazing deeply at her reflection, to Angel, sweating and delirious, to Faith, hitting a punching bag with abandon; the dramatic images establish these three characters, rather than the mayor and the hero team, as the participants in the season's vital battle. With the viewers, Faith recognizes the symbolism of Buffy's leather pants and jacket, taunting, "Look at you, all dressed up in big sister's clothes." Faith then initiates the lengthy, expansive fight scene with one final verbal blending of sexuality and violence: "C'mon, give us a kiss." This final physical blending of sex and violence and the ultimate discipline for crossing borders comes as Buffy thrusts Faith's own knife into Faith's lower abdomen. Faith confirms this finality: "You did it, B. You killed me." [27]

Faith's fall from the roof provides Buffy with one more opportunity to transgress: she forces her own body and blood on Angel in a scene that Whedon characterizes as the most sexual of the season.[28] This sexual/blood sacrifice places Buffy unconscious in the hospital, once again parallel to and yet opposite of Faith, who is in a coma. This positioning allows a final contrast between the slayers and once more privileges Buffy's restrained, reluctant violence.

In a dream sequence, the two slayers try to make sense of the scene and coming events. For some viewers, the sequence symbolizes Faith's redemption as she provides clues that allow Buffy to defeat the mayor. Other viewers posit that the dream is Buffy's alone, with Faith's presence symbolizing a subconscious knowledge of the mayor's weakness. Several posters read the end of the dream as indicating Faith's death. Even comatose, Faith maintains an openness and ambiguity that invites meaning making.

Whedon has acknowledged that Faith's coma serves two purposes: most practically, it allows the actor to follow other projects while keeping all options open, but it also keeps Buffy from violating the code that unraveled Faith— Buffy has not killed and so has not become Faith.[29] The parallels between the two characters can mask the vital difference that Buffy is not and will never be Faith. Even with the most urgent and heteronormative exigence of saving not just the world but also her true love, Buffy falls short of crossing the border.

The coma serves a third function, however, as Faith ends the season suspended on the ultimate border. Physically she is neither living nor dead, the absence of her usual extreme makeup emphasizing her corpselike appearance. Morally and socially she may have been either punished or redeemed. Having first appeared as a warrior with no past, she exits as a motionless, colorless figure with no future.

Early in the season, Faith offers her own understanding of her place in Buffy's world: "You need me to toe the line because you're afraid you'll go over it." [30] At the end of the season, that borderline has been marked by Faith's transformation from warrior to killer, and Buffy has been characterized not as transgressor, but as responsible, restrained, and reluctant warrior woman. The narrative is reducible neither to a complete rejection of feminine roles and adoption of warrior power nor to an insidious reassertion of hegemonic structures. Rather, as postings and poachings indicate, the show presents authored messages that can be read within and against each other from a variety of positions. Viewers' responses to Faith illustrate both the complexities of the female warrior figure and the myriad opportunities for meaning making among active readers. *Buffy the Vampire Slayer* belongs to Whedon, but viewers increasingly can advocate and circulate their own explanations of its world.

7

"Action, Chicks, Everything"

On-Line Interviews with Male Fans
of *Buffy the Vampire Slayer*

LEE   PARPART

When my husband of eight years suddenly became obsessed with *Buffy the Vampire Slayer* a few years ago, I could not help wondering about his fascination with the series and its vivacious, often hyperfeminine woman warrior figure, Buffy Summers. I already knew why I had started to crave my weekly visit to the Buffyverse. As an early thirty-something, third-wave feminist graduate student in film studies, I was tantalized by the spectacle of a female hero who combined beauty and brawn, physical strength with stoicism, who could both "kick ass" and joke about it, both go it alone and nurture close relationships. Here, finally, was an appealing action hero, a flawed, funny, wise-cracking justice fighter whose gender mattered and whose violent ways could be savored because they formed part of a larger metaphorical context having to do with female empowerment.

Although my attraction to the show seemed clear enough, why was my husband interested in *Buffy?* As a writer and editor whose main allegiance is to language and narrative, my partner, Ron Wadden, insists that Buffy's woman warrior status is of little more than passing interest. He says he is drawn to the show's clever dialogue, believable characters, and engaging mix of realistic situations and pure fantasy, not to its politics.

Part of me sympathizes with this approach. *Buffy the Vampire Slayer* is a complex phenomenon that should not be reduced to a polemic on gender. Yet, for me and, I suspect, for many women, the issue of female empowerment remains a central and indispensable part of the show's appeal. It is Buffy's status as a young woman doing what typically has been considered a man's job—

leading her troops, fighting evil, saving the world—that arguably provides much of the show's visceral satisfaction for female fans. Moreover, *Buffy*'s woman warrior motif is a constant reminder of the debt the program owes to a populist and liberal version of feminism. As series creator Joss Whedon has acknowledged in interviews, part of his hope for *Buffy* lies with the possibility that it will help shift male attitudes about women through the figure of a capable but nonthreatening action heroine. "If I can make teenage boys comfortable with a girl who takes charge of a situation," he is quoted as having said, "that's better than sitting down and selling them on feminism." [1]

What concerns me here is the degree to which that modest but important political objective may be either getting through to male fans or getting lost in transit. Beginning at home and continuing in my conversations with other male fans, I have been struck by the number of men who seem able to enjoy the series while feeling no need to concern themselves directly with issues of female empowerment or the gendered implications of Buffy's warrior role. Who are these male fans, and what are they getting out of the series, if not an enlarged sense of the possibilities for female action, leadership, and heroism? Is *Buffy the Vampire Slayer* really such a free-floating phenomenon that fans who wish to read it nonpolitically can do so, perhaps even without a loss of interpretative subtlety in other areas? [2] Looking closely at these questions promises to open up new avenues for thinking through the show's already contested status as a political text. [3] We also might raise questions about the shifting basis for interpreting woman warrior narratives in general at a time when the cultural meanings surrounding *Buffy* and other female-centered action episodics increasingly are inflected by the competing discourses of second- and third-wave feminism and postmodern perspectives founded on "gender skepticism." [4]

As part of a preliminary approach to these questions, this chapter looks at the viewing practices, interpretative tendencies, and beliefs of two different groups of *Buffy* fans contacted separately in June 2001, shortly after Buffy's death by high dive at the end of season five (2000–2001). The first group consists of nine male *Buffy* fans who regularly take part in discussions about the show at the Bronze, a threaded discussion board maintained on *Buffy*'s official Web site (www.buffyslayer.com). The second group consists of twenty-eight highly educated, for the most part academically oriented, professional and preprofessional men who watch the series regularly and who responded to a call for subjects posted on three academic listserves.

Both groups were contacted by e-mail and were asked to complete separate questionnaires. The first survey was brief and open-ended and invited respondents to state in their own words why they watch the series and what they think of its treatment of issues of girl power or female empowerment. The responses tended to be brief, rushed, and colloquial, in keeping with the discursive style of many electronic bulletin-board messages. The second group filled out a more lengthy, multipart questionnaire dealing in various ways with the respondents' beliefs about female empowerment, their opinion of Buffy's status as a woman warrior, and their views on whether the show can be considered feminist. The term *feminism* was left undefined, but possibilities for interpretation were set out in a series of multiple-choice questions dealing with respondents' attitudes regarding appropriate rights and privileges for women. The questionnaire also gave respondents several opportunities to discuss the term *feminism,* the feminist movement, and its applicability to *Buffy* in their own words. This part of the survey proved to be both revealing and problematic. Respondents had a certain amount of freedom of interpretation (limited, in some cases, by the vocabulary and parameters set out in the multiple-choice questions), but they lacked a consistent sense of the way the term *feminism* was being used by the author of the questionnaire. Not surprisingly, every respondent approached the questionnaire with a different understanding of feminism, making comparisons difficult.

In its use of subjects found on-line, this study superficially resembles Daniel Bernardi's work with members of the *Star Trek* discussion group STREK-L in his "cyberspace ethnography" Star Trek *and History,* which devotes a chapter to fan understandings of the series' treatment of race. Whereas Bernardi positioned himself as a "lurker" analyzing messages by fans, I chose to contact fans directly and attempted to treat them as I would ethnographic subjects. Bernardi's method has the advantage of avoiding researcher bias, at least at the data-collection phase, because the responses are always unprompted and expressed in the participants' own words. The approach I take here is closer to a journalistic exercise in its use of self-completed interviews.

Both approaches are vulnerable to a host of problems associated with self-reporting. In both cases, the researcher has no way of knowing whether respondents are telling the truth about their age, occupation, sexual orientation, or, for that matter, anything else. (One of my respondents appeared to misrepresent his age by more than a decade, a discrepancy I discovered only when his partner, who submitted a separate survey, reported a different age for him.) On-line communities are well known for supporting fluid identities, and bulletin-board participants are obviously free to engage in strategic play with such categories as race, age, and gender because of the anonymity provided by the medium. I had hoped to reduce the danger of outright misrepresentation by contacting subjects directly, developing a rapport via e-mail, and engaging them in lengthy self-directed interviews, but one obviously cannot verify certain basic features of identity when subjects are interviewed from afar. For all of these reasons and for other reasons having to do with the design of the questionnaire, this study must be considered preliminary and its results treated as anecdotal. Even given these blind spots and constraints, however, the results suggest a number of fascinating patterns in the way different groups of men approach the series and read its woman warrior figure; they also indicate that these patterns warrant more careful and systematic study.[5]

My overall aim in this study has been to begin to assess the heterogeneous viewing patterns of fans who appear divided on whether to emphasize or deemphasize Buffy's gender or the political implications of her warrior role. I became increasingly interested in these sorts of macrolevel interpretative divisions after communicating with the mentioned nine *Buffy* fans on the official Web site. In a preliminary attempt to learn more about why males were watching the show, I sent out a call for subjects and posted a brief, general survey on the Bronze. As mentioned, respondents were asked to state in their own words how they became interested in the show, why they keep watching, and what, if anything, they think of its theme of female empowerment or girl power.

Though this foray into Buffy's male fan base yielded many different threads, the most striking finding has to do with the detachment many respondents seemed to feel from the show's handling of gender issues. Of those who responded, more than half indicated either through direct statement or through omission that although they are drawn to the show for various reasons, they have no particular interest in its girl-power themes and no opinion about Buffy's status as a woman warrior or as a role model for girls and women. Furthermore, those who addressed this question explained that they cannot be expected to hold opinions about this aspect of the show because they themselves are not female. As one fan calling himself "rh" wrote: "This part I can't speak for because I'm not a girl."[6]

Two other respondents indicated what I call "weak interest" in the show's theme of female empowerment: they address the issue but in such a way that it does not always appear to be a genuine concern for them. One respondent using the on-line nickname "Faith's Mr. Pointy" stated that Buffy is "a good role model and stuff." But this lukewarm assent to a question about the show's empowerment appeal seems less persuasive when considered alongside his reply to an earlier, more general question about why he loves the show: "Everything, chicks, action, and funny." Another fan known as "eyeofnewt" addressed the issue of female empowerment by recasting it in general, non-gender-specific terms, then diverted attention with a tangential critique of Buffy's love life: "Anybody on TV is a 'role model' at some level," he wrote. "Buffy is a hero in the Buffy world, but her track record with guys is not one that I'd hope a lot of girls would follow." This latter comment, which appears to represent a particularly slippery example of gender indifference in a male fan's response to the show, tends to erase gender as an element in Buffy's heroism while simultaneously portraying her as typically feminine in her susceptibility to romantic chaos.[7]

Other participants in the first group responded defensively to the idea that *Buffy the Vampire Slayer* might be described as a girl-power series. One fan calling himself "Idiot Savant" wrote: "i guess it works as a female empowerment show but i think it also works as a PEOPLE empowerment show. . . . i think it transcends simplistic gender-based analyses."[8] Among other things, this reply seems interesting for the way it combines defensiveness about the notion of girl power with a potentially sophisticated suggestion that gender is only one of several possible routes along which identifications might be formed within the Buffyverse. Though the opinion is expressed in nontheoretical terms, one can read into it a submerged call for what has been described as postmodernism's core assumption: "radical and decentered attention to multiple differences, none of which merit theoretical privileging over others."[9]

Even those who acknowledged that Buffy might serve as a model for young women did so by drawing attention to less-threatening aspects of her warrior role. Endorsing the show's suggestion that female power can and should coincide with being conventionally sexy, one fan called "xanderh79" wrote: "id [*sic*] say it is a good role model for girls that u can be cute and still have a smart head [and] be strong." Only one respondent, Sasha, a gay high school student, identified female empowerment as an important theme within the series, discussed this theme independently of Buffy's physical attractiveness, and positively identified Buffy's woman warrior role as an aspect of his enjoyment of *Buffy the Vampire Slayer*.[10]

Similar patterns (and some significant differences) emerged when I conducted an expanded version of the survey, this time focusing on the mentioned group of older, media-literate, and, in most cases, professional male fans. As in the first survey, all respondents came to the study via the Internet. This time, however, I began by restricting the search to three academic listserves: Film-Philosophy (for academics and others interested in film studies and philosophy), Q-Study (a queer studies site), and the Film Studies Association of Canada (the listserve of my local film studies organization).[11] As part of a "snowball" process, the call also went out to selected newspaper readers who had voted *Buffy* the "best show on TV" in a *National Post* poll conducted in early June 2001.[12]

Of the twenty-eight men who participated in the second leg of the study, seventeen identified themselves as heterosexual and eleven as gay or bisexual. Interestingly, sexual orientation emerged as an important predictor of whether respondents, in discussing their reasons for watching the series, would focus significant attention on Buffy's gender or on the political implications of her warrior role. At the risk of simplifying what were often complex replies to the questions posed in the self-completed questionnaire given to all participants, I established three basic categories for thinking about the responses: "gender conscious," "gender blind or neutral," and "mixed." As these admittedly tendentious labels imply, the first group consists of replies strongly attuned to Buffy's status as a woman warrior and highly conscious of and interested in the gendered implications of her warrior role. The second group consisted of subjects who, like eyeofnewt, showed either a marked lack of interest in Buffy's gender or an active desire to suppress any reading of the show or of her character that would emphasize political meanings attached to her status as a woman warrior. (Included in this category are respondents who were clear about their desire to read Buffy's challenges and accomplishments in general, humanistic terms rather than as an effect of or a commentary on her gender.) The third group tended to combine the two positions, acknowledging Buffy's gender and reflecting on its significance within the narrative, but withdrawing from a full engagement with the show's protofeminist significance or its handling of female empowerment.

The many shades of gray within these categories should become clearer as I report on the comments in detail, but for the moment I would like to maintain these divisions and explore the mentioned patterns that emerged through examination of the respondents' sexual orientation. Of the seventeen heterosexual men who completed the questionnaire, four fell clearly into the gender-conscious group; seven fell clearly into the gender-blind or neutral group; and another six gave responses that were best classified as mixed. Among the eleven gay respondents, the pattern was reversed, with seven subjects offering gender-conscious replies and four taking a mixed position. None of the gay or bisexual participants gave responses that fell clearly into the gender-blind or neutral category.

Of the gender-conscious gay participants, thirty-year-old librarian Steve Sposato (subjects had the option of using their real name or a pseudonym) offered a fairly typical but unusually detailed set of responses. Though he identified many reasons for watching the show, including Buffy's " 'Scooby gang' [of friends and helpers] and the clever pop-cultural California-influenced wordplay," he cited Buffy's character and the show's woman warrior theme as the key to his interest. Linking this leitmotif to a lifelong attraction to female heroes dating back to his childhood fascination with Wonder Woman in the 1970s, he wrote that it is "more exciting to see women triumph (and kick ass) because society teaches us to expect women to be weak/victims/rescued." In contrast to respondents who resisted defining the show as centrally concerned with girl power, Sposato stressed that this has always been part of the series' appeal and that if he initially resisted the show at all, it was because he worried *Buffy* would not take the issue of female empowerment seriously enough. "Not at all threatened" by the spectacle of a female action hero, Sposato noted that he would have "a harder time seeing a male character in the same way," in part because male heroes always present the possibility of sexual attraction. "With Buffy I can relate," he writes. "Angel is always more of a sex object to me (while being simultaneously a hero), while Buffy is someone I can empathize with." [13]

Though their answers tended to classify them as gender conscious, many gay respondents nevertheless cited a complex variety of reasons for watching the show. Wendell, a forty-two-year-old writer based in the United States, explained his attraction to the Buffyverse in terms of both genre and gender: "I'm mad for horror flicks and Stephen King and the whole, messy genre, so that was the first thing. If it was 'Buffy the Florist,' I wouldn't be watching at all. I like it because it's campy and because it has a sense of humor about itself. I like that Buffy is both deeply spiritual and kind of stranded, a klutz and a superwoman, all at the same time." [14]

Despite such complexity in most of the replies, virtually all of the gay respondents in the sample referred in various ways to the pleasure of watching an unlikely action hero take charge and become physical with opponents. Mike and Nick, a gay couple in their twenties, agreed that they "kinda like the fact that a whole bunch of macho guys have to depend on a girl to save their lives."

Another respondent, Mike H., a forty-three-year-old researcher living in Canada, wrote that the " 'girl power' premise has always been part of his attraction" to the show and that he has found it "cleverly done." Hugh, a twenty-three-year-old health educator living in the United States, wrote that he enjoys the show's "depiction of a kick-ass, tough young woman." He initially shared Sposato's concern that the show would trivialize the issue of female empowerment but wrote that he has been pleased with the complex way the show has dealt with Buffy's evolution from airhead former cheerleader to accomplished and heroic slayer. Displaying what turned out to be a common tendency in this part of the sample to cross and combine identificatory positions, Hugh wrote that he finds both Angel and Buffy "totally hot": "Buffy is totally hot too, and her 'I'm gonna kick your ass!' tough-as-nails poses bring me lots of viewing pleasure." [15]

Gay respondents in the mixed category had few serious objections to reading Buffy's character as gendered or the show itself as political. For Neil, a thirty-one-year-old consultant, part of the trouble is semantic. He has difficulty thinking of *Buffy* as a girl-power show because the term *girl power* reminds him of trivial examples such as the Spice Girls. But he admitted the term has some usefulness and stated that Buffy "paints the model (true) picture of girl power, or at least what it should be about." In a sophisticated version of the move to universalize Buffy's powers and to mark the show's humanist tendencies, Neil wrote that *Buffy* cannot be read simply in terms of gender because the series often concerns itself more broadly with issues of intolerance: "On many deep and pervasive levels, the show explores intolerance (whether of demons or lesbians or strong women or authority figures), and says to the viewer, 'Think and decide for yourself.' " Only two gay respondents in the sample, a thirty-three-year-old clerk named Michel and his partner Doug, a medical doctor, offered what might be considered an evenly mixed response to the show's gender concerns. Although Michel acknowledged that girl power is "part of the show's interest," he wrote that this is the case "not so much because it is a feminist view as because it is a play on expectations (which happens to push things in a feminist direction)." [16]

Heterosexual participants were, as indicated, far more likely to focus on non-gender-related aspects of the show, often downplaying Buffy's status as a woman warrior or reading the show's themes in generic, broadly humanistic terms. Comments such as "a quality show speaks to both genders" and "I don't give much thought to the feminist movement" or descriptions of Buffy as a "flawed, complex person who *happens* to be a young woman" were relatively common in this part of the sample, particularly among the seven subjects whose replies put them into the gender-blind or neutral category. Clayton, a twenty-four-year-old office worker to whom all of the these comments belong, wrote that the show is not feminist because it "doesn't have an agenda to force any ideals upon its viewers . . . it's just telling a story." (Straight respondents who rejected the idea of *Buffy the Vampire Slayer* as belonging to any kind of feminist framework tended implicitly to define feminism as a singular and highly polemical phenomenon concerned with "pushing an agenda.") Daniel, a thirty-year-old systems administrator living in the United States, argued that "*Buffy* speaks to me as human, not as pick-your-gender." He acknowledged that the series has feminist tendencies, most of which center on the fact that it does not "lock women into traditional roles," but he joined others in arguing that this pattern is "secondary to the storytelling." In keeping with this pattern, James, a twenty-two-year-old Australian, wrote that although the show has respect for females, this respect does not necessarily translate to feminism. Like Clayton and others, he privileged narrative structure and downplayed the presence of strong female characters as a coincidental effect of the writers telling the story they want to tell.[17]

When asked to comment on Buffy's role as an action hero, several respondents suggested the main value of such reversals lies in their ability to surprise viewers and to keep narratives fresh. "Aside from titillation," Daniel wrote, "it's good to [see] women in the action hero archetype [because] it keeps the stories from getting stale."[18] For such viewers, the novelty and entertainment value attached to the show's key gender reversal holds more importance than any potential for cultural or ideological shifts in the construction of femininity. The move to a woman warrior figure becomes a matter of narrative surprise, not of political efficacy.

Perhaps the most telling results in this part of the sample occur in the few cases where male respondents' surveys were accompanied by separate surveys completed by their female partners or spouses. I initially collected this data hoping to focus a portion of the study on the issue of how couples together consume and make meaning about the series, but I suspended this part of the research when it proved difficult to secure enough participants. Though the "couples" portion of this research will have to wait, it is useful to look at the differences in tone and substance between the few male and female fans who did fill out matching questionnaires. Perhaps the most striking contrast occurs in the responses from Kim, thirty-nine, and from his wife Megan, thirty-seven, both administrators living in Australia. Their differences of opinion about the show and its woman warrior figure were matched by a high level of self-awareness about their viewing practices. Although Kim acknowledged that Megan is "more attracted to [the series] because . . . Buffy is a girl kicking butt," he noted that he "doesn't care who is doing the butt kicking" but feels "robbed" when the occasional show does not include slaying or action sequences. His comments about Buffy's status as a woman warrior and the show's girl-power appeal were highly mixed, suggesting that he approves of the gender reversal on ideological grounds, but that he also thinks about the show in more instrumental terms as straightforward entertainment: "I have never had any problem with the idea of *Buffy* as a 'girl power' thing," he wrote. "I think that was one of the appealing factors—the main female character wasn't window dressing for the boys." By contrast, Megan voiced strong support for the idea that *Buffy* represents an opportunity for female viewers to blow off steam through the figure of a woman warrior: "For years guys have been able to sublimate their aggression by watching an action hero 'kick ass,' so it's great that the girls finally get a turn!"[19]

The substantial number of mixed replies in the heterosexual part of the sample seems to indicate a preference for reading the series in global terms and for conceptualizing Buffy's warrior role as both gendered and general. For Darian, a fifty-two-year-old senior civil servant living in Canada, the show's feminist leanings are "subtle and indirect," but "its message is more global: do the right thing and stand by your friends." Buffy's status as a woman warrior provides an interesting reversal, and "she is clearly a role model," Darian wrote, but he gets more "long-term enjoyment out of the fact that Buffy needs her friends to survive" than from watching her function as an independent action hero.[20]

A small number of straight male respondents (four, as mentioned) showed a pronounced tendency to read the series from within a feminist framework and in some cases offered detailed reflections on the gender-related implications of Buffy's woman warrior role. None of these respondents suggested that the series be considered unproblematically feminist. In fact, straight, gender-conscious respondents were among those most likely to identify limitations in the show's approach to gender. They noted, for example, the show's tendency to work within standard notions of feminine beauty and pointed out that Buffy's superhero status inherently sets her apart from other women, making her strengths seem fantasy based and remote and her achievements impossible to duplicate. Thus, although the subjects in this group often had reservations about the program, their criticisms generally were informed by an awareness of gender politics and a desire to read Buffy's warrior status in complex relation to her femininity.

Thus, for Ted, a thirty-nine-year-old, self-described socialist-feminist teaching in Boston, the show's girl-power appeal is something to be acknowledged but innately distrusted as a potentially compromised version of feminism. Admitting to having "erotic investments" in the show that are not shared by his wife, also a *Buffy* fan, he wrote: "I actually find the whole 'girl power' cultural phenomenon sexually exciting—which is one reason that I tend to distrust it as feminism. It seems like—in part at least—a marketing creation of dirty old capitalists to let young women have their feminism and let the guys have their T&A eye candy at the same time." He noted that the notion of girl power easily can be used to lock women in a double bind: "you can (i.e. must) be strong and competitive, and you can (i.e. must) still be 'feminine,' pretty, thin, interested in clothes and cosmetics, etc."[21]

Ted is married to Amy, a thirty-six-year-old editor, whose response to the show's woman warrior figure is more unequivocally enthusiastic than his own and more clearly tied to the vicarious thrill of watching another woman take action and extend herself into the world: "The visceral thrill of a woman kicking ass—after decades of seeing them hang on the sidelines and wait to be saved by men, etc. etc.—is fantastic," she wrote. "I'm a bit used to it now, but at first, it was shockingly great." Watching Buffy's intense physicality has given her "a way of connecting to and feeling my own aggressiveness, competitiveness, etc.— those 'masculine' characteristics that were/are undesirable in a woman, and that many girls, including myself, learned to suppress."[22]

For other gender-conscious heterosexual male fans, such as MZ, a thirty-seven-year-old Canadian university professor, Buffy offers a guilt-free opportunity to consume what typically are considered masculine genres: "I enjoy action/science fiction genres because they are often more conceptual or allegorical (rather than psychological, the tendency of much typical 'drama')," he wrote. "But these genres are often male-dominated in a reactionary way, and stunted (e.g., *Star Trek,* with its remarkably infantile or non-existent sexuality). Having even halfway progressive gender politics frees up my enjoyment of their genres, allowing them to become a relatively non-offensive entertainment." Summing up what he gains from being a fan, he writes: "I get male and female figures with whom to 'identify' and a relatively non-sexist narrative world to care about and in which to imaginatively play." Part of that sense of "play," for MZ and another straight, gender-conscious respondent, twenty-two-year-old Los Angeles writer Matthue Roth, involves the show's tendency to side-step creatively orthodoxies of all kinds, including rigid assumptions about gender. Although Roth pointed out that "one of the most important aspects of *Buffy* is that it explores the female condition, and the condition of femininity," he also noted that this process of discovery is held in suspension, never finalized. Part of the show's success, he argued, lies in "not statement-izing its statements." As a result, "*Buffy* is unbound from a lot of feminist type causes célèbres. She's not afraid to kick ass, but she's still afraid to go outside without makeup."[23]

How can we begin to think about this diverse collection of views about the Buffyverse and its woman warrior? With Mr. Pointy's "chicks, action, everything" quip still hovering over the discussion, one might conjecture that young, straight men are simply "getting off" on the spectacle of Sarah Michelle Gellar chewing up the scenery in her famously sexy vamp-hunting outfits. In a mediascape saturated with images of physically violent and highly sexualized women such as Xena and Nikita, it seems likely that heterosexual men and video game-playing boys are developing a heightened erotic taste for this new postmodern and postfeminist version of the femme fatale. Buffy's particular combination of moral goodness and kick-boxing prowess may even have a tendency to ratchet up the sexual tension for some straight male viewers because, as a long line of fictional characters suggests, for a certain type of "cultured" heterosexual male reader there is nothing quite so titillating as a young woman with sound moral principles.[24]

But lingerie sightings and sexy female morality are clearly not the only sources of fascination for the show's growing number of male fans.[25] As the preliminary findings here suggest, male viewer response to *Buffy the Vampire Slayer* and its warrior figure is more varied and complicated than one might expect. Sexual orientation, in particular, emerges as a key element in the way male fans read the show's gender politics. To borrow an insight from one of my respondents, gay and bisexual fans of the show do seem to take particular pleasure in the spectacle of another cultural outsider or marginalized figure, in this case a young woman, wielding power over opponents.[26] Whether or not such viewers "identify" with Buffy, this small anecdotal study suggests that some gay fans are more attuned than their straight counterparts to both the novelty and the political implications of a woman holding authority and using physical violence to achieve just ends. Along with her attractiveness to gay male viewers as a campy figure of pleasurable feminine excess, Buffy also may represent a sign that gender politics are moving in a desired direction.[27]

Straight males' responses to the show were more varied and ultimately more difficult to read. Although this group supplied some of the most theoretically informed and gender-conscious readings of the series' feminist promise and limitations, as heterosexual men they were more inclined than gay fans to gloss over or actively to repress any sense of the show as having political content. Straight men also were more inclined to look to the series for genre satisfaction and to read its key gender reversal as a novelty rather than as a political phenomenon. Numerous male fans went out of their way to read *Buffy* as simple entertainment, and some categorized Buffy as a politically inert figure rather than as a woman warrior whose very existence challenges patriarchal assumptions about female passivity.

Months after beginning this research, I must admit to being strongly divided about the overall significance of this pattern. On the one hand, all fans of *Buffy the Vampire Slayer* have an obvious right to nurse their own forms of *Buffy*-related viewing pleasure. Surely, Joss Whedon's call for viewers to "Bring Your Own Subtext!" extends its generous reach to all fans, even those who might read the series in ways that risk draining the program and its woman warrior figure of one of its intended subtexts: an engagement with feminism. Moreover, some of the responses that I have chosen to classify as gender blind or neutral clearly border on the increasingly defensible postmodern position of "gender skepticism," with its tendency to resituate gender in relation to other features of identity, such as class, race, and sexual orientation. Even considering this possibility complicates many of the assumptions operating within this chapter and tends to recast woman warrior narratives as contradictory cultural texts in need of readings that extend beyond a simple emphasis on one feature of identity.

As feminist cultural critics begin to make room for such perspectives, however, it seems worthwhile to bear in mind Susan Bordo's warning about the limits of postmodern versions of feminism. Offering a corrective to the idea that unreconstructed second-wave feminism has become its own metanarrative, Bordo argues that the theoretical impulse to diminish gender's role in the production of identities and cultural texts can become a sophisticated way of dismissing gender altogether. Although the male/female duality is a social construction, Bordo points out, "like it or not, in our present culture, our activities are coded as 'male' or 'female' and will function as such within the prevailing system of gender-power relations." Within this system, Bordo suggests, one cannot be gender neutral without "operating in the service of the reproduction of white, male knowledge/power."[28]

Though the postmodernist in me wants to relax and leave all *Buffy* fans to their polymorphous pleasures, I am suspicious of the impulse, dominant within the heterosexual portion of my sample, to downplay Buffy's role as a woman warrior and to look past the program's interest in female empowerment. Although the larger motives behind this insistence on reading Buffy's warrior status as a metaphor for general human achievement may be difficult to assess, the immediate payoff seems fairly clear. A gender-neutral reading creates more room for straight male fans to enjoy the show's action and fantasy sequences without considering those few aspects of the series (and the woman warrior genre in general) that actually might be unsettling to patriarchal structures and values. If Buffy is not a girl but a warrior for all genders and all ages, viewers are under no particular obligation to think about her character's impact on the social construction of femininity or to consider the symbolic or real-world implications of her appropriation of violence. In this respect, Whedon may have succeeded a little too well in making male fans comfortable with the idea of a girl who takes charge: for those who wish to read the series as simple entertainment, the Chosen One's transgressive force can be made simply to disappear.

8

Buffy? She's Like Me, She's Not Like Me—She's *Rad*

VIVIAN CHIN

How can a woman of color be a fan of the blond and very white Buffy the vampire slayer? In order to enjoy *Buffy the Vampire Slayer,* how might an Asian American female viewer watch this show? What kinds of mental gymnastics must she perform to see herself as both like and unlike Buffy? Such questions arose for me when an Asian American fan introduced me, also an Asian American woman, to Buffy. How can Buffy appeal to us? How might race and gender affect the ways one views a mainstream television serial? One way to begin to address these questions is to take up the notion of masquerade. Viewers know that Buffy masquerades as a dumb blond but is secretly a powerful vampire slayer. Similarly, a viewer can choose to identify with Buffy by masquerading as Buffy, at the same time recognizing that she is not like Buffy. This kind of viewing permits an individual to place herself within the narrative and still maintain a distance from the imaginary world of *Buffy.*

Masquerade can do more than cover a hidden identity or permit vicarious involvement in a given situation. As feminist film studies scholar Mary Anne Doane theorizes, masquerade also can reveal the artifice of gendered identities, specifically the way the concept of "femininity" serves in Western culture to define what it means to be a "woman." According to Doane, who is interested in understanding how individuals resist socially imposed identities, masquerade "constitutes an acknowledgement that it is femininity itself which is con-

Thanks go to Dziep Nguyen, Buffy fan, and to Akira Chin for watching *Buffy* now and then. Thanks also to the Mills College Women's Studies Program for the Meg Quigley Summer Fellowship.

structed as a mask."[1] From this point of view, gender—or, more specifically, femininity—can be construed to comprise, in part, a performed element of identity that can be manipulated, applied, and, in certain circumstances, removed at will.[2]

One form of masquerade that is useful to consider in relation to Doane's theory is the performance of blackface. As scholar Houston Baker describes it, "blackface is a space of habituation not only for repressed spirits of sexuality, ludic play, id satisfaction, castration anxiety, and a mirror stage of development, but also for that deep-seated denial of the indisputable humanity of inhabitants of and descendants from the continent of Africa."[3] In this definition, blackface enables the masked actor to enact what cannot be effected without the mask, to play at being the "other." At the same time, blackface upholds a racist agenda. Blackface allows white actors to "put on blackness" and, in doing so, to maintain racial hierarchies.[4] Whiteness has the privilege of masquerading in blackface.

This privilege of assuming a mask of "otherness" extends beyond that of blackface. At times within *Buffy*, vampire characters don an "Oriental" mask, an "orientalface," that serves to distance vampires further from "normal" humans.[5] This masking can be read as an enactment of a phenomenon known as Orientalism. Cultural critic Edward Said has expounded on the mechanics of Orientalism, a complex strain of Eurocentrism that has bearing on how otherness is sometimes presented in *Buffy*.[6] Orientalism is a way of constructing "the Orient" so that it serves as the "evil twin" of the West. The West can exist because "the Orient" is foreign and everything that the West is not. Although vampire characters in *Buffy* are not altered physically to look Oriental, they are placed in contexts that render them quasi-Oriental by association. This vampiric affiliation with the Oriental demonstrates some of the racial politics at work in *Buffy*. Certain vampires have the ability to play at being Oriental without actually being Oriental. This play may seem to be inclusive of things Oriental, but it may not challenge preexisting racial hierarchies where whiteness dominates. Although racial masking, like masquerade involving gender, can expose the constructed artifice of race and gender, it may not reposition or make something new of these elements of identity.

Although *Buffy* is just a television show, there are ways in which television and real life feed off of each other. *Buffy the Vampire Slayer* can reveal attitudes and beliefs about gender and about race, not just as presented in the series, but as enacted in the everyday world. A critical stance that allows for a recognition of "othering" permits one to see how certain viewers are excluded and how whiteness is presented as the norm. At the same time, by seeing Buffy as masquerading a certain type of femininity that is intertwined with race and by joining her in this masquerade, one can find pleasure in viewing. By being privy to insider knowledge, by knowing that Buffy is more than what she seems, a viewer can experience a certain pleasurable sense of superiority and authority. Moreover, an additional lesson can be learned from Buffy's masquerade: gender and race can be understood as masks that, to a certain extent, can be manipulated playfully. But, one might ask, how does this playfulness work?

The character Buffy can be read as "feminist" when she is seen as a powerful young woman who refuses to let anyone push her around.[7] On the other hand, she wears miniskirts, shows cleavage, and does not challenge the idea that a television actress must be "conventionally" attractive to a heterosexual male viewer. Joss Whedon, the creator of *Buffy the Vampire Slayer* explains, "If I can make teenage boys comfortable with a girl who takes charge of a situation without their knowing that's what's happening, it's better than sitting down and selling them feminism."[8] In an interview, he describes how he envisions Buffy as countering a certain blond and helpless horror-genre stereotype: instead of being a victim of a violent man, a "beautiful blonde girl walks into an alley, and not only is she ready for him she trounces him."[9] In a somewhat subversive manner, he uses an antifeminist model, the helpless blond, to present an alternative, feminist possibility: the kick-ass blond.

This alternative possibility, however, must be blond. Because blond hair is a trait considered to be a racially white characteristic, blondness equals whiteness. In an episode where Buffy appears to be the perpetrator of a crime, a (blond, white) policewoman reports, "All units . . . we have a homicide suspect, female, blond, approximately sixteen years old."[10] Here, the description *blond* is sufficient: the police officer does not need to mention race because *blond* means *white*. This kind of silence is significant because it demonstrates how race is there and yet not there in *Buffy*.

In a similar manner, some Asian Americans might choose to identify themselves as simply "American" without mentioning a specific ethnicity or race. However, with this type of identification, race does not simply drop out. Instead, it is subsumed by whiteness. Like *blond,* the term *American* can be synonymous with *white*. When *Asian* means *foreign* and when nonwhite U.S. citizens are called on to use a qualifier to name what type of American they are, then *American* means *white*. To be an Asian American citizen, then, and to identify as only an American can require wearing a mask of whiteness.

Buffy's masquerade operates differently. After all, underneath the mask, Buffy is white. Although Buffy is meant to put a spin on the dumb-blond stereotype, she must be not only blond but also white in order to accomplish this feat. Buffy's blue eyes are brought to attention when Buffy wears baby blue clothing, and her squeaky cleanness and affinity with whiteness are shown in scenes in which she wears all-white apparel and in which she is seen snuggling with her mother on a pristine white sofa. The point of reference is whiteness, and in this context Buffy celebrates a new kind of feminine, possibly feminist, blond whiteness.

Critic bell hooks argues that viewers do not always join in this kind of celebration. In an essay entitled "The Oppositional Gaze," hooks quotes Julie Burchill, another critic who considers the meaning of the artificial blond: " 'What does it say about racial purity that the best blondes have all been brunettes (Harlow, Monroe, Bardot)? I think it says that we are not as white as we think.' " Hooks continues, "Burchill could easily have said 'we are not as white as we want to be,' for clearly the obsession to have white women film stars be ultra-white was a cinematic practice that sought to maintain a distance, a separation between that image and the black female 'other'; it was a way to perpetuate white supremacy."[11] The suggestion that films and television programs might serve as tools of white supremacy is provocative. Working from this presumption, does *Buffy* challenge or reinscribe white supremacy? Or, perhaps, does the program function at both levels? Although such questions cannot be answered definitively, hooks's point that there exists a white screen presence and a nonwhite absence suggests the necessity for nonwhite viewers to engage in masquerade in order to write themselves onto the screen.

Buffy is both a blond icon presented to be looked at and a potent "shero." When we first meet Buffy, she is a high school student who cannot avoid her destiny to become a vampire slayer. A lollipop-licking, apparently ditzy, yet wise-cracking blond, she has been chosen to be a protector of humanity. She lives in middle-class, suburban Sunnydale, California, which just happens to be built over a portal to a demonic netherworld. As we become familiar with the vampire, demon, and human population of Sunnydale, we notice that most characters are neither entirely good nor entirely evil.[12] Following this ambiguity, vampires can feel love, as Spike does for Drusilla and, later in the series, for

Buffy, and humans can be driven by revenge, as in the case of the gypsies' curse on Angel. Moreover, vampires can pass as humans; they do not always have blood-dripping fangs and alien-looking faces. In her essay, "Feminist Icon? *Buffy the Vampire Slayer* and Postfeminist Television," Rosie White claims that in *Buffy* "there are no 'authentic' identities . . . anything can change."[13] In a show where the entire regular cast is white, can it be possible that some are meant to be symbolically nonwhite? Can some characters, the evil characters, be serving as stand-ins for absent, nonwhite people, representing what might be most horrifying to white suburbia?

In horror films, the object of horror is often alien and sometimes black. The evil enemy can symbolize anything that is different from a white middle-class norm. For example, in the film *Rosemary's Baby* (1968), the devil who rapes Rosemary is black-skinned, unlike anyone else in the movie, and the crowd who welcomes the baby is not just from her apartment building but is an international set made up of men in turbans and camera-toting Japanese tourists—in other words, aliens.[14] On occasion, this model can be reversed, as in the movie *Blade* (1998), in which Wesley Snipes plays a black vampire-slaying hero.[15] Although Buffy is a white vampire slayer and her friends are white, the evil forces that Buffy fights are entities perceived as "alien" to a predominately white suburban town. In this context, one might argue that evil as personified in *Buffy* signifies people of color in general.

How do fans and purveyors of North American youth culture perceive Buffy's whiteness? In a movie created to appeal to teenagers, *Bring It On* (2000), a cheerleading squad unwittingly steals a routine from another squad in a rivalry between a predominantly white suburban high school and a predominantly black inner-city high school. When this theft is discovered, one of the black cheerleaders says, "Let's kick Buffy's ass."[16] This comment is an inside joke—one of the actors who portray the white cheerleaders appeared on *Buffy*—but it also demonstrates how Buffy is synonymous with being a generic "white girl" who is unlike the speaker. The cheerleader who names Buffy as a symbol of white femininity demonstrates a consciousness of racial politics at work in *Buffy*. She recognizes that Buffy is not someone with whom she can identify, despite the pretext that everyone can identify with Buffy. In this sense, *Buffy* fails to confront a variant of white supremacy in which whiteness is a universalized concept. This form of white supremacy erases difference and maintains that everyone is the same as long as everyone assumes or aspires to whiteness as their fundamental consciousness of self.

Is Buffy both different and not different? For a nonblond, is Buffy "like me"? In order for a fan to cheer for Buffy, does that fan need to identify as white? To enjoy the show, does a viewer need to look through the eyes of a male viewer and desire whiteness? Not necessarily. As bell hooks notes, "women can construct an oppositional gaze via an understanding and awareness of the politics of race and racism." [17] Although specifically referring to a black woman's ability to see the mechanics of racism at work on screen, hooks's remark can apply to women of color in general. With regard to *Buffy*, Asian American women can interrogate representations of women of color in the program, as well as consider their absence. This way of looking permits us to critique notions of women of color as powerless, irrelevant, or absent. With this critical gaze, how can a viewer continue to enjoy watching *Buffy?*

When the cheerleader in *Bring It On* remarks on Buffy's whiteness, she conforms to a phenomenon that occurs in other mainstream U.S. movies—the actor of color bringing attention to racial dynamics. In the movie *Evolution* (2001), a black character states that the black man always becomes an object of ridicule, and then he himself later becomes a fool when a bug gets caught in his suit. In *Scary Movie 2* (2001), a young black woman wonders why the black characters always get stranded and attacked just prior to being abandoned by their white friends.[18] Likewise, the black cheerleader in *Bring It On* is called on to draw attention to Buffy's whiteness. It is difficult to imagine a white character in *Buffy* explicitly discussing matters of race, and it is difficult to remember significant characters in *Buffy* who are not white.

When people of color do make appearances in Sunnydale, they are not so memorable. They are extras in shopping malls; they pass through the halls of the high school; or they represent "firsts." For instance, with regard to the last category, in "The Harvest," a vampire orders, "bring me the first," and the black doorman at the Sunnydale teen hangout, the Bronze, is apprehended and presented to the vampire to be killed and devoured.[19] Interestingly, vampires of color occasionally appear on *Buffy*, but only briefly. In "Becoming, Part 2," an Asian vampire jumps out at Buffy, only to be swiftly staked without much of a fight.[20] Counter to stereotypes, this Asian character is not skilled at martial arts. In general, nonwhite characters are not strong enough to have lasting power.

When Kendra, a second vampire slayer, first appears in "Becoming, Part 1," it is dark and difficult to tell by sight that she may be of color.[21] In a subsequent scene, she stands stiffly, chest out, and when she speaks, we notice she uses *t* in place of *th*. The brighter light and her speech reveal her as someone who is different from Buffy. Kendra is black and is supposed to be Jamaican by virtue of her accent. She is more voluptuous than Buffy, but her dimensions do not make her sufficiently powerful. Having given to Buffy her favorite stake, a weapon that she has named "Mr. Pointy," Kendra succumbs to the vampire Drusilla's hypnotic control. After swaying with the vampire in an almost sexualized dance, Kendra is slashed across the throat and dies. One might say she is punished for having a G-rated lesbian interlude with Drusilla. In addition, through an act of generosity toward Buffy, Kendra, in effect, has castrated herself by relinquishing Mr. Pointy. In *Buffy*, Anglo-Europeans are positioned at the top of the human and vampire hierarchy.

The Anglo-Eurocentrism so prevalent in *Buffy* has a long history in Western thought. We can recognize how *Buffy* participates in one form of this racial and cultural ordering—that is, Orientalism. From an Orientalist point of view, the Orient is completely objectified, and there are no Oriental subjects who can speak for themselves. Oriental objects are exotic things that can impart some of their desirable exotica to a non-Oriental collector.

Orientalism is woven into the fabric of *Buffy* in identifiable ways. For instance, Angel, the slayer's tortured vampire love interest, lives in an apartment where the decor is steeped in Orientalism. Featuring a rice-paper screen and Asian art, the "otherness" of Angel's furnishings contrast with the strictly whitebread furniture of Buffy's house. Living in a space surrounded by Oriental objects, Angel becomes quasi-Oriental by association. He is supposed to be Irish, and underscoring this ethnic identity, he holds dear an Irish object, a Claddaugh ring he gives to Buffy. However, unlike the Oriental objects that make his apartment exotic, this ring has a special power to restore him to life. The Oriental objects are merely decorative, serving to highlight Angel's difference from the population of Sunnydale.

Orientalia also is employed to accentuate the otherness of vampires in relation to the citizens of Sunnydale. Angel's Orientalist bent apparently is shared by the vampire Darla. In one episode, Angel taunts Darla with the words, "last time I saw you it was kimonos." [22] For the blond Darla, a kimono does not mark a continuation of tradition, but rather a connection with the exotic or the bizarre. Conjuring Darla in a kimono presents only an absurd image, but at the same time it shows her desire to be associated with exotica, a desire akin to the use of blackface. She can put on a kimono and take it off; she can become Oriental at whim. Another "Oriental connection" extends to the vampire Spike, who, in an episode entitled "The Yoko Factor," compares himself to Yoko Ono. [23]

An Orientalist perspective of Yoko Ono names her as an evil dragon lady who, out of selfishness, destroyed a significant part of modern white popular culture. Although Spike explains that everyone blamed Ono for the break up of the Beatles, when in actuality she just happened to be there when they disbanded, he strategizes to break up Buffy and her friends. He is a dragon lady, not the boy next door. He chooses to align himself with a disparaged "other."

However, in the episode "Fool for Love," Spike distances himself from an Asian character, a Chinese slayer.[24] As she lies dying in his arms from wounds he has inflicted, her speech is subtitled to read, "Tell my mother. I'm sorry." Spike responds, "Sorry, luv, I don't speak Chinese." Spike's cosmopolitanism is not far-reaching enough to enable him to understand a simple request spoken in Chinese. Spike is not able to cross over into a space of Chinese language ability, and the slayer is not able to shed her Chineseness. Although viewers receive a translation, Chinese is indecipherable and unknowable to Spike. A masking that would enable Spike to understand the slayer's speech would not be advantageous to him and would benefit the slayer. Simply understanding Chinese would not make him exotic; he would have to respond in Chinese in order to attain such status. Spike is represented as decidedly European because he has no knowledge of Chinese. In this example of Orientalism at work, Chinese is simply too strange for him to understand.

To further stress the concept of Asia as completely "other" to that which is defined as the West, Angel is called on to take a demonic body part far from Sunnydale, and he tells Buffy, "I've got to get this to the remotest region possible. . . . I've gotta catch a cargo ship to Asia, maybe trek to Nepal."[25] Although Asia is not equated with a demonic otherworld, it is the most distant imaginable earthly location from Sunnydale. Asia is a place that is different both from what is given to us as normal, Sunnydale, and from what is given to us as abnormal, the demonic world. One might argue that Angel thinks of Asia as neither good nor bad, but simply far away and perhaps unimaginable. He ultimately is thwarted from taking a trip to Asia. Thus, this vast geographic region remains an abstraction, a symbol of "otherness" rather than a real place. In his study on vampire fiction, *Reading the Vampire,* Ken Gelder notes that "Dracula is a character whose . . . ability to circulate freely—to traverse national boundaries signif[ies] nothing less than his irreducible Otherness."[26] Angel's plan to travel underscores his special ability to journey to a faraway, "exotic" place, while Buffy remains in suburban Sunnydale.

Just as Asia is constructed as a place that is different, the vampires also must be shown as different. Joss Whedon has described his fascination with vampires: "I've always been interested in vampires, I think, because of the isolation they feel. They're in the world, but not of it. As a child I always felt the same way."[27] Whedon compares his own sense of isolation with that of vampires, and in this sense he is not different from the average vampire, but rather the same. Similarly, Buffy experiences a certain isolation. Her distinction as a vampire slayer separates her from her peers. She can never return to a normal life. Although she may seem to be nothing but a blond high school girl and, later, a college co-ed, she is something other. She can pass as normal, but she is anything but normal.[28]

Certain vampires share Buffy's ability to pass as normal. Because many of the vampires have faces that look inhuman only when they are about to feed, they can pass as normal humans. Their identifying features are not always obvious. Although Buffy points out that a vampire's outdated clothing can be used to identify them, the slayer's friend Willow is also prone to wearing unstylish clothes; unfashionable outfits are not always a reliable way of outing a vampire. Because vampires may not be easily recognizable, they can assimilate into Sunnydale, making them all the more insidious and powerful. If outsiders cannot be recognized as such, then maintaining boundaries between insiders and outsiders can be difficult, if not impossible. What a horror if those who do not really belong in white suburbia cannot be identified.

In *Buffy*, it appears that vampires are made, not born. This vampiric feature contrasts with other vampire narratives—for instance, *Blade* (1998), in which vampires may be "pure blood" (born as vampires) or "turned" (once human). Nonetheless, even in *Buffy* not all vampires are alike. Some vampires lead, and others follow. Furthermore, one distinguishing feature that a number of vampires share, notably Spike and Drusilla, is an "un-American" accent. In contrast, by the time Angel arrives in Sunnydale, he has shed his Irish brogue. Giles, a librarian and Buffy's watcher or mentor, has an upper-class British accent; slayer Kendra speaks with some semblance of a Jamaican patois, and an indeterminate accent marks an errant gypsy. Even in Sunnydale not everyone with a noticeable accent is evil. Clear signs of outsider status may not mark a character as necessarily bad. Although Buffy was born to be a slayer, an essential, inborn difference for any character may be less important than having undergone a transformation that has made that character an outsider who is different or evil.

Is it reasonable to assert that despite her appearance and the privileges it brings, Buffy is also in some respects an outsider? The ambiguity that makes it difficult to tell who is one of "us" in *Buffy* extends to Buffy herself. Angel struggles with a lost and found soul that makes him act like and not like a vampire, and Buffy struggles with a duplicitous life because only a select group knows she is a vampire slayer. She looks at first like a typical teenager and then, as she matures, like a typical co-ed—signified here by blond and white—but her actions prove she is also atypical. Buffy, then, is both typical and atypical.

Buffy exhibits ambiguous characteristics both in her presentation of self and in her physical prowess. Although she is "tough" because of her ability to beat up and kill vampires and monsters, she conforms to notions of femininity that require her to be desirable to men or to male vampires and that require her to display a certain vulnerability. Her attractiveness and her emotional weaknesses may be read as artificial masks that she uses to hide her slayer powers, but they also may be read less as masks and more as evidence of her "true" femininity. For example, when she cries, especially when she is alone, her tears are meant to demonstrate her real feelings, not to show that she is manipulating those around her. Although the Buffy character challenges the stereotype of the helpless female and may suggest the possibility that femininity is a construct rather than a collection of essential, inborn traits, it is not difficult to dismiss her as yet another female character who acquiesces to preconceived ideas of femininity.

In addition to the ambiguity surrounding her enactment of gender, a measure of ambiguity resides in her enactment of whiteness. Buffy has martial arts skills that lend her a certain "Oriental" flavor, and yet she is unmistakably blond and certainly not Asian. One *Buffy* critic points out that "the principal question that arises when attempting any analysis of the presentation of martial arts in *Buffy* is why they are there at all." [29] Buffy's use of martial arts is yet another example of masquerade and cultural appropriation. The slayer's fighting methods allow her to act exotic without having to be exotic.

Buffy's ambiguity provides some space to grant her the benefit of the doubt. In *Tough Girls: Women Warriors and Wonder Women in Popular Culture*, Sherrie Inness notes "how impossible it is to perceive the depiction of the tough girl in the popular media as entirely positive or negative; instead, like most popular culture characters, she is a multivalent representation that can be read in numerous and even paradoxical ways." [30]

In addition to this indistinctness, Buffy may have certain powers beyond those of a slayer, powers that reiterate a racial hierarchy. If we accept that her masquerade reasserts the superiority of a blond icon, then viewing the show can become less than pleasurable. A viewer may not wish to participate in such a racial ordering and may not wish to identify with Buffy. In the essay "Not You/Like You: Post-Colonial Women and the Interlocking Questions of Identity and Difference," filmmaker and critic Trinh T. Minh-ha asserts: "To raise the question of identity is to reopen again the discussion on the self/other relationship in its enactment of power relations."[31] Must a certain disavowal of racial politics occur in order for a viewer to sit back and just enjoy the show? Perhaps what saves *Buffy* from this fate is a certain "campy" factor. The play that takes place when Buffy feigns being a dumb blond highlights the superficiality or silliness of the blond icon and reveals a certain fear of not being white enough. However, such a fear provides evidence of a racial hierarchy where whiteness reigns supreme. As noted earlier in bell hooks's remark, the artificial blond may voice the anxiety that " 'we are not as white as we want to be.' " Even Buffy is vulnerable, and she may harbor an "inappropriate other" within herself.[32] This other within herself can be enough to allow for transracial identifications or to allow for an Asian American woman to be a continually skeptical fan of *Buffy*.

PART THREE

La Femme Nikita

Like Buffy Summers, Nikita made her debut in a feature film. *La Femme Nikita* (1991) and its American remake *Point of No Return* (1993) followed the exploits of a drug addict and murderer who is recruited by a covert antiterrorist organization. But to make Nikita a more sympathetic character, the television show, *La Femme Nikita* (aired 1997–2001), portrays a young woman wrongly accused of a hideous crime who is nonetheless forced to join Section One, whose cause, loosely defined, is to protect Western governments from a variety of threats. As the most covert of all government agencies, it is not bound by law and moral codes. As Nikita tells the audience at the beginning of every show, "their ends are just, but their means are ruthless." And because the agency operatives are former criminals and other disposable individuals, the leaders of Section One sacrifice and torture them with impunity.

La Femme Nikita traces Nikita's quest to escape from Section One with her soul intact. Although Nikita develops into Section One's most talented operative, her rejection of its utilitarian morality and its leaders' ambitions leave her loyalty in question. Like Xena and Buffy, she must negotiate the meaning of justice in a world in which violence and evil exist.

9

"The Most Powerful Weapon You Have"

Warriors and Gender in *La Femme Nikita*

LAURA NG

Nikita is just one of the new woman warriors who recently have been receiving high ratings on prime-time television. At first glance, it seems simple enough: beautiful blond woman defeats the terrorists and saves the day. However, it is never that simple. The idea of the woman warrior is one surrounded by debate. Key questions in this discussion are, Can a woman hold both positions of woman and warrior, or does one role necessarily negate the other? The territory of the warrior has long been the domain of the tough guy. He is the one society sends into danger, the one behind whom everyone rallies. Women have been waiting for him either to come home or to come to their rescue. With a decisively female sheriff in town, more questions arise: How does a woman navigate this traditionally masculine field? What changes does a woman bring to the role? What tensions and obstacles must she negotiate? How can she escape being considered a man in drag?

Within academics, most criticism of *La Femme Nikita* is focused on the French and the American films that preceded the television program. At first, reception of the series appeared hesitant, as exemplified by Susan Isaacs's reluctant assignment of hero status to the television Nikita. Isaacs argues that the ambiguity surrounding both gender and the moral markers of right and wrong in the series makes that assessment difficult for her.[1] This ambiguity has both plagued and stimulated critics.[2] In "A Pygmalion Tale Retold: Remaking *La Femme Nikita*," Laura Grindstaff concludes that although Nikita does rebel against the social order and the Lacanian idea of the Law of the Father, she is trapped within it and cannot escape.[3] As compelling as her point is, Grindstaff fails to realize fully the power of ambiguity on the designation of the female warrior and the resistant agency these gray areas grant the woman warrior.

In the dark world of covert operations and professional lies, Nikita takes strong, aggressive, and violent actions in order to create her own role as warrior. Along the way, in order to retain her power, agency, and identity as one of the new women warriors, she deftly confronts backlash stereotypes associated with aggressive women and threats of victimization.

As Jean Bethke Elshtain explains in *Women and War,* the male warriors are "avatars of a nation's sanctioned violence." They are the ones who protect and inscribe the order of the society they defend. Because they fight for the values placed at the center of society, in the eyes of society they are untouched by the negative associations of the violent action. They are in the trenches fighting for Mom and apple pie; it is part of the hero's job description. The violence is seen as a necessary, although perhaps distasteful, part of the role, if it is considered at all. Few ever accuse Rambo of murdering any of the villains who roll across the screen. This view, as Elshtain points out, is far too simple and misleading,[4] a willful social blindness to the dark aspects of violence embedded in the role of hero. It is these aspects, however, that the television show *La Femme Nikita* brings to the forefront. This show problematizes the easy validation of the warrior hero by obscuring those clearly marked moral boundaries typically used to validate the hero.

Nations possess a core set of values to which systems of religion, society, and government are bound. These values, whether termed *patriotism* or *morality,* are what warriors ideally fight to uphold. Many critics have commented on the way the morally ambiguous premise of *La Femme Nikita* slips away from these easy moral markers. Susan Isaacs comments: "So while I admire the boldness of *La Femme Nikita,* the moral compass of the main character spins too fast for me to consider her a brave dame."[5] The clear boundaries of morality used for a simple judgment call of either hero or villain are obscured in the murky darkness of Nikita's world.

Section One, the group for which Nikita works, presents itself as an antiterrorist organization; however, it strays from the path of socially acceptable action by inflicting violence on the innocents whom society desires to protect. In the episode "Into the Looking Glass" of season four (2000–2001), threats to arms dealer Dante's unborn child prove to be the point of needed persuasion. While Madeline (the lead strategist for Section One) questions Dante, she shows him the stressed heartbeats of his girlfriend and unborn offspring:

WOMAN: Please, Horst, give them what they want!

MADELINE: Are you ready to talk?

DANTE: She doesn't mean anything to me.

MADELINE: She's pregnant.

DANTE: You are lying.

MADELINE: Your girlfriend's is the one that sounds stressed. The other is your unborn son.[6]

By threatening the same innocent life that society values, *La Femme Nikita* also threatens the role of the warrior. Madeline, charged with protecting society, is ignoring mainstream society's drive to protect an innocent life and instead threatens the unborn child in order to defend the society against a terrorist threat. One must ask if the show has fallen so far from the moral core or if it is merely revealing the dark facts of a reality that the audience does not want to acknowledge.

Presented vividly are the harsh means used to produce the just end. Although in theory society protects the innocent, the series brings to light the darker side of justice. When can one life be spared at the risk of losing many? The myth of America's democratic majority is torn asunder by the realization that where there is a choice, a minority may be silenced or sacrificed. The simple breakdown of warrior-hero versus terrorist-villain often works to obscure the hostile choices and frightening actions taken to preserve the nation as a whole. Society utilizes a willing belief in the rightness of the hero's actions to ignore the darker parts of justice. However, *La Femme Nikita* brings the sacrifices and choices to the viewers' attention. It does not cover up the more frightening aspects forming the foundation of the solid moral compass of social values. It displays the harsh choices on which survival may hinge.

In other nuanced ways, the show deviates and defies traditional value systems embodied by the ideology of the warrior. Its physical representation of the world is often unclear. The backgrounds and landscapes for the conflicts are not marked by any recognizable monuments. There is no Eiffel Tower or Statue of Liberty to inspire patriotism and to identify the threat as one poised against a specific government or nation. This absence of geographical marking keeps the audience from associating Nikita and Section One with any direct political or national allegiance that might be used to redeem them and thus place them into the ranks of the heroes. Patriotism cannot be used to rescue Nikita's actions from moral questioning. This same stark landscape ironically keeps the audience from abandoning Nikita. As Edward Said astutely notes in *Culture and Imperialism,* most societies project their fears on the unknown or the exotic other.[7] This barren land, where the viewers are kept disorientated, is threatening. It is a place between the familiar and the foreign, like part of a dream or vision that one cannot remember clearly. There is always a sense of a lurking danger from which the viewers need protection. Nikita provides that sense of protection.

However, the blurring of morality does not mean there are no villains in Nikita's world. Section One fights against many terrorist organizations, but none is as powerful as the Collective in the fourth and final season. The similarity between Section One and the Collective is striking. In "The Man Behind the Curtain," the Collective attempts to destroy an important factory.[8] Section One's objective is to prevent the destruction. As both sides work to achieve their goals, the camera switches from Section One's headquarters to the Collective's command center. What stands out in these scenes are the similarities. Both sets of control centers are dark, allowing light to flow from the screens of computers and other forms of identical technology filling the stark rooms. Both organizations have support, and an individual operating a computer and one focused on tactics issue orders. Thanks to Michael, Nikita's lover and a former Section One operative, both associations even use similar strategies. He left Section One and sold its plans and protocols to the Collective. As the camera cuts from one base to another, the dominant impression of the scenes is one of sameness. The technology is the same. The orders issued are similar in direction and nature. The drive to succeed at all costs is the same. The goals are the thin difference between the two groups, a slim line in an ill-lit world.

To complicate matters further, Section One has no clear-cut hero. The carefully crafted group of agents is not united by the martyrlike drive to die for the protection of the culture. Rather, Section One is marked with suspicion, paranoia, and power plays. The actions it undertakes often have less to do with conducting antiterrorism operations than with securing power for the individual plots unfolding from within the organization. Paul (the leader of Section One and better known to fans as "Operations") and Madeline constantly battle Nikita for control over the lives of the agents and the direction Section One will take in the future. The constant internal struggles are marked with malicious tactics from all sides. The often brutal power struggles keep the audience from unconditionally accepting any of the characters as the clearly defined and fully sympathetic hero.

In "Up The Rabbit Hole," Paul and Madeline engineer the death of a supervisor named George to protect Section One and their own agendas.[9] Even the protagonist, Nikita, is embroiled in power plays. In "Four Light Years Farther," the audience learns that Nikita has been spying on Section One for a superior, Mr. Jones, who is head of a fellow agency known as the Center.[10] All learn that three years of friendships, conflicts, and missions have been recorded and related to the mysterious Mr. Jones. There is more concern for the personal rank and file of power than for the nation Section One was designed to protect. This focus on the internal dysfunction of Section One undercuts Nikita as hero. The audience, like weapons designer Walter and computer specialist Birkoff, begins to wonder how much of the agency's operatives shared past experiences have constituted a true bond and how much has been a performance to gain information. Is Nikita the hero we see? Or is she just another version of Paul, waiting to use her information to break the last resistance to her plans for gaining power?

In this murky world where the markers of the warrior are destroyed, how does Nikita fit into our quest for discovering the *just* woman warrior? Psychologist Michael Ventura finds this ambiguity a redeeming aspect of *La Femme Nikita*. He feels that it is this uncertainty, this escape from sharply defined categories, that the audience finds attractive about the show.[11] The lack of a rigidly defined social process of validation leaves open doors of possibility. It is in these possibilities that Nikita the warrior may be found. *La Femme Nikita* avoids the conflict with the land of the male warrior by removing itself from mainstream society's domain. On the border, it creates a new order.

Gloria Anzaldúa offers a clear and versatile definition of borders and borderlands: "A border is a dividing line, a narrow strip along a steep edge. A borderland is a vague and undetermined place created by emotional residue of an unnatural boundary. It is a constant state of transition. The prohibited and forbidden are its inhabitants."[12] In this domain of outcasts, society's rules and desires hold little bearing on the power struggles and identities arising from the mysterious unstable ground. Section One and the world of *La Femme Nikita* exist in this nebulous untamed border region. As Ventura aptly phrases it, "Nikita lives in hell."[13] The key is the lawlessness of the situation. Where there is chaos, the familiar rules of the world can be left behind. Does this mean there is no ideal, no great moral truth to reach for? On the contrary, the show displays the compromises that occur when the moral codes of society are not applied in the lawless land of the border.

With the removal of the overarching moral construction society uses to validate the warrior's violent actions, the fringe area exposed is a ground ripe for transgression. The obscuring of the clear boundaries gives those transgressive characters on the fringe the ability to explore this new ground and to construct their own codes. Nikita is such a character. Her actions, beliefs, expectations, values, and agendas become the standard the audience uses to measure good and bad, success and failure. Utilizing this filter of the chaotic gray, Nikita avoids becoming a drag stereotype of a male warrior in a female shell.

Another obstacle Nikita must battle comes from viewer expectations. In *Gender Trouble,* Judith Butler explains that the gender division of people and roles is based on the validation and suppression of body parts and actions. Although Butler is theorizing about sexuality, her ideas can be extrapolated to include violence. According to her, society sanctions or denies pleasures or access to specific body parts based on the idea of gender. It sanctions women's use of their hands to nurture or prepare food but not to inflict harm. Butler explains that denial and access function as social power structures designed to privilege and oppress,[14] hence the male warrior's dominance and the considerable conflict surrounding the idea of a female warrior. Although the setting of *La Femme Nikita* does not attempt directly to incorporate society's privileging, such privileging is nevertheless present if in no other form than the cultural and social baggage the viewer brings to the show.

The woman warrior also must confront the threat from the myth of essentialism. Diana Fuss explains essentialism as "a belief in true essence—that which is most irreducible, unchangeable, outside of history and time." Extending this definition of essentialism to gender is problematic, according to Fuss, because of the unstable categories of "masculine" and "feminine." [15] Throughout history, the markers of masculinity and femininity have not stayed constant. We are not the women our grandmothers would have considered ideal. The idea of the female warrior becomes problematic if one views a woman as essentially nurturing and passive. Nikita then is either an abnormal monster or an androgynous figure, stuck between the biological and behavioral makeup of masculine and feminine. She thus is limited in her transgressive power. Her genetic makeup dictates behavior and may prohibit her utilization of violence in aggressive ways. This essentialism, then, works only to diminish Nikita's agency and does not account adequately for her existence or for the existence of other women warriors. In contrast to Fuss's perspective, Butler's constructionist view of humanity presents a much more useful tool for examining the power and potential of Nikita as a woman warrior.

Owing to the gender privileging of the body, roles, and access to violence, the image of a violent woman brings additional social fears to the forefront. As Ann Jones documents in *Women Who Kill*, the idea of even abused women engaging in violent actions creates the backlash fear of an "open season on all men,"[16] with the underlying fear of a lawless, unconstrained, uncontrolled woman. The female warrior must meet directly the broad and negative connection between one violent relationship and a threat against all men if she wishes to avoid becoming lost in the land of the monster woman. Apparent in the concept of the monster woman is the idea that the violence the female monster embodies is lacking in thought, rational motivation, or principle. Her motivation is seen as chaotic, and she randomly targets the male gender. She is then the modern-day gorgon, out to get whatever man she can. Nikita, in her practiced violence, must deal with this cultural baggage.

The blurred nature of the show helps to explain how Nikita avoids exile as monster. With no clear boundaries, she does not have to worry about crossing them. However, the viewer brings to the show these cultural threats—the monster woman and stereotypically gendered feminine passivity. So although the show does not present Nikita as personifying the monster woman killer, it must make her go through other necessary steps to diffuse and dismiss the backlash stereotypes.

Nikita defeats this backlash connected to her violent actions through cognitive dissonance. Through the first two seasons of the show (1997–98 and 1998–99), she is forced to consider her violent escapades as well as her emotional and psychological well-being. In episodes such as "Choice" and "Charity," she explores her own soul and the question "Am I still human?"[17] This emotional exploration allows viewers to empathize with her and keeps them from easily dismissing her as an immoral killer. Nikita is not necessarily apologizing for her actions or begging for redemption. Instead, she takes the "reality" in which she is trapped and studies the effect it has on herself. Viewers can hold Nikita up as their protagonist because she can feel pain and still has a loose concept of right and wrong. Though they may not always approve of Nikita's choice and actions, they find it is easier to deal with them because of the ambiguity permeating the show.

In "Half Life," Nikita decides to reveal the identity of the bomber, knowing that Michael's connection to the bomber will be revealed and that her revelation will force an emotionally painful and potentially deadly confrontation for Michael.[18] The bomber, Rene, knew Michael when they both were idealistic antiterrorist student protestors in the 1980s. When Nikita falls, she becomes human. Her actions show the compromises she must make to survive. Her mental agonizing also works to display her control. She is not the untamed, irrational monster woman. She is calm. As she weighs each of her choices and the possible outcomes, she displays her considerable control and rationality. Nikita is an individual who is trying to navigate an extraordinary world, where right and wrong are not clear and where most choices become a question of who should suffer.

Whenever there is violence, there is usually a victim. It is not a concept one can deny. Nikita, however, artfully avoids woman's traditional role of victim in the violence equation. Scattered throughout the show are many opportunities for victimhood into which Nikita might escape, thereby alleviating her angst. The victim potential begins in the first episode, "Nikita." The television Nikita, unlike the French film Nikita, did not commit the crime she was imprisoned for originally. Based on society's unjust and incorrect condemnation of her, she is forced into her life at Section One, with the promise of death if she tries to escape.[19] This premise and Nikita's innocent origin work to invoke sympathy from the viewer and to provide Nikita with a possible way out of accepting responsibility for her violent actions. If the situation is to kill or be killed, Nikita might absolve herself with the obvious answer, "They made me do it. I did not want to." However, along with absolving herself of the responsibility for her actions, this choice also absolves her of her agency. Once she relinquishes to Section One the repercussions of her actions, she admits to herself and to the audience that she has no power. She then becomes a tool and a victim.

Instead, Nikita acknowledges these events, but in carrying out her own agendas she refuses to allow circumstances to take away her agency and to render her a victim, as implied by Laura Grindstaff's analysis of the television show.[20] She accomplishes this goal by implementing her own plans. At times, she must act as the conduit for the power of Section One and the Center, but she often undercuts that power. In "Four Light Years Farther," she is forced to evaluate the Section One operatives.[21] Although passing judgment on Operations and on Madeline instills in her a sense of justice or at least revenge, it is the sentencing of her lover, Michael, to death that provides the pivot point for Nikita's agency and the audience's empathy. Nikita does issue the "cancellation" order for Michael, as the Center and Mr. Jones demand, but she later rescues

Michael from his death sentence and provides him with a window of escape from Section One. These later actions help to illustrate that however often she is maneuvered into undesirable situations, she refuses to relinquish her power and acts only to uphold her own desires. Like all events in the series, though, even forms of agency are compromised.

In the series finale, "A Time For Every Purpose," Nikita appears to have achieved the ultimate form of agency by being made leader of Section One.[22] This appearance, like most features of the show, is deceiving. Her freedom and power are still limited by her inability to leave behind the violent world of Section One. Her personal goal to make Section One a better place for the agents is formulated incompletely. She is still caught in the paradoxes marking this covert world.

Another element lessening the threat of victimhood for Nikita is the fact that all of the residents of Section One are potential victims. Michael, Birkoff, and Walter are subject to the same death threats as Nikita. All will be killed if they try to escape. Nikita is not singled out because of her gender. She is equal to her colleagues. This aspect of equality also forges a bond between Nikita and her Section One comrades.

On a strictly American level, Nikita's position as the besieged and besieging underdog strikes a resounding chord. America has long had a special love for individuals who work against oppressing systems. The very roots of the country are entwined with the myth of the rebel. Seeing Nikita as a light struggling against an overwhelming dark draws on this cultural currency for American viewers. Being designated the rebel grants Nikita a culturally recognizable role on which to build her identity, while at the same time garnering for her the audience's patience and understanding. It is one of the few readily recognizable mainstream symbols represented in *La Femme Nikita*, where otherwise little is clearly identifiable.

Nikita's one incontestable attribute is her biological sex. It is impossible to escape her physicality. Feminists have long been in conflict about how important the role of the body is in constructing identity and in performing roles in society. This debate does not look as if it will come to an end in the near future, but in the meantime Nikita's body is a central focus in this particular show. Her looks are emphasized from the very beginning of the show with Madeline's purr, "they are the most powerful weapon you have."[23] Nikita is the only blond primary character on the program, played by Pita Wilson. This fact is emphasized by the settings on the show. They are often dark, cast with shadows, and inadequately lit with pale lights. The characters are clothed in black or equivalent dark colors and blend into the shadowed background. In contrast, Wilson's golden hair always manages to gleam. It catches the light and makes her noticeable and distinct among the shadows. Even when Nikita wears a cap or hat, chunky strands of her bright golden hair stick out or trail from behind in a ponytail-a visual bright spot drawing the viewer's attention. Nikita's clothing plays a part in juxtaposing her biological gender and the role she acts out for Section One. Her outfits are usually tight around her torso, displaying her athletic figure. It is not unusual for her undercover wardrobe to be low cut across the chest. This focus on Nikita's biological body just might threaten to underscore all of society's potential problems with the woman warrior, but Nikita once again turns this factor in her favor.

Paired with this emphasis on her body is Nikita's use of her own physical beauty to distract the potential target of her mission. In "There Are No More Missions," an underwear-clad Nikita attempts to distract Michael with kisses and a provocative display of skin, while she covertly reaches for her gun. When Michael escapes before she can shoot him, she chases him out into the street still in her state of partial undress.[24] This emphasis on her body does contain a threat to reduce Nikita's power. As Laura Mulvey notes in her essay "Visual Pleasures and Narrative Cinema," images of women often are constructed to pander to the male gaze of the audience. Therefore, the woman exists only to represent and gratify the masculine construction of the feminine.[25] On the other hand, the one who does the constructing controls the power. It is Nikita who is presenting her image to Michael. She controls what he sees and how he sees. In constructing herself in a specific way and by carrying out the alternative agenda of attempted murder, Nikita clearly is the one using the power of the gaze, not Michael or the audience. Her body is no longer a potential hazard; it is a tool she presents and utilizes for her own designs.

In an examination of the power struggles in which Nikita engages as she drives herself to remain in control, it becomes clear that she is most certainly a woman warrior. Society is largely sidelined in the battles, leaving her free to construct herself and her power as she can in the dangerous world of Section One. Her own agendas often place her in direct confrontation with the orders that structure her job and existence in the section. However, her ability to subvert Section One's aims and to outmaneuver the other agents pitted against her is a testament to Nikita's power, status, and ability.

The figure of Nikita as a woman warrior reflects a breakdown in traditional gendered social roles in which the man is the hero and the woman is the faithful sidekick or damsel in distress. Although the woman warrior's role may seem designed to uphold mainstream social norms with the imposition of order upon the criminal fringes, it brings to light the power found in the borderlands of society and allows the woman (such as Nikita) to protest these norms. This protest also reveals the instability of such roles and is a step toward new role models for women. Flickering on the small screen is the image of an empowered woman. However, Nikita is also a warning. With this new, violent role come the issues of responsible use and abuse of authority that will not disappear simply because the hero is an empathic woman. The woman warrior demands from us the reexamination of cultural roles and agencies of authority.

PART FOUR

Star Trek: Voyager

Star Trek: Voyager (aired 1995–2001) is one of several spin-offs of the original *Star Trek* television series. The program follows the crew of *Voyager*, who are stranded far from home with no immediate prospects for rescue. The crew's quest is to find a technology that will enable them to return home as quickly as possible without jeopardizing the existence of other civilizations. In their travels, the crew assimilates a Borg, Seven of Nine, and her quest to discover the meaning of being human takes center stage. Her quest is often used as a foil for the moral dilemmas faced by the crew and their captain, who, cut off from Star Fleet, must make complicated decisions about the moral use of alien technology, the formation of alliances, and the cost of appropriating the means to return home.

10

We Who Are Borg, Are We Borg?

EDRIE SOBSTYL

Readers may recognize in my title an allusion to Hélène Cixous's Amnesty lecture, "We Who Are Free, Are We Free?" [1] Addressing poets in particular, Cixous's answer is "no"; poets are a threat to established order and must work against forces of oppression to free themselves and others. In the spirit of Cixous, I offer an unqualified "yes" to my own title question: we are Borg, although not in the sense typically advocated by cyborg feminists. Donna Haraway originally introduced the figure of the cyborg, a hybrid of human and machine, "as a blasphemous anti-racist feminist figure reshaped for science-studies analyses and feminist theory alike." Her hope was that cyborgs would be used in "defying their founding identities as weapons and self-acting control devices, thus trying to trouble U.S. cultural commitments to what counts as agency and self-determination." [2] My argument contrasts Haraway's ideal with Cixous's scrutiny of the individual as still inextricably linked to freedom for women. In particular, I use my examination of the cyborg warrior to address issues of autonomy, justice, and violence in an era of expanding corporate globalization and to raise questions about feminist theorists' use of popular culture.

Haraway calls the cyborg "the illegitimate offspring of militarism and patriarchal capitalism." She acknowledges that the cyborg can be read in terms of global control, military apocalypse, and "the final appropriation of women's bodies in a masculinist orgy of war." [3] But she hopes for a different perspective: "a cyborg world might be about lived social and bodily realities in which people are not afraid of their joint kinship with animals and machines, not afraid of permanently partial identities and contradictory standpoints." [4] It once may have been true that, as Haraway claims, "the cyborg is our ontology; it gives us our politics," but my examination of Seven of Nine in *Star Trek: Voyager* will ask what those politics have become and suggest that feminism may now wish to give them back.

In a different vein, Cixous asks, "[D]oes the individual self, such as it was defined in the eighteenth century by the ideology of human rights, still exist?" She wonders, "[I]f it does not, whose freedom are we at such pains to protect?"[5] She argues that although the philosophy of individual freedom has had liberating effects, it also has been undermined by its own unforeseeable consequences. Therefore, she suggests that it is now necessary "to do two things at once: to emphasize both the permanent value of the philosophy of rights, and simultaneously, the inadequacy, the limits of the breakthrough it represented."[6]

It is the limits of these breakthroughs for women that I wish to relocate, not in terms of cyborg transgression or even in terms of the discourse of individual rights, but in terms of the lives of women. The Borg are a natural starting point for such an analysis. Their very existence poses an "extreme narrative danger" that threatens to exceed the limits of Star Trek: Voyager's liberal ideals.[7] These are the very limits to which Cixous refers. The Borg's original appearance on the Star Trek: The Next Generation series locates them at "the confrontation of the most deeply rooted values of the Star Trek universe, the values of human freedom and self-determination, with something like their pure opposite."[8] They are a "nightmare vision of technological progress from which the concept of a self has been eliminated."[9] At first, the Borg are genderless. It is reported that the species appears to have no females. But by the time we reach the Star Trek: Voyager series, because the ship is stranded in the depths of space, the program "must address every value of the Federation anew in almost every episode."[10] Although Star Trek: Voyager does not intend to question the value of liberal individualism for women, gendering the Borg clearly allows us to do so.

The disassimilated Borg character Seven of Nine, Tertiary Adjunct of Unimatrix Zero One (played by Jeri Ryan), might not seem to belong in a collection of essays about just warrior women. Seven does not fit the same mold as characters such as Buffy, Xena, or Nikita, but in many ways she is an exemplary woman warrior. Few would challenge her status as a woman; one need only look at her. The sensuality of the new women warriors—who are beautiful, often buxom, and frequently tall and blond—indicates that violent female transgression is constrained strictly by the demands of commercial success. It is not surprising that sex sells. What is interesting is the way that Seven's subject position *as woman* has eclipsed her liberation from the Borg.

Ryan joined the cast of Star Trek: Voyager in 1997, at the end of the program's third season (1996–97). Although Seven's earliest episodes did not make much of Ryan's femininity, other than to dress her in form-fitting clothing, her character gradually became more stereotypically feminine, but in most respects less warriorlike. At the outset, she referred to herself in the plural or third person, spoke in clipped military phrases, and demonstrated little personal initiative. Despite her exterior appearance, she was quite "masculine," exhibiting strength, reason, and emotional detachment. As she finds a niche on *Voyager*, however, things change. What began as a plausible mother-daughter relationship between Seven and the ship's captain, Kathryn Janeway, grows into a constellation of maternal relationships. Seven becomes a substitute mother for young Naomi Wildman and later for a group of liberated Borg children. When Seven is frustrated at her inability to deal with the Borg children, Janeway blithely tells her to "use her maternal instincts," never considering that someone who was captured, enslaved, and turned into a human-machine hybrid at age six would not have any maternal instincts. The implication is clear: these instincts are a matter of biological destiny, no matter how they may have been suppressed by her upbringing in a Borg military hive. Once she is free, her maternal instincts will surface. Janeway's assumption illustrates that underneath the implants and modifications, the cyborg figure of Seven is still a woman.

The problem of maternalism is reinforced by what Anne Cranny-Francis calls Seven's infantilization. When her ties to the Borg are severed, Seven begins to remember her childhood, her parents, and her capture. These memories are seldom pleasant, but rather demonstrate her helplessness as a human female. Her increasingly exaggerated femininity also "robs her of any authority and constructs her resistance to humanization as a childish dependency and fear." [11] Neither fear of the family nor the undermining of female authority with revealing costumes are unusual on *Star Trek*, but they take on a new significance for Seven. As Thomas Richards has shown, unwelcome family members are a common plot on *Star Trek: The Next Generation*. He argues that, like the Borg, the family is a direct threat to the sacred autonomy of the individual. [12] On *Star Trek: Voyager* this plot device is limited by the ship's location in the Delta Quadrant, but Seven's childhood memories still highlight her trade-off between Borg power and feminine weakness.

This inescapable femininity is one of the unusual paradoxes Seven faces as a just warrior woman. In order to enjoy the masculine privilege of the Borg warrior, she must denounce or efface all but the most superficial aspects of her gender. But on *Star Trek: Voyager* the exchange is exposed as a dirty trick because the military-industrial entertainment complex will not let her efface her gender. Indeed, the program continually goes to lengths unmotivated by plot or character to exaggerate her femininity. In one episode, for example, Seven wants to use her technical skills to help her fellow crewmen win a space race. She also wishes to develop a better social relationship with pilot Tom Paris, one of the racers. Seven's efforts do not elicit the gratitude of *Voyager's* aggressive Klingon chief engineer, B'Elanna Torres, who is Paris's love interest. Instead, we are treated to a soap opera-style jealous glare at Seven.[13] Such pointlessly feminine behavior fits neither character and illustrates an important way in which Seven differs from other female warrior characters. They are women warriors, whereas Seven must clearly choose one role or the other. In the Borg hive, she is a powerful drone. For her to become an individual, she must become an individual woman, with all the drawbacks that entails. Although on the surface she has been offered a choice between freedom and captivity, her real choice is between captivity and femininity. It is a poor bargain, for, as Cixous attests, one cannot be both a woman and free.[14]

Cixous's point is driven home when we contrast Seven's experience with another captured Borg on *Star Trek: The Next Generation.* Third of Five, later known as Hugh, embraces his humanity quickly and easily and regards the prospect of masculine individuality with wonder and delight. He even persuades Captain Jean-Luc Picard not to attack the Borg. Hugh, of course, is male, so it seems natural that he should wish to step easily into the role of free individual for which our cultural context already has prepared him.[15] Picard himself previously was captured and assimilated by the Borg, although he was ultimately rescued. The enthusiasm with which his experience has been interpreted reveals a serious barrier to the possibility of reading the cyborg in the way Haraway wished.

Cynthia Fuchs writes that Picard's assimilation shows us that the Borg are "*exemplary* mass media cyborgs." She insists that the Borg offer "an alternative, nonbinary model of subjectivity, one that allows self-relation and self-transgression in the creation of a new, incongruous, and multiple subjectivity."[16] Fuchs misses the heavy-handedness with which the screenwriters hold the viewer's nose to the similarities, not the differences, between the Federation and the Borg. Hugh's human name is chosen for him because he does not understand the way crew members refer to one another as *I* and *you.* These pronouns indicate individuality, in contrast to the Borg's *we.* Commander La

Forge thus decides to call him "Hugh" because it sounds like "you." Hugh responds, "we are Hugh," and must be corrected immediately, but the implication is clear: "we"—the Borg—are "you"—the Federation. Now that we have both male and female Borg characters to compare, we can see that the possibilities of which Fuchs writes are realizable only in the figure of the male cyborg. This limitation, in turn, suggests that cyborg status can be only a thin and distracting veneer for human bodies marked by differences of sex and race. In both cases, the military might behind both Federation and Borg is unchallenged.

The notion of individual autonomy *for women* is therefore central to our understanding of Seven's position. Warrior women such as Buffy, Xena, and Nikita are lone actors, largely isolated from their communities. They have friends and sidekicks, but only they are "chosen." Thus, these women warriors are not just individuals; they are special individuals, set apart by skills and burdens most women lack. Seven, in contrast, is out of place on a Federation starship and terrified by her disconnection from the Borg collective. Unlike Hugh, she does not wish to be an individual at all. Her first postliberation words to Janeway are, "you will return this drone to the Borg." Why might a warrior woman reject liberal freedom and agency? Is Borg solidarity so attractive to women that it makes the liberal ideal of atomistic individualism seem undesirable? Even Janeway recognizes the appeal of the Borg, telling Seven, "you were part of a vast consciousness, billions of minds working together, a harmony of purpose and thought, no indecision, no doubts—the security and strength of a unified will, and you've lost that." [17]

The rejection of the liberal ideal is a stock theme in science fiction. A couple of years before *Star Trek* hit our television screens, Susan Sontag observed that whenever science fiction uses Borg-like invaders, "they obey the most rigid military discipline, and display no personal characteristics whatsoever. And it is this regime of emotionlessness, of impersonality, of regimentation, which they will impose on the earth if they are successful." [18] She added that the humans in these stories typically are satisfied with their improvements once creatures with no emotions, who think and act as a group, have colonized them. The Borg recapitulate this sci-fi trope, with a gender-biased twist. Picard was deeply scarred by his assimilation, and Hugh leaps at the chance to be free of the Borg. But as a woman, Seven prefers her Borg efficiency, lack of volition and emotion, and blind obedience to the tyranny over the individualistic liberal will. As Anne Cranny-Francis points out, the cyborg tends to confirm the "position of women as excluded from authority, as powerless, as primarily sexual beings, as of interest only in terms of their (sexual) uses/value to men. Not surprisingly, women have not rushed to fill this role." [19]

In the third episode in which Seven appears, tellingly titled "The Gift," she clearly articulates the weakness of the liberal model of individual autonomy:

> JANEWAY: I've met Borg who were freed from the collective. It wasn't easy for them to accept their individuality, but in time they did. You're no different. Granted you were assimilated at a very young age and your transition may be more difficult, but it will happen.
>
> SEVEN: If it does happen, we will become fully human?
>
> JANEWAY: Yes, I hope so.
>
> SEVEN: We will be autonomous, independent?
>
> JANEWAY: That's what individuality is all about.
>
> SEVEN: If at that time we choose to return to the collective, will you permit it?
>
> JANEWAY: I don't think you'll want to do that.
>
> SEVEN: You would deny us the choice, as you deny us now. You have imprisoned us in the name of humanity, yet you will not grant us your most cherished human right, to choose our own fate. You are hypocritical, manipulative. We do not want to be what you are. Return us to the collective.

Janeway's response to Seven's scathing observation is typically heavy-handed:

> JANEWAY: You lost the capacity to make a rational choice the moment you were assimilated. They took that from you, and until I'm convinced you've gotten it back, I'm making the choice for you. You're staying here.
>
> SEVEN: Then you are no different than the Borg.

In rejecting Seven's choice, the *Voyager* crew is simply applying classical liberal principles. Each individual is free to rationally choose what he or she wishes, subject to the constraints that no one be harmed and that no one else's right to exercise their freedom be limited. But clearly forces external to the chooser determine the standard of rational choice for the crew. The Borg collective cannot remain free to roam the galaxy assimilating cultures because doing so would promote harm and limit freedom and therefore is deemed irrational. If we pay attention to Seven's preference for the collective rather than for the Borg's techno-imperialism, however, we see, initially at least, how she stands poised to subvert the ideal of freedom offered by the Federation, as Haraway hopes the cyborg might do. The ideal in question is, of course, the Western liberal ideal. Seven's withering remark that the Federation is "no better than the Borg" is clear evidence of both her rational prowess and her subversive/critical power.

The notions of agency and autonomy that underpin the liberal ideal have long been upheld as promising goals for the oppressed. They remain goals toward which many feminists strive, despite much well-deserved criticism.[20] Seven therefore embodies an important objection to liberal feminism. The view of human nature that goes along with Federation (that is, U.S. liberal) politics is not promising for women. As Cranny-Francis warns us, we should not be surprised by this limitation. But Cranny-Francis also holds out some small hope that a more deconstructive reading of the Borg is available to the "resistant reader."[21] From the point of view of feminist cultural studies, however, we see that the Borg are right: resistance is futile, and Seven's preference for the Borg turns out to be hideously correct. Haraway might say that she would rather be a cyborg than a goddess, but Seven's rejoinder would be that she would rather be a cyborg than a woman. The speed with which she is assimilated into a new militaristic collective, the United Federation of Planets, and turned into an inadequate mother/frightened daughter can be read as a rebuff to the liberal feminist. The figure of her cradling a rescued Borg infant is a potent image, reinforcing the closure of the gap in which she once stood between Borg warrior and liberal woman.[22]

Seven becomes an icon of popular culture whose job it is to remind women that we cannot win. The distinctly liberal promises of freedom and the importance of agency and subjectivity for women are illusions. They obscure the multileveled dominance and inescapability of patriarchy by telling us that if we are on the "right" team—that is, the one with the right ends—we can be recognized as fully human. But as long as we continue to seek these ends, we will suffer Seven's fate. As Borg, Seven is part of the powerful but evil scourge of the galaxy. As an outsider in two camps, she possesses some power to destabilize existing structures but is always subject to pressure to conform, to sacrifice her subversive status. As a woman, her power will always be traded off against the empty promise of freedom.

Reading Seven as a racially marked character, Robin Roberts insists that she retains her transgressive power. She argues that the working triad of Seven, Janeway, and Torres shows how "women can create new rules and new understandings among themselves; they have an opportunity to confront racism and work out how to practice science without being constrained by a white, male-dominated hierarchy such as Starfleet."[23] But this optimistic interpretation does not withstand scrutiny for at least a couple of reasons. First, it is questionable that Seven "shows how 'white' can be reconstructed as another race through her mechanical appliances."[24] This seems to trivialize the notion of race. Second, Roberts's optimism hinges on her assertion that this triad conducts cooperative, "feminist" science. But there is nothing unusual in a team approach to problem solving in Starfleet. Roberts is mistaken that Janeway "bends hierarchical structures to work with B'Elanna and Seven."[25] Janeway is accessible to all of her crew only as long as it suits her interests as captain. Whenever there is a difference of opinion, Janeway prevails and typically reflects the will of Starfleet. The militarist hierarchy does not yield to women.

Being fooled by the value of being on the "right" team raises the issue of justice. First, let us note the ways in which Seven contrasts with other just women warriors. Buffy and Xena are warriors of a much older tradition. Their battles utilize weapons that are primitive by today's standards: stakes, crossbows, bullwhips, and occasionally magic. (Ancient Greeks do not have guns, and bullets will not kill vampires.) Buffy and Xena fight at close range, often in hand-to-hand combat. Their battles showcase their strength, agility, and quick wit. Nikita uses a modern arsenal and dispatches her enemies with less direct physical confrontation, promoting the idea that a big handgun is a great equalizer for women. But only Seven participates in battles that are fought as military engagements and waged in the present using high-tech weapons of mass destruction launched without direct physical contact with the enemy. One might say that she is more soldier than warrior, but this claim would miss the extent to which the masculine ideal of the "good soldier" is continuous with the older ideal of the just warrior. All of the *Star Trek* series have a Homeric feel to them, and on *Star Trek: Voyager,* with an *Odyssey* at its core, this atmosphere is especially palpable.

When *Voyager* liberates Seven, she nominally is transferred from captivity to freedom. It is tempting to see Seven's release from the Borg as a triumph of righteousness over the forces of evil. However, one might argue that she merely trades one military hierarchy for another. (The Federation is actually more hierarchical than the Borg collective, which is modeled on an anthill or beehive.) The battles she fights as Federation crew member are not notably different from those she waged with the Borg. The program returns frequently to the tension surrounding Seven's adjustment to her individuality in tacit recognition of her bad bargain. In "One," for example, the crew is placed in stasis to avoid radiation poisoning that, as Borg, she is able to withstand. Completely isolated, she ultimately breaks down and hallucinates Borg taunts of her individuality and Federation condemnation of her genocidal Borg past.[26] In "Infinite Regress," she experiences the Borg equivalent of multiple-personality disorder, as she tries to cope with her lingering attachment to the collective.[27] "Survival Instinct" puts her in contact with three of the other eight Borg who made up her unimatrix, and she must grapple with the dilemma of whether to return them to the collective or to sever their link and probably kill them.[28] In "Human Error," she begins to explore her emotions in depth, even creating a holodeck program of a passionate affair with the ship's first officer, Chakotay. She experiences an emotional overload, eventually found to be a built-in failsafe of her Borg modification. When the doctor offers to remove the failsafe so she can enjoy emotions, she declines, wryly observing that she has had enough humanity for the time being.[29] Finally, in the series' concluding episode, time travel is used to show Seven that her future will contain wedded bliss with Chakotay, but at the cost of the greater good of the ship. She cuts off the blossoming relationship between herself and Chakotay, sacrificing love for *Voyager*'s speedy return home.[30] Her constant ambivalence about her individuality warps the moral compass of the program and demonstrates that the notion of justice is more up for grabs for Seven than it is for Buffy, Xena, or Nikita, who are more clearly aware of who the "enemy" is. But Seven's struggles are always played out against the backdrop of her femaleness.

The Federation is ambivalent about the ideal of justice, sliding from military absolutism to wishy-washy relativism as the current plot demands. In midseries, Seven often interjected incisive observations that good and evil seemed to be in the eye of the beholder on *Voyager,* in keeping with her early subject position as outsider-transgressor. In "Nothing Human," for example, when the crew confirms that a famous Cardassian doctor performed Mengele-like experiments on captive human subjects, Seven comments, "it is curious. The Borg are accused of assimilating information with no regard for life. This Cardassian did the same, and yet his behavior is tolerated."[31]

In later episodes, Seven is co-opted into the moral instrumentalism that pervades the show, further diminishing her seditious promise. As argued previously in this essay, it is odd that a character whose aptitudes and experience encompass everything but the maternal would be made into a mommy. But Seven is often used instrumentally as Borg per se and not just as a maternal substitute.

Her Borg knowledge is valuable to Starfleet, and she is expected to share it without question, as though she were a mere appendage to the ship's computer. She does not just store knowledge: she instantiates it. She *is* engineered, she *is* technological, and the crew does not hesitate to use her *as* a machine when the occasion demands it. Using Seven's knowledge or even altering one of her Borg implants to deal with some mechanical or military crisis is a technical panacea for the crew. Seven becomes a combination database and toolbox for *Voyager*, but hardly a *person*. As previously noted, Seven's trade-off between Borg enslavement and Federation individuality is no great bargain because it reinforces the constraints of gender. A similar point can be made about the moral weight of the exchange. The moral autonomy that is supposed to go along with the liberal ideal of individual personhood is regularly withheld from Seven.

Star Trek: Voyager is at best inconsistent in respecting the moral autonomy of its characters. When Seven is first brought aboard the ship, the implants linking her to the Borg collective deteriorate quickly, and she refuses treatment, preferring to die. The following exchange between Janeway and the ship's doctor ensues:

> DOCTOR: If a patient told me not to treat them, even if the situation were life threatening, I would be ethically obligated to honor that request.
>
> JANEWAY: This is no ordinary patient. She may have been raised by Borg, raised to think like a Borg, but she's with us now. And underneath all that technology she is a human being, whether she's ready to accept that or not. And until she is ready, someone has to make decisions for her. Proceed with the surgery.[32]

Similarly, in "Nothing Human," previously cited, a hologram of the Cardassian Mengele-like doctor is created in order to perform lifesaving surgery on Torres. But Torres fought against the Cardassians in their war with Bajor, and she refuses to let a war criminal—even a hologram of a war criminal—treat her. Janeway autocratically intervenes and forces Torres to undergo treatment. Her justification is that her ship cannot function without its chief engineer, showing that within the confines of a military hierarchy, morality is instrumental, not categorical. In a later episode, the family of one of the Borg children, Icheb, is located. He does not wish to return to his primitive home planet. Janeway again quashes his choice, justifying herself this time by Icheb's status as a minor.[33] Later still, after it has been revealed that Icheb's parents used him as

"Borg bait", he returns to *Voyager*. Another of Seven's Borg implants has begun to deteriorate, and she is dying. Icheb, who has grown attached to his Borg surrogate mother, confronts Janeway to force Seven to accept risky treatment. Janeway replies that she cannot make a decision for Seven, yet she certainly made decisions for Seven and for others in the past.[34] Such examples make it difficult to establish the kind of clear moral superiority that would place the Federation decisively on the side of justice. The "might makes right" morality of the Borg may be objectionable, but Federation military discipline is not obviously a superior alternative.

When we attend to the moral messiness of Seven's warrior status, we notice parallels between *Voyager's* world and our own. One might argue that a "good" military operation must be structured hierarchically to preserve the ends of the vessel and her crew even at the expense of individuals. Yet as Haraway insists, we live within the confines of a military-industrial hierarchy now. She says, "I do not think that most people who live on earth now have the choice not to live inside of, and not to be shaped by, the fiercely material and imaginative apparatuses for making 'us' cyborgs."[35] But one must then wonder whether our cyborg status adds anything to cyborg feminism that is not already present in our status as women. From the patenting of our gene sequence to everyday consumer choices, the warped moral compass of *Star Trek: Voyager* is part of our world, too. Reading Seven as a just warrior woman obliges us to notice the ground we hold in common with Seven and to articulate a feminist response. We therefore can interpret Seven as a signpost to the inhumane, instrumental moral reasoning that victimizes women and can recognize that the sources of their victimization are largely the same as they are for Seven. Although the figure of the cyborg is an appealing pop culture figure, the arguments given show that one need not scratch very hard on the Borg icon to reveal the intractable signs of gender beneath its surface. The "permanently partial identities" Haraway advocates are shown to collapse under the cultural weight of being female. This collapse is key to using Seven as a critical resource for feminism.

Much of contemporary discourse is marked by excessive enthusiasm for the newest technology, but shallow consideration of the history and philosophy of technology plagues studies of popular culture. Every emergent technology is treated as though it holds fundamentally new potential for human freedom. Yet the claim that "this device will change everything" is mundane from the standpoint of history. Optimism about the potential for the Internet to build new, more democratic communities has been heard earlier in similar discussions about railroads, radio, telephones, and even television.

Richard Sclove notes that when we ignore the history of technology, we overlook the social origins and consequences of technology. We thereby increase the ease with which technology exerts and reinforces social, physical, and political limitations on us.[36] Cyborg feminism simply facilitates this ease. There are many tensions at work in Seven's character: Borg/human, drone/soldier, woman/individual, and instrument/agent. In light of Sclove's observation, we need to add another antagonism. Seven is not just technological; she is delivered via technology. Because she is a television character in a flashy adventure, pat resolutions to the paradoxes she presents are especially threatening. The moral quagmire of *Star Trek: Voyager* is not just a product of bad screenwriting or chance; it is an inevitable consequence of the program's ambivalence about violence and its place in popular culture. Similarly, the unease with which the series handles Seven's transgressive potential is an inevitable manifestation of this ambivalence.

Gary Westfahl claims that the dichotomized character of the *Star Trek* series points to a serious problem: "Episodes might conclude with a ringing affirmation of the dangers or evils of armed conflict, but before that message emerged, viewers were invited to vicariously enjoy the thrill and excitement of armed conflict. All these scenes can be read as encoded endorsements of warfare and as an appropriate, even pleasurable, method for resolving human problems."[37] Gene Roddenberry is known to have struggled with NBC executives over violence in the original series, and Westfahl asserts that Roddenberry's only real option was to conceal the program's violence behind the smokescreen of last resort.[38] The same claim can be made for the show's disregard for moral autonomy, which is always for a character's own good as determined by paternalistic Starfleet authority.

Star Trek: Voyager is also constrained by audience demands. Violence and sex sell, and in Seven the program's producers have a juicy commercial opportunity. But popular culture creates the desire for violence and sex and uses its power over the consumer to fulfill and reinforce that desire. Women bear the physical, political, and economic brunt of these practices. Sexy, violent cyborg characters delivered to us through the politically opaque medium of television make it difficult to identify the still untouched limits imposed on women simply because they are women. As Seven's subversive potential wanes over the course of the series' run, we see the tremendous force with which the cyborg's potential to "trouble" U.S. cultural commitments to what counts as agency and self-determination can be crushed. A female Borg is easy to defeat; we already know how to oppress women. This is surely one of the unforeseen limiting consequences of the eighteenth-century rhetoric of rights alluded to by Cixous.

We are bound in a network of global capitalist, military, and patriarchal forces, even without technologies such as the Internet and cybernetics. Women, especially outside of the United States, are renewable resources for transnational capital.[39] In Seven, we see the idea of woman as resource extrapolated almost without alteration into the twenty-fourth century. Seven as database, toolbox, and mother is a symbol of popular culture's failure to imagine a world in which the freedom promised by the philosophy of rights is available to women, no matter how potent the figure of the cyborg may once have been. Instead, popular culture offers military and gender hierarchies as commodities. The problem is not just that we are able to purchase oppressive forces in the form of television programs and licensed goods. It is the way in which, by willingly suspending our disbelief, we tacitly assent to and promote these hierarchies. In decoding a character such as Seven in terms of her diabolical imperialist origins and her status as liberal soldier, we pander to consumerism and the culture industries that sustain it,[40] and, in turn, we participate in our own oppression. How can feminist studies of popular culture resolve this dilemma?

There is another sense in which today's technologies are qualitatively different from older ones. They hold the potential for more serious forms of enslavement. Bill Joy argues that "the most compelling 21st century technologies—robotics, genetic engineering, and nanotechnology—pose a different threat than the technologies that have come before."[41] They are the very same technologies Seven embodies and makes appealing. They are a different threat because they will be capable of self-replication, thereby increasing the risk of substantial damage to our physical world. Furthermore, Joy indicates that although nuclear, biological, and chemical weapons are obscenely powerful, they also require access to "rare—indeed effectively unavailable—raw materials and highly protected information." For the first time, he points out, our new technologies "will not require large facilities or rare raw materials. Knowledge alone will enable the use of them." When we combine these two factors, the result is knowledge-enabled mass destruction, multiplied by the power of self-replication. As Joy puts it, "we are on the cusp of the further perfection of extreme evil."[42] Programs such as *Star Trek: Voyager* therefore continue to play the role Susan Sontag attributed to science fiction nearly forty years ago: they "provide a fantasy target for righteous bellicosity to discharge itself, and for the aesthetic enjoyment of suffering and disaster." [43] If, as Sontag claimed, science fiction of the 1950s and 1960s was in complicity with the abhorrent, then contemporary sci-fi films and television programs are even worse, normalizing as they do our "perfection of extreme evil." The distinctive place of gender in this evil must be examined.

Similarly, Kevin Robins and Les Levidow argue that the intersection of real-world military technology with representations of it on television promotes in us an infantile desire for omnipotence combined with paranoid fear. The televised cyborg is powerful, but this power is accompanied by the constant dread of counterattack. [44] The initial tenuousness of Seven's freedom is thus to be expected because her very existence is a constant threat. In Seven's case, this dread is complicated by her gender, and the program ultimately channels this complication into the "safe" roles of dutiful daughter, surrogate mother, lover, and wife. Not even her cyborg status can protect Seven from being trampled by the weight of her sex.

Can feminist cultural theorists overcome the gap between theory and popular/consumer consciousness? We seem to be caught in an endless feedback loop. Popular culture offers us reinscriptions of the limited ideals of U.S. liberalism, and we respond, "Look! There they are again!" By now, we understand these limits all too well. In reading popular culture in this way, feminist theorists risk submerging their political impact in what I call the "infinite egress of representation": we create multiple layers of appraisal, each more sophisticated and abstract than the last, which reproduce themselves ad infinitum. Difficult questions about why these readings matter retreat further into the background. The character Seven of Nine reminds us that being cyborg women leaves untouched the problems of being woman.

What is required, then, is a return to Cixous's recommendation that we do two (or more) things at once. While continuing to acknowledge the permanent value of the philosophy of rights and challenging any limits to the philosophy of rights, feminist cultural theory must return the female, in all her diversity, to center stage. Reading Seven as a just warrior woman lets us see that her transgressive power was taken from her in exchange for the false lure of freedom. It also enables us to identify the capitalist, patriarchal, and military hierarchies that reinforce the lure of freedom and to see those forces at work in our own lives. Making the cyborg a *female* demonstrates that the problem for feminism is not lack of freedom, individuality, and agency; nor is it fear of permanently partial identity. It is that we are *women,* and there is no cure for that.

NOTES

BIBLIOGRAPHY

INDEX

Notes

Foreword: Out Far or In Deep

1. "Tabula Rasa," Nov. 13, 2001.
2. See Richard Dyer, "White," *Screen* 29, no. 4 (1989): 44–64, for his discussion of the minatory identification of whiteness as default mode.
3. See note 2, chapter 7.
4. I thank Jackie Stacey for giving me a model of personal relation to the text, in her case a visual one, with her analysis of her own teen photograph in the "How Do I Look?" chapter of *Star Gazing: Hollywood Cinema and Female Spectatorship*, 1–18 (New York: Routledge, 1994).
5. My third *Buffy* essay, for example, includes a meditation on John Donne and the double and starts with a quotation from one of his poems. See " 'Every Night I Save You': Buffy, Spike, Sex, and Redemption," *Slayage: The Online International Journal of Buffy Studies* 5 (2002), available at: www.slayage.tv. See also " 'Who Died and Made Her the Boss?' Patterns of Mortality in *Buffy*," in *Fighting the Forces: What's at Stake in* Buffy the Vampire Slayer? edited by Rhonda V. Wilcox and David Lavery, 3–17 (New York: Rowman and Littlefield, 2002).

1. Introduction: Athena's Daughters

1. Donna Haraway, *Modest_Witness@Second_Millennium. FemaleMan©_Meets_Onco-Mouse™: Feminism and Technoscience* (New York: Routledge, 1996), 44.
2. Jean Elshtain, *Women and War* (New York: Basic, 1987).
3. According to feminist critic Marilyn R. Farwell, "the female functions as the boundary figure, the frontier or the object from which the narrative subject must separate himself, [and as such] encodes violence and oppression as part of the narrative"; see *Heterosexual Plots and Lesbian Narratives* (New York: Columbia Univ. Press, 1996), 31.
4. Teresa de Lauretis, *Technologies of Gender: Essays on Theory, Film, and Fiction* (Bloomington: Univ. of Indiana Press, 1987), 42–43.
5. Marina Warner, *Joan of Arc: The Image of Female Heroism* (1981; reprint, New York: Penguin, 1987), 176.
6. Farwell, *Heterosexual Plots,* 30.
7. Ibid., 58.
8. Sharon MacDonald, "Drawing the Lines—Gender, Peace, and War: An Introduction," in

Images of Women in Peace and War: Cross-cultural and Historical Perspectives, edited by Sharon MacDonald, Pat Holden, and Shirley Ardener (Madison: Univ. of Wisconsin Press, 1987), 22–23.

9. Michael Ventura, "Warrior Women: Why Are TV Shows Like *Buffy the Vampire Slayer, La Femme Nikita,* and *Xena, Warrior Princess* So Popular, Especially among Teens?" *Psychology Today* 31, no. 6 (Nov.-Dec. 1998), 62.

10. Sherrie A. Inness, *Tough Girls: Women Warriors and Wonder Women in Popular Culture* (Philadelphia: Univ. of Pennsylvania Press, 1999).

11. With regard to this point, one can point to Yvonne Craig as Batgirl as an apt example. Her fights were choreographed carefully to imitate the moves of a Broadway showgirl through the use of a straight kick to her opponent's face rather than the type of kick a martial artist would use. When the woman warrior of the 1960s and 1970s did use martial arts, she usually was restricted to a karate chop to the back of her opponent's neck or a single kick. She seldom engaged in prolonged hand-to-hand combat and rarely, if ever, was shown taking a punch herself.

12. See, for example, "Buffy the Vampire Slayer," *The Nation* (Apr. 6, 1998): 35–36; Mike Flaherty, "Xenaphilia," *Entertainment Weekly* (Mar. 7, 1997): 39–42; Donna Minkowitz, "Xena: She's Big, Tall, Strong—and Popular," *MS.* (July-Aug. 1996): 74–77; Jennifer Pozner, "THWACK! POW! YIKES! Not Your Mother's Heroines," *Sojourner: The Women's Forum* 23 (Oct. 1997): 12–13; and Debbie Stoller, "Brave New Girls: These T.V. Heroines Know What Girl Power Really Is," *On the Issues* (fall 1998): 42–45.

13. For example, Charlie's Angels were employed by and answered to a paternalist playboy and unseen boss. Agent 99 was Maxwell Smart's sidekick, and Batgirl and the Bionic Woman were inferior versions of their male counterparts.

14. One notes in this context that Agent 99 married Maxwell Smart, Wonder Woman fell in love with Steve Travis, and the Bionic Woman with Steve Austin; the program *Charlie's Angels* placed as much emphasis on the heterosexual allure of their characters as on their fighting skills and intellectual abilities.

15. See Susan Faludi, *Backlash: The Undeclared War Against American Women* (New York: Crown, 1991), 138, and James William Gibson, *Warrior Dreams: Paramilitary Culture in Post-Vietnam America* (New York: Hill and Wang, 1994).

16. Elyce Rae Helford, "Introduction," in *Fantasy Girls: Gender in the New Universe of Science Fiction and Fantasy Television,* edited by Elyce Rae Helford (Lanham, Md.: Rowman and Littlefield, 2000), 7.

17. Elyce Rae Helford, "Feminism, Queer Studies, and the Sexual Politics of *Xena, Warrior Princess,*" in *Fantasy Girls,* edited by Helford, 138.

18. Kent A. Ono, "To Be a Vampire on *Buffy the Vampire Slayer:* Race and ('Other') Socially Marginalizing Positions on Horror TV," in *Fantasy Girls,* edited by Helford, 165.

19. Two scholarly essay collections on *Buffy the Vampire Slayer* appeared just as *Athena's Daughters* was being submitted for publication; several contributors to this anthology have cited these edited books. See Rhonda V. Wilcox and David Lavery, eds., *Fighting the Forces: What's at Stake in* Buffy the Vampire Slayer? (New York: Rowman and Littlefield, 2002), and Roz Kaveney, ed., *Reading the Vampire Slayer: An Unofficial Critical Companion to* Buffy *and* Angel (London: Tauris Parke, 2002).

20. Haraway, *Modest Witness,* 45.

2. The Baby, the Mother, and the Empire: Xena as Ancient Hero

1. Some recent considerations of the meaning of ancient tropes in popular culture include Maria Wyke, *Projecting the Past: Ancient Rome, Cinema, and History* (New York: Routledge, 1997), and Sandra R. Joshel, Martha Malamud, and Don McGuire, eds., *Imperial Projections: Ancient Rome in Modern Popular Culture* (Baltimore, Md.: Johns Hopkins Univ. Press, 2001).

2. Robert Jewett and John S. Lawrence, *The American Monomyth* (New York: Doubleday, 1977), xx. See also Richard Slotkin, *Gunfighter Nation* (New York: Atheneum, 1992), and his emphasis on "purifying" violence.

3. See Deborah Lyons's effort to find independent agency for Greek mythic heroines in *Gender and Immortality* (Princeton, N.J.: Princeton Univ. Press, 1996). Jennifer Pozner discusses Xena's female heroism in "THWACK! POW! YIKES! Not Your Mother's Heroines," *Sojourner: The Women's Forum* 23 (Oct. 1997), 12; and Sherrie A. Inness discusses female heroism in relation to constructs of the masculine hero in action-adventure films and similar mass-media productions in her book *Tough Girls: Women Warriors and Wonder Women in Popular Culture* (Philadelphia: Univ. of Pennsylvania Press, 1999).

4. "Destiny," Jan. 27, 1997. (All dates for episodes cited in the endnotes refer to the original U.S. airdates.) The incident is loosely based on an experience of the historical G. Julius Caesar: in 75 B.C.E., he was kidnapped by pirates. After insisting on an increase in the amount of ransom asked, the freed Caesar hunted down his former captors to crucify them at Pergamum. See Suetonius, "Caesar," in *Lives of the Caesars*, translated by John C. Rolfe (New York: Macmillan, 1914), 4 and 74, and Plutarch, "Caesar," in *Parallel Lives*, translated by B. Perrin (New York: Macmillan, 1914), 1–2.

5. Severed heads in "The Debt, Part I," Nov. 3, 1997. Crucifixions in "Past Imperfect," Nov. 4, 1999. "Scourge of God" is an allusion to Attila the Hun in "The Debt, Part II," Nov. 10, 1997.

6. "Past Imperfect," Nov. 4, 1999. See also emphasis on motherhood in Esther Mitchell, "Xena: Warrior Goddess," *SageWoman* 45 (1999), 28. In contrast, see Inness's claim in *Tough Girls* (161) that the maternal is deliberately downplayed in the formation of Xena's heroism.

7. "Deliverer," Oct. 20, 1997.

8. "Destiny," Jan. 27, 1997.

9. The *Oresteia* trilogy was performed at the City Dionysia festival of 458 B.C.E., a few short years before the so-called Golden Age of Athens under Pericles. For more on the political and social impact of Greek theater, see John J. Winkler and Froma Zeitlin, eds., *Nothing to Do with Dionysus?* (Princeton, N.J.: Princeton Univ. Press, 1990).

10. For discussion of the reciprocity of crimes against gender throughout the *Oresteia*, see Michael Gagarin, *Aeschylean Drama* (Berkeley and Los Angeles: Univ. of California Press, 1976), 87–118, and Froma Zeitlin, *Playing the Other* (Chicago: Univ. of Chicago Press, 1996), 87–113.

11. See the description of the Furies in Aeschylus, *Eumenides*, in *Works*, translated by Herber Weir Smith (Cambridge, Mass.: Harvard Univ. Press, 1963), 46–59, 68–77, 183–97, and 245–54. For commentary, see Maud Gleason, "The Semiotics of Gender," in *Before Sexuality*, edited by D. Halperin, J. Winkler, and F. Zeitlin, 389–415 (Princeton, N.J.: Princeton Univ. Press, 1990), and Lesley Dean-Jones, "The Cultural Construct of the Female Body in Classical Greek Science," in

Women's History and Ancient History, edited by Sarah Pomeroy, 111–37 (Chapel Hill: Univ. of North Carolina Press, 1991).

12. Mother blood as *philtatos,* "most-beloved," in Aeschylus, *Eumenides,* 608; as essential, *Eumenides,* 653–56. Main importance of the marriage bond, *Eumenides,* 217–18. Mother as stranger, *Eumenides,* 606 and 658–61.

13. Aechylus, *Eumenides,* 600–602. The multiply horrifying nature of Clytaemnestra's action is expressed slightly differently, at 625–39, where she kills (1) a male ruler, (2) as a woman, (3) in a sneaky way, and (4) right after he returns from manly military success.

14. Aeschylus, *Eumenides,* 734–41. This, despite her declaration that justice should always be impartial.

15. "The Furies," Sept. 29, 1997. Acknowledgment of Xena's world as one dominated by specifically female justice also can be found in Deirdre Neilen, "Review: *Xena, Warrior Princess,*" *Hera* 17 (1997): 1–3.

16. Implied throughout "The Furies" is divine jealousy, especially Ares' desire for Xena's undivided loyalties.

17. For an ancient interpretation of this crisis period that similarly emphasizes personal greed and lust for power, see Sallust, "Catilinarian Conspiracy," in *Works,* translated by John C. Rolfe, 10–13 (New York: J. P. Putman's Sons, 1931).

18. British freedom fighters in "Deliverer," Oct. 20, 1997, here fighting under the leadership of Boadiccea, the *XWP* version of Boudicca, who led a revolt against Nero's Rome in the early 60s B.C.E. Gallic nationalism in "When in Rome," May 2, 1998: Vercinix speaks here, a character derived from the historical Vercingetorix, leader of the last, most dangerous opposition in Caesar's Gallic Wars. Ethnic cleansing in "Legacy," Oct. 30, 2000, where the goal is protection of Roman trade in Arabia, North Africa.

19. "When in Rome," May 2, 1998.

20. "A Good Day," Oct. 26, 1998.

21. "Endgame," May 3, 1999.

22. "Antony and Cleopatra," Apr. 17, 2000. For consideration of the Cleopatra myth in greater depth, see, among others, Lucy Hughes-Hallett, *Cleopatra: Histories, Dreams, and Distortions* (London: Bloomsbury, 1990), and Mary Hamer, *Signs of Cleopatra* (London: Routledge, 1993).

23. Joanne Morreale considers the use of masquerade, or "camp," in *XWP,* noting its repeated importance in the series' deconstruction of feminine stereotypes; see *"Xena, Warrior Princess* as Feminist Camp," *Journal of Popular Culture* 32, no. 2 (fall 1998): 79–86.

24. Note that the *XWP* character is called "Octavius," the birth name of the historical figure; after his adoption by the will of the deceased dictator in 44 B.C.E., Octavius legally became Gaius Julius Caesar Octavianus, commonly abbreviated as "Octavian." He would be known widely as "Augustus" after 27 B.C.E., when the Senate granted him this honorific title in recognition of his pacification of the Roman world and restoration of Roman republican tradition.

3. Tall, Dark, and Dangerous: Xena, the Quest, and the Wielding of Sexual Violence in *Xena* On-Line Fan Fiction

1. Marija Gimbutas, *Language of the Goddess* (New York: Harper and Row, 1989), xx.

2. Sir James Frazier, *The Golden Bough* (New York: Macmillan, 1922), 420–27; Joseph Campbell, *The Hero with a Thousand Faces* (Princeton, N.J.: Princeton Univ. Press, 1972), 92–93; David Adams Leeming, *Mythology: The Voyage of the Hero* (New York: Harper and Row, 1981), 231–33.

3. Sherrie A. Inness, *Tough Girls: Women Warriors and Wonder Women in Popular Culture* (Philadelphia: Univ. of Pennsylvania Press, 1999), 171.

4. Ibid.

5. E-mail message to Helen Caudill from Ella Quince, Jan. 15, 1999.

6. Henry Jenkins, *Textual Poachers: Television Fans and Participatory Culture* (New York: Routledge, 1992), 205, 18.

7. Annis Pratt, *Archetypal Patterns in Women's Fiction* (Bloomington: Univ. of Indiana Press, 1981), 172–73. Both Carl Jung and Joseph Campbell, the appointed mainstream authorities on the quest, assume that women have a secondary role in the quest, often as the prize at the end. Yet Pratt—quoting Jesse Weston's excellent book on the grail, *From Ritual to Romance* (Garden City, N.Y.: Doubleday, 1957)—notes the central role that women play in ancient quests.

8. "The Price," Apr. 28, 1997. This date and all subsequent episode dates refer to the original U.S. airdates.

9. "The Bitter Suite," Feb. 2, 1998.

10. Elyce Rae Helford, "Feminism, Queer Studies, and the Sexual Politics of *Xena, Warrior Princess*," in *Fantasy Girls: Gender in the New Universe of Science Fiction and Fantasy Television*, edited by Elyce Rae Helford (Lanham, Md.: Rowman and Littlefield, 2000), 152–56.

11. E-mail message from Ella Quince to Helen Caudill, Jan. 15, 1999.

12. "The Crusader," Nov. 16, 1998.

13. Ibid.

14. "Forgiven," Feb. 16, 1998.

15. Jenkins, *Textual Poachers*, 120–51.

16. This process of negotiation between fans and creators is well documented in Jenkins, *Texual Poachers*.

17. Inness, *Tough Girls*, 168.

18. All quotations in this paragraph come from an e-mail message from Catherine M. Wilson to Helen Caudill, Apr. 12, 2000.

19. Camille Bacon-Smith, *Enterprising Women* (Philadelphia: Univ. of Pennsylvania Press, 1992), 262.

20. Helford, "Feminism, Queer Studies," 148–49.

21. Jenkins, *Textual Poachers*, 176; Bacon-Smith, *Enterprising Women*, 45.

22. "One Against an Army," Feb. 9, 1998.

23. Pratt, *Archetypal Patterns*, 8.

24. Ibid.

25. Catherine Wilson, "Wedding Night," in *Catherine M. Wilson's Xena Fan Fiction*, Nov. 12,

1996, available on-line at: www.tsoft.com/~cmwilson/Stories/WeddingNight.html; accessed Apr. 18, 2000.

26. Ella Quince, "Well of Sighs," in *The Australian Xena Information Page,* n.d., available on-line at: www.ausxip.com/fanfic2/sighs.html; accessed Apr. 14, 2000, p. 28.

27. Ibid., 37.

28. Pink Rabbit Productions, "Blood for Blood," in *Pink Rabbit Consortium,* n.d., available on-line at: www.altfic.com; accessed Apr. 14, 2000.

29. Sharon Bowers, *Lucifer Rising* (Tacoma, Wash.: Justice House, 1999), 39.

30. E-mail message from Catherine Wilson to Helen Caudill, Mar. 25, 2001.

31. E-mail message from Ella Quince to Helen Caudill, Mar. 19, 2001.

32. Marilyn R. Farwell, *Heterosexual Plots and Lesbian Narratives* (New York: Columbia Univ. Press, 1996), 60.

33. Karl Kroeber, qtd. in Farwell, *Heterosexual Plots,* 60.

34. Farwell, *Heterosexual Plots,* 53.

35. Helford, "Feminism, Queer Studies," 138. Helford gives *Xena* as an example of a "polysemic text—a text for multiple interpretations" (138).

36. Jenkins, *Textual Poachers,* 24.

37. Helen Caudill, "Appropriation of a Hero: The World of *Xena, Warrior Princess* Alternative Fan Fiction Online." Paper presented at the Popular Culture Association Conference, San Diego, Calif., Apr. 1, 1999.

38. Bacon-Smith, *Enterprising Women,* 240–41.

39. Inness, *Tough Girls,* 166. In fact, Inness believes that "Xena questions and changes what it means to be a hero" and "represents one of the strongest 1990's challenges to the dominance of the male hero" (166).

40. Ibid., 102.

41. Pratt, *Archetypal Patterns,* 8.

42. Leeming, *Mythology.*

43. Paulina Palmer, *Lesbian Gothic* (London: Cassell, 1999), 118.

44. Ibid.

45. Bowers, *Lucifer Rising,* 325.

46. Friedrich Nietzsche, *The Birth of Tragedy* (New York: Doubleday Anchor, 1956).

4. Love Is the Battlefield: The Making and the Unmaking of the Just Warrior in *Xena, Warrior Princess*

1. Elyce Rae Helford, "Feminism, Queer Studies, and the Sexual Politics of *Xena, Warrior Princess,*" in *Fantasy Girls: Gender in the New Universe of Science Fiction and Fantasy Television,* edited by Elyce Rae Helford (Lanham, Md.: Rowman and Littlefield, 2000), 135–39.

2. Susan Stanford Friedman, *Mappings: Feminism and the Cultural Geographies of Encounter* (Princeton, N.J.: Princeton Univ. Press, 1998), 84.

3. This literature often is referred to as commonwealth literature or second-world literature.

4. I am defining *imperialism* as both the "advocacy and glorification of military force to both expand and maintain empire" and "the practice, the theory, and the attitudes of a dominat-

ing metropolitan center ruling a distant territory." For the former definition, see M. Daphne Kutzer, *Empire's Children: Empire and Imperialism in Classic British Children's Books* (New York: Garland, 2000), xviii. For the latter definition, see Edward W. Said, *Orientalism* (New York: Vintage, 1978), 9.

5. "Unchained Heart," *Hercules, The Legendary Journeys,* May 5, 1997 (original U.S. airdate).

6. "Destiny," Jan. 27, 1997, and "The Debt, Part I," Nov. 3, 1997. (All references to *XWP* episodes cite the original U.S. airdates.) A fairly literal example of this power takes place when Xena briefly dies in the show's second season and is visited by M'lila's spirit, who explains to her the purpose of her painful past: "Now that you know evil, you can fight evil" ("Destiny"). And Lao Ma chooses to rescue Xena from certain death because Xena is "a remarkable woman, capable of greatness" ("Debt, Part I").

7. For the Western hero's investment in maintaining clear boundaries between the West and other parts of the world, see Donna J. Haraway, *Modest_Witness@Second_Millennium. Female-Man©_Meets_OncoMouse™: Feminism and Technoscience* (New York: Routledge, 1996), 23–118, and Said, *Orientalism.*

8. "Friends in Need, Part II," June 18, 2001.

9. Helford, "Feminism, Queer Studies," 139–42.

10. Friedman, *Mappings,* 77.

11. Joanne Morreale, *"Xena, Warrior Princess* as Feminist Camp," *Journal of Popular Culture* 32, no. 2 (fall 1998), 86.

12. The literature on queer theory is extensive. For an introduction to queer theory, see Marilyn R. Farwell, *Heterosexual Plots and Lesbian Narratives* (New York: Columbia Univ. Press, 1996), and Teresa de Lauretis, "Queer Theory: Lesbian and Gay Sexualities: An Introduction," *differences: A Journal of Feminist and Cultural Studies* 3, no. 2 (1991): iii–xviii.

13. "Looking Death in the Eye," Apr. 24, 2000.

14. "Seeds of Faith," Jan. 10, 2000.

15. For a discussion of this problem, see Kathleen Kennedy, "Writing Trash: Truth and the Sexual Outlaw's Reinvention of Lesbian Identity," *Feminist Theory* 1, no. 2 (Aug. 2000): 151–72, and Katie King, "The Situation of Lesbianism as Feminism's Magical Sign: Contests for Meanings and the U.S. Women's Movement, 1968–1972," *Communications* 9 (1986): 65–91.

16. Helford, "Feminism, Queer Studies," 157. Historian Alison Futrell, who has contributed an essay to this volume (chap. 2), suggested to me that Xena's dragging of Gabrielle may be an allusion to Achilles' dragging of Hector around the walls of Troy, perhaps signifying the death of love and the rage of the hero.

17. "The Bitter Suite," Feb. 2, 1998.

18. Lynda Hart, *Between the Body and the Flesh: Performing Sadomasochism* (New York: Columbia Univ. Press, 1998), 79.

19. "Seeds of Faith," Jan. 10, 2000.

20. Like most stories in the Xenaverse, Eve's birth also subverts Judeo-Christian myths.

21. "The God You Know," Jan. 29, 2001.

22. Said, *Orientalism,* 25.

23. Joanna Liddle and Shirin Rai, "Feminism, Imperialism, and Orientalism: The Challenge of the 'Indian Woman,' " *Women's History Review* 7, no. 4 (1998), 500. See also Leela Gandhi, *Post-*

colonial Theory: A Critical Introduction (New York: Columbia Univ. Press, 1998), 81–101, and Regina Lewis, *Gendering Orientalism: Race, Femininity, and Representation* (New York: Routledge, 1996). Of course, Western feminism is more diverse than sometimes portrayed here or than sometimes is portrayed in postcolonial theory. Many Western feminists are engaged in compelling critiques of racism and colonialism. Many postcolonial critics point out that Western ways of knowing incorporate and have built on racialist constructions and consequently that Western thought inevitably reproduces such constructions.

24. Said, *Orientalism*, 1.

25. "The Debt, Part I," Nov. 3, 1997.

26. "The Debt, Part II," Nov. 10, 1997.

27. Ibid.

28. "Forget Me Not," Mar. 9, 1998.

29. "The Debt, Part II," Nov. 10, 1997.

30. Ibid.

31. "The Debt, Part I," Nov. 3, 1997.

32. Meyda Yegenoglu, *Colonial Fantasies: Towards a Feminist Reading of Orientalism* (Cambridge, Eng.: Cambridge Univ. Press, 1998).

33. Gandhi, *Postcolonial Theory*, 87.

34. Robert G. Lee, *Orientals: Asian Americans in Popular Culture* (Philadelphia: Temple Univ. Press, 1999).

35. Robert J. C. Young, *Colonial Desire: Hybridity in Theory, Culture, and Race* (New York: Routledge, 1995), 22.

36. A rather literal example of this point is Xena's rescue of Grinhilda, whom she previously turned into a monster when she stripped her of her ability to love. To regain her human form, Grinhilda must let go of her hatred for Xena and rediscover the heroic woman she was before Xena corrupted the Valkyrie. See "The Return of the Valkarie," Nov. 27, 2000.

5. The Female Just Warrior Reimagined: From Boudicca to Buffy

1. Joss Whedon, qtd. in Ginia Bellafante, "Bewitching Teen Heroines," *Time* 149, no. 18 (May 5, 1997), 83. Journalistic commentary on *Buffy* abounds.

2. Sherrie A. Inness, *Tough Girls: Women Warriors and Wonder Women in Popular Culture* (Philadelphia: Univ. of Pennsylvania Press, 1999).

3. Scholarship on *Buffy* is mushrooming. See, for instance, Rhonda V. Wilcox, "Buffy and the Monsters of Teen Life: 'There Will Never Be a Very Special Buffy,' " *Journal of Popular Film and Television* 27, no. 2 (summer 1999): 16–23; A. Susan Owen, *"Buffy the Vampire Slayer:* Vampires, Postmodernity, and Postfeminism," *Journal of Popular Film and Television* 27, no. 2 (summer 1999): 24–31; and Rachel Fudge, "The Buffy Effect or, a Tale of Cleavage and Marketing," *Bitch: Feminist Response to Popular Culture*, no. 10 (1999): 18–21 and 58. Two scholarly anthologies have appeared recently: Rhonda V. Wilcox and David Lavery, eds., *Fighting the Forces: What's at Stake in Buffy the Vampire Slayer?* (New York: Rowman and Littlefield, 2002), and Roz Kaveney, ed., *Reading the Vampire Slayer: An Unofficial Critical Companion to* Buffy *and* Angel (London: Tauris

Parke, 2002). A scholarly on-line journal devoted to *Buffy* studies also exists: *Slayage,* at www.slayage.tv.

4. Elizabeth Grosz, *Space, Time, and Perversion: Essays on the Politics of Bodies* (New York: Routledge, l995), 16, emphasis in the original.

5. Sharon MacDonald, "Drawing the Lines—Gender, Peace, and War: An Introduction," in *Images of Women in Peace and War: Cross-cultural and Historical Perspectives,* edited by Sharon MacDonald, Pat Holden, and Shirley Ardener (Madison: Univ. of Wisconsin Press, 1987), 22–23.

6. In this narrative, the male "just warrior" fights and possibly dies for the greater good, whereas the female "beautiful soul" epitomizes the maternal war-support figure in need of male protection. Jean Elshtain has coined these terms, and her analysis of the gendered constructs of war is the starting point for many feminist studies of gender and war making; see *Women and War* (New York: Basic, 1987).

7. Cross-dressing female soldiers of seventeenth- and eighteenth-century European society provide a case in point. See Diane Dugaw, *Warrior Women and Popular Balladry, 1650–1850* (Cambridge, Eng.: Cambridge Univ. Press, 1989).

8. See, in particular, Marina Warner's books *Joan of Arc: The Image of Female Heroism* (1981; reprint, New York: Penguin, 1987) and *Monuments and Maidens: The Allegory of the Female Form* (New York: Atheneum, 1985). Also useful are Elise Boulding's *The Underside of History: A View of Women Through Time* (Boulder, Colo.: Westview, 1976); Linda Grant De Pauw's *Battle Cries and Lullabies: Women in War from Prehistory to the Present* (Norman: Univ. of Oklahoma Press, 1998); Margarita Stocker's *Judith: Sexual Warrior* (New Haven, Conn.: Yale Univ. Press, 1998); Megan McLaughlin's "The Woman Warrior: Gender, Warfare, and Society in Medieval Europe," *Women's Studies* 17, nos. 3–4 (1990): 193–209; and Natalie Zemon Davis's brilliant essay on the subversive power of the disorderly woman in early modern European society, "Women on Top," in *Society and Culture in Early Modern France,* 124–51 (Stanford, Calif.: Stanford Univ. Press, 1975).

9. Mary R. Beard was a pioneer in this recovery process; see her classic study *Woman as Force in History* (1946; reprint, New York: Collier, 1971); also consult De Pauw, *Battle Cries and Lullabies.*

10. Elshtain, *Women and War,* 180.

11. Warner, *Monuments and Maidens,* 176.

12. Michel Foucault, *The History of Sexuality,* vol. 1 (New York: Vintage, 1980), 101.

13. Joss Whedon, qtd. in Kathleen Tracy, *The Girl's Got Bite: The Unofficial Guide to Buffy's World* (Los Angeles: Renaissance, 1998), 6.

14. Joss Whedon, qtd. in Barbara Lippert, "Hey There, Warrior Grrrl [*sic*]," *New York* (Dec. 15, 1997): 24–25.

15. Dorothy E. Smith, "Femininity as Discourse," in *Becoming Feminine: The Politics of Popular Culture,* edited by Leslie G. Roman and Linda K. Christian-Smith, with Elizabeth Ellsworth (London: Falmer, 1988), 38 and 55. See also Vivian Chin's essay in this anthology, "Buffy? She's Like Me, She's Not Like Me—She's *Rad*" (chap. 8). Chin argues that it is possible to read *Buffy* critically from a postmodern Asian American feminist perspective as a dialogue about constructed notions of whiteness, gender, and race in U.S. society. Other related studies that problematize the handling of gender and race in *Buffy* include Kent A. Ono, "To Be a Vampire on *Buffy the Vampire*

Slayer: Race and ('Other') Socially Marginalizing Positions on Horror TV," in *Fantasy Girls: Gender in the New Universe of Science Fiction and Fantasy Television,* edited by Elyce Rae Helford, 163–86 (Lanham, Md.: Rowman and Littlefield: 2000), and Lynne Edwards, "Slaying in Black and White: Kendra as Tragic Mulatta in *Buffy,*" in *Fighting the Forces,* edited by Wilcox and Lavery, 85–97.

16. Grosz, *Space, Time, and Perversion,* 36. In her study *Real Knockouts: The Physical Feminism of Women's Self-Defense* (New York: New York Univ. Press, 1997), Martha McCaughey presents an extended reflection on the pleasures of female physical aggression in relation to male violence against women. For the race and class dimensions of the expression of girls' aggression and anger in the *Buffy* series, see Elyce Rae Helford's nuanced essay, " 'My Emotions Give Me Power': The Containment of Girls' Anger in *Buffy,*" in *Fighting the Forces,* edited by Wilcox and Lavery, 18–34. Up through season four, Sophia Crawford served as a stunt double for the actor playing Buffy, Sarah Michelle Gellar, and handled all the fight sequences. See Dave West, "Concentrate on the Kicking Movie: *Buffy* and East Asian Cinema," in *Reading the Vampire Slayer,* edited by Kaveney, 182.

17. Quotes in this paragraph are taken from the following *Buffy* episodes: "When She Was Bad," Sept. 15, 1997; "Ted," Dec. 8, 1997; "Welcome to the Hellmouth/The Harvest," Mar. 10, 1997; and "Enemies," Mar. 16, 1999. All dates for episodes cited in the endnotes refer to the original U.S. airdates.

18. "Bad Girls," Feb. 9, 1999.

19. "Consequences," Feb. 16, 1999.

20. "Lie to Me," Nov. 3, 1997.

21. Interestingly, evil creatures are not always slain; sometimes they cause their own deaths by inadvertently falling against a spiked fence or landing against a high-voltage electrical outlet or playing a part in some other misadventure. Joss Whedon has remarked that "Buffy vampires" crumble into dust because he does not want every episode to show Buffy killing beings that look like humans. Interview with Joss Whedon, preceding "Angel" episode, Apr. 14, 1997.

22. "The Puppet Show," May 5, 1997.

23. "Earshot," Sept. 21, 1999. This show ironically was one of the two episodes that the television networks delayed in the wake of the Columbine tragedy because of its perceived violent content and possible negative influence on youth. "Earshot" initially was scheduled to be shown in May 1999. For a thoughtful scholarly exploration of the problem posed by the Columbine massacre in relation to *Buffy,* see Kathleen McConnell, "Chaos at the Mouth of Hell: Why the Columbine High School Massacre Had Repercussions for *Buffy the Vampire Slayer,*" *Gothic Studies* 2, no. 1 (2000): 119–35.

24. "Helpless," Jan. 19, 1999.

25. "Goodbye Iowa," Feb. 15, 2000.

26. "This Year's Girl," Feb. 22, 2000.

6. "If You're Not Enjoying It, You're Doing Something Wrong": Textual and Viewer Constructions of Faith, the Vampire Slayer

1. Debbie Stoller, "The Twenty Most Fascinating Women in Politics," *George* 8 (Sept. 1998): 110–13.

2. Kent A. Ono, "To Be a Vampire on *Buffy the Vampire Slayer:* Race and ('Other') Socially Marginalizing Positions on Horror TV," in *Fantasy Girls: Gender in the New Universe of Science Fiction and Fantasy Television,* edited by Elyce Rae Helford (Lanham, Md.: Rowman and Littlefield, 2000), 179.

3. Since I completed this essay, three articles have appeared that discuss Faith. See Elyce Rae Helford, " 'My Emotions Give Me Power': The Containment of Girls' Anger in *Buffy*"; Donald Keller, "Spirit Guides and Shadow Selvers: From the Dream Life of Buffy (and Faith)"; and Rhonda V. Wilcox, " 'Who Died and Made Her the Boss?' Patterns of Morality in *Buffy.*" All appear in *Fighting the Forces: What's at Stake in* Buffy the Vampire Slayer? edited by Rhonda V. Wilcox and David Lavery, 18–34, 165–77, and 3–17 (New York: Rowman and Littlefield, 2002).

4. John Fiske, *Television Culture* (London: Methuen, 1987), 132.

5. Ibid., 134.

6. Henry Jenkins, *Textual Poachers: Television Fans and Participatory Culture* (New York: Routledge, 1992), 25–28.

7. Nancy K. Baym, *Tune In, Log On: Soaps, Fandom, and Online Community* (Thousand Oaks, Calif.: Sage, 2000).

8. "Faith, Hope, and Trick," Oct. 13, 1998. This date and subsequent episode dates refer to the original U.S. airdates.

9. "Bad Girls," Feb. 9, 1999.

10. Mitch Persons, "Eliza Dushku, Vampire Slayer," *Femmes Fatales* 9, no. 1 (June 30, 2000): 24–27.

11. Joss Whedon, interview, *Buffy the Vampire Slayer: The Slayer Chronicles,* vol. 1, *Bad Girls/Consequences,* videocassette, Twentieth Century Fox Home Entertainment, 2000.

12. "Bad Girls." Feb. 9, 1999.

13. "Dopplegangland," Feb. 23, 1999.

14. Mitch Persons, "Marti Noxon—Supervising Producer—On Teen Angst, the Dark Side, Sex, Censors," *Femmes Fatales* 9, no. 1 (June 30, 2000): 12–16.

15. "The Zeppo," Jan. 26, 1999.

16. Joss Whedon, qtd. in Keith Topping, *Slayer: The Totally Cool Unofficial Guide to Buffy* (London: Virgin, 2000), 153. This post is attributed to Whedon, via the WB network's www.buffyslayer.com posting board.

17. "Consequences," Feb. 16, 1999.

18. Ibid.

19. Ibid.

20. "Enemies," Mar. 16, 1999.

21. Topping, *Slayer,* 56.

22. "Choices," May 4, 1999.

23. Persons, "Marti Noxon," 15.

24. A. Susan Owen, *"Buffy the Vampire Slayer:* Vampires, Postmodernity, and Postfeminism," *Journal of Popular Film and Television* 27, no. 2 (summer 1999): 24–31.

25. "Choices," May 4, 1999.

26. Carol J. Clover, *Men, Women, and Chainsaws: Gender in the Modern Horror Film* (Princeton, N.J.: Princeton Univ. Press, 1992), 47.

27. "Graduation Day, Part 1," May 18, 1999.

28. Joss Whedon, interview, *Buffy the Vampire Slayer: The Slayer Chronicles,* vol. 3, *Graduation Day, Parts 1 and 2,* videocassette (Twentieth Century Fox Home Entertainment, 2000).

29. Ibid. See also Nancy Holder, *The Watcher's Guide,* vol. 2 (New York: Simon and Schuster, 2000).

30. "Bad Girls," Feb. 9, 1999.

7. "Action, Chicks, Everything": On-Line Interviews with Male Fans of *Buffy the Vampire Slayer*

1. Joss Whedon, as cited on "Buffy the Patriarchy Slayer," available on-line at http://darin-givens.home.mindspring.com/btps.html; accessed June 20, 2001.

2. Joss Whedon has been quoted as saying that part of the attraction of the Buffyverse is that it lends itself to "polymorphously perverse" readings: "It encourages it. I personally find romance in every relationship (with exceptions), I love all the characters, so I say Bring Your Own Subtext!" The Bronze VIP archive through Dec. 3, 1998, as cited in Esther Saxey, "Staking a Claim: The Series and Its Slash Fan-Fiction," in *Reading the Vampire Slayer: An Unofficial Critical Companion to* Buffy *and* Angel, edited by Roz Kaveney (London: Tauris Parke, 2002), 208.

3. Feminist critics in the popular press have disagreed about whether Buffy should be considered a feminist icon or a detriment to women everywhere. For a brisk summary of recent debates, see Mary Spicuzza, "Bad Heroines," *Metro: Silicon Valley's Weekly Newspaper,* Mar. 15–21, 2001. Meanwhile, recent academic debates dealing with the series' political merits have focused on issues such as *Buffy*'s anti-institutional investments and conservative approach to race. For the former, see Brian Wall and Michael Zryd, "Vampire Dialectics: Knowledge, Institutions, and Labour in *Buffy the Vampire Slayer* and *Angel,*" in *Reading the Vampire Slayer,* edited by Kaveney, 53–77. For the latter, see Kent A. Ono, "To Be a Vampire on *Buffy the Vampire Slayer:* Race and ('Other') Socially Marginalizing Positions on Horror TV," in *Fantasy Girls: Gender in the New Universe of Science Fiction and Fantasy Television,* edited by Elyce Rae Helford, 163–86 (Lanham, Md.: Rowman and Littlefield, 2000).

4. For an influential argument in favor of gender skepticism, see Christine di Stefano, "Dilemmas of Difference: Feminism, Modernity, and Postmodernism," in *Feminism/Postmodernism,* edited by L. J. Nicholson, 63–82 (New York: Routledge, 1990). For a recent, readable discussion of the gap between second- and third-wave feminisms, see Marysia Zalewski, *Feminism after Postmodernism: Theorising Through Practice* (New York: Routledge, 2000).

5. In retrospect, I believe the best way to approach this study may be through a combination of Daniel Leonard Bernardi's anonymous "lurker" method—what he calls "cyberspace ethnography" (Star Trek *and History: Race-ing Toward a White Future* [New Brunswick, N.J.: Rutgers Univ. Press, 1998], 154)—and in-person interviews with selected subjects using established methods

for grounded theory research. For a sampling of recent, more systematic work on television audiences and fans, see Henry Jenkins, *Textual Poachers: Television Fans and Participatory Culture* (New York: Routledge, 1992); John Tulloch and Henry Jenkins, *Science Fiction Audiences: Watching* Doctor Who *and* Star Trek (New York: Routledge, 1995); and David Gauntlett and Annette Hill, *TV Living: Television, Culture, and Everyday Life* (New York: Routledge, 1999). Grounded research methods are discussed in John W. Creswell, *Qualitative Inquiry and Research Design* (Thousand Oaks, Calif.: Sage, 1997). For a discussion of the Internet specific to *Buffy,* see Amanda Zweerink and Sarah N. Gaston, "www.buffy.com: Cliques, Boundaries, and Hierarchies in an Internet Community," in *Fighting the Forces: What's at Stake in* Buffy the Vampire Slayer? edited by Rhonda V. Wilcox and David Lavery, 239–50 (New York: Rowman and Littlefield, 2002).

6. "Calling All Buffy Boys," available on-line at http://board.buffy.com/bronze/mboard/ thread; accessed June 13–14, 2001.

7. "Calling All Buffy Boys." Faith's Mr. Pointy, June 13, 2001, and e-mail message to Lee Parpart from eyeofnewt, June 13, 2001.

8. E-mail message to Lee Parpart from Idiot Savant, June 13, 2001.

9. Di Stefano, "Dilemmas of Difference," 75, cited in Sue Thornham, *Passionate Detachments: An Introduction to Feminist Film Theory* (London: Arnold, 1997), 165.

10. E-mail messages to Lee Parpart from xanderh79, June 13, 2001, and from Sasha, June 13, 2001. Xanderh79's reading of the show does seem justified, given ample textual evidence that Buffy's acceptability as a woman warrior rests on her having qualities that reinforce rather than unsettle patriarchal assumptions about femininity. All quotations from e-mail correspondents appear verbatim.

11. QSTUDY-L's Web site is: www.qempire.com/qstudy. Film Philosophy's salon address is: filmphilosophy@jiscmail.ac.uk. The Film Studies Association of Canada's listserve address is: fsac@yorku.ca. My reasons for restricting the study to these particular listserves were in part a concern for strategy and in part a matter of convenience. I wanted to focus on highly educated, potentially pro- or proto-feminist male Buffy fans in order both to provide a contrast with the first sample and to give the second group the best possible chance of reading Buffy's warrior status in relation to ideas about gender. The film listserves are two to which I belong, though I would not describe myself as an active participant on either one. Knowing that *Buffy* has a large gay following, I also felt it was important to direct at least one call for subjects to a gay-specific site. (I am indebted to Tom Waugh for suggesting QSTUDY-L.)

12. Scott Feschuk, " 'It's Awesome . . . There Is a God,' " *National Post* (June 13, 2001): B1–B2. Those *Post* readers who took part in this study in most cases had written detailed letters to accompany their votes for *Buffy,* leading me to speculate that their responses could be studied alongside those of the other respondents.

13. E-mail message to Lee Parpart from Steve Sposato, July 11, 2001.

14. E-mail message to Lee Parpart from Wendell, July 4, 2001.

15. E-mail messages to Lee Parpart from Mike and Nick, June 15, 2001, and June 18, 2001, respectively; from Mike H., June 24, 2001; and from Hugh, June 28, 2001.

16. E-mail messages to Lee Parpart from Neil W., June 27, 2001, and from Michel and Doug, June 25, 2001, and June 26, 2001, respectively.

17. E-mail messages to Lee Parpart from Clayton S., June 28, 2001 (emphasis in original); from Daniel, June 27, 2001; and from James, July 6, 2001.

18. E-mail message to Lee Parpart from Daniel, June 28, 2001.

19. E-mail message to Lee Parpart from Kim and Megan, July 10, 2001.

20. E-mail message to Lee Parpart from Darian, June 26, 2001.

21. E-mail message to Lee Parpart from Ted, June 29, 2001.

22. E-mail message to Lee Parpart from Amy, June 28, 2001.

23. E-mail messages to Lee Parpart from MZ, July 7, 2001, and from Matthue Roth, June 24, 2001.

24. Apropos of this point, my favorite example is Henry Crawford's often overtly erotic obsession with the morally upright Fanny Price in Jane Austen's *Mansfield Park*.

25. Female *Buffy* fans have outnumbered male fans since the show's debut in 1997, but the gap is gradually closing for older male viewers ages eighteen to forty-nine, whose numbers rose from 725,000 to 1,072,000 between season one and the end of season five (1999–2000). *Buffy* had 1,523,000 female fans in the same age group at the end of season five. I derived figures from round number data contained in the "Nielsen TV National People Meter," Nielsen Media Research, 2001. Charts provided by the WB network. E-mail message to Lee Parpart from David Eckelman, June 27, 2001.

26. E-mail message to Lee Parpart from Marc Brennan, June 26, 2001: "I do think it's possible to speculate that gay male viewers or nontraditional males may gain pleasure from seeing other 'marginal' members of society (women, gays, nerds, etc.) being heroes for a change."

27. For a discussion of the intersections of queer identity and camp aesthetics, see Fabio Cleto, ed., *Camp: Queer Aesthetics and the Performing Subject: A Reader* (Ann Arbor: Univ. of Michigan Press, 1999).

28. Susan Bordo, "Feminism, Postmodernism, and Gender-scepticism," in *Feminism/Postmodernism,* edited by Nicholson, 149, 152, as cited in Thornham, *Passionate Detachments,* 167.

8. Buffy? She's Like Me, She's Not Like Me—She's *Rad*

1. Mary Ann Doane, "Film and the Masquerade: Theorising the Female Spectator," *Screen* 23, nos. 3–4 (Sept.-Oct. 1982), 81.

2. See also Judith Butler, *Gender Trouble: Feminism and the Subversion of Identity* (New York: Routledge, 1990). Butler asks, "Does being female constitute a 'natural fact' or a cultural performance, or is 'naturalness' constituted through discursively constrained performative acts that produce the body through and within the categories of sex?" (viii). Definitions of *woman* and *female* are not necessarily based on "natural fact," but on historically and culturally specific notions of femininity.

3. Houston Baker, *Modernism and the Harlem Renaissance* (Chicago: Univ. of Chicago Press, 1987), 17, cited in Saidiya V. Hartman, *Scenes of Subjection* (New York: Oxford Univ. Press, 1997), 212, n. 37.

4. Hartman, *Scenes of Subjection,* 26–29.

5. See Yen Le Espiritu, *Asian American Women and Men: Labor, Laws, and Love* (Thousand Oaks, Calif.: Sage, 1997), 92. In another example of this masking, Espiritu explains, "heedful of the

larger society's taboos against Asian male–white female sexual union, white male actors donning 'yellowface'—instead of Asian male actors—are used in these 'love scenes' " (92). Here I use the term *Oriental* rather than *yellow* or *Asian* to stress that this category is constructed with the specific goal of rendering all that is "Oriental" strange, dangerous, and inferior, if at times also desirable.

6. See Edward Said, *Orientalism* (New York: Vintage, 1978).

7. For a similar argument, see Rachel Fudge, "The Buffy Effect or, a Tale of Cleavage and Marketing," *Bitch: Feminist Response to Popular Culture*, no. 10 (1999): 18–21 and 58. Although Fudge's article provides a substantial discussion of feminism, marketing, and "girl power" in *Buffy*, it neglects to consider how race is a part of the show's style of feminism. For an article that does consider race, see Lynn Edwards, "Slaying in Black and White: Kendra as Tragic Mulatta in *Buffy*," in *Fighting the Forces: What's at Stake in* Buffy the Vampire Slayer? edited by Rhonda V. Wilcox and David Lavery, 85–97 (New York: Rowman and Littlefield, 2002).

8. Joss Whedon, qtd. in Ginia Bellafante, "Bewitching Teen Heroines," *Time* 149, no. 18 (May 5, 1997), 83.

9. Joss Whedon, interviewed in *Buffy the Vampire Slayer: Welcome to the Hellmouth/The Harvest*, videocassette (Twentieth Century Fox Home Entertainment, 1998).

10. *Buffy the Vampire Slayer: The Buffy and Angel Chronicles*, vol. 3, *Becoming, Parts 1 and 2*, videocassette (Twentieth Century Fox Home Entertainment, 1998).

11. bell hooks, "The Oppositional Gaze," in *Black Looks* (Boston: South End, 1992), 119. Hooks quotes from Julie Burchill, *Girls on Film* (New York: Pantheon, 1986).

12. See also Asim Ali, "Community, Language, and Postmodernism at the Mouth of Hell," available on-line at www.wam.umd.edu/~asimali/buffnog.html; accessed Mar. 13, 2001.

13. Rosie White, "Feminist Icon? *Buffy the Vampire Slayer* and Postfeminist Television," in *Millennial Visions: Feminisms into the 21st Century*, edited by Carolyn Brina, Carolyn Britton, and Allison Assiter (Cardiff, Eng.: Cardiff Academic, 2001), 156.

14. *Rosemary's Baby*, directed by Roman Polanski (Paramount, 1968).

15. *Blade*, directed by Stephen Norrington (New Line Studios, 1998).

16. *Bring It On*, directed by Peyton Reed (Universal, 2000). A thank you to Dziep Nguyen for pointing out this scene to me.

17. hooks, "The Oppositional Gaze," 123.

18. *Evolution*, directed by Ivan Reitman (Umvd/Dreamworks, 2001). *Scary Movie 2*, directed by Keenan Ivory Wayans (Dimension Films, 2001).

19. *Welcome to the Hellmouth/The Harvest.*

20. *Becoming, Parts 1 and 2.*

21. Ibid.

22. "The Puppet Show," May 5, 1997. Dates for all cited *Buffy* episodes are the original U.S. airdates.

23. "The Yoko Factor," May 9, 2000.

24. "Fool for Love," Nov. 14, 2000.

25. *Welcome to the Hellmouth/The Harvest.*

26. Ken Gelder, *Reading the Vampire* (New York: Routledge, 1994), 13.

27. Joss Whedon interview, qtd. in Ali, "Community," 4.

28. See also Rhonda V. Wilcox, "Buffy and the Monsters of Teen Life: 'There Will Never Be a Very Special Buffy,' " *Journal of Popular Film and Television* 27, no. 2 (summer 1999): 16–23.

29. Dave West, "Concentrate on the Kicking Movie: *Buffy* and East Asian Cinema," in *Reading the Vampire Slayer: An Unofficial Critical Companion to* Buffy *and* Angel, edited by Roz Kaveney (London: Tauris Parke, 2002), 180.

30. Sherrie A. Inness, *Tough Girls: Women Warriors and Wonder Women in Popular Culture* (Philadelphia: Univ. of Pennsylvania Press, 1999), 179.

31. Trinh T. Minh-ha, "Not You/Like You: Post-Colonial Women and the Interlocking Questions of Identity and Difference," in *Making Face, Making Soul,* edited by Gloria Anzaldúa (San Francisco: Aunt Lute, 1990), 371.

32. Trinh, "Not You/Like You," 375.

9. "The Most Powerful Weapon You Have": Warriors and Gender in *La Femme Nikita*

1. Susan Isaacs, *Brave Dames and Wimpettes* (New York: Ballantine, 1999). Isaacs offers a popular commentary on the women of U.S. television. Academics are now entering into debates on topics formerly the domain of journalists such as Isaacs.

2. Michael Ventura, "Warrior Women: Why Are TV Shows Like *Buffy the Vampire Slayer, La Femme Nikita,* and *Xena, Warrior Princess* So Popular, Especially among Teens?" *Psychology Today* 31, no. 6 (Nov.-Dec. 1998): 58–63. Ventura addresses this problematic uncertainty from the perspective of audience engagement. He mentions the ambiguity in *Nikita* in contrast to *Buffy* and *Xena.* Though he ultimately finds that ambiguity disturbing, he does note that the blurring of such lines is an attractive feature for most viewers, especially teenagers. His analysis does not approach the topic of Nikita as a warrior or hero.

3. Laura Grindstaff, "A Pygmalion Tale Retold: Remaking *La Femme Nikita,*" *Camera Obscura* 47 (Dec. 2001): 133–43. Grindstaff mainly focuses on the politics of remakes from the French culture to the American, with some discussion of the Japanese. She does examine the television show, but her discussion of the film versions is much more extensive.

4. Jean Bethke Elshtain, *Women and War* (New York: Basic, 1987). Also of interest are Renée R. Curry and Terry L. Allison, eds., *States of Rage: Emotional Eruption, Violence, and Social Change/(Rage)* (New York: New York Univ. Press, 1996), and Susie M. Jacobs, Ruth Jacobson, and Jen Marchbank, eds., *States of Conflict: Gender, Violence, and Resistance* (New York: Zed, 2000). These works offer discussion on gender, war, and military service.

5. Isaacs, *Brave Dames and Wimpettes,* 119.

6. "Into the Looking Glass," Jan. 23, 2000. This date and dates for other cited episodes in the series are original U.S. airdates.

7. Edward W. Said, *Culture and Imperialism* (New York: Vintage, 1993). Said's work is a watershed piece for cultural studies and for imperialism and colonization theory. Western society tends to demonize the exotic, foreign "other" for being different from "the West" with respect to culture, religion, and appearance. This process, Said insists, reveals more about the fearful colonizer than about the demonized "other."

8. "The Man Behind the Curtain," Feb. 11, 2001.

9. "Up the Rabbit Hole," Aug. 27, 2000.

10. "Four Light Years Farther," Aug. 27, 2000.

11. Ventura, "Warrior Women," 58–61.

12. Gloria Anzaldúa, *Borderlands = La Frontera,* 2d ed. (San Francisco: Aunt Lute Books, 1999), 3. Anzaldúa's work primarily centers on cultural differences among societies. The borderland is the gray area in which immigrants attempt to adjust to a new country while preserving their own unique ethnic and cultural identities. This text pairs well with Said's work.

13. Ventura, "Warrior Women," 58–61.

14. Judith Butler, *Gender Trouble: Feminism and the Subversion of Identity* (New York: Routledge, 1990). This work focuses on the performance of gender in culture, but Butler's ideas can be extended to issues of violence and power. Other works by Butler that may be of interest in the discussion of identity, performance, and individual power are *Bodies That Matter* (New York: Routledge, 1993) and *Excitable Speech* (New York: Routledge, 1997). For a more in-depth look at how cultures control access to the body and dialogues of power, see Michel Foucault, *The History of Sexuality,* vol. 1 (New York: Vintage, 1980). Lois McNay's *Foucault and Feminism: Power, Gender, and the Self* (Cambridge, Eng.: Polity, 1992) offers a balanced view of Foucault's theory and takes into account the agency of the individual.

15. Diana Fuss, *Essentially Speaking: Feminism, Nature, and Difference* (New York: Routledge, 1989), 2–3. Fuss examines the close connection between theories of essentialism and theories of constructionism with regard to gender and identity. She concludes that these two allegedly polar opposites depend on and utilize each other. Therefore, both approaches, when used with critical awareness, yield valuable insights. For further exploration of the connection between the body and the mind, see Elizabeth Grosz, *Volatile Bodies: Toward a Corporeal Feminism* (Bloomington: Indiana Univ. Press, 1994), and Anne Fausto-Sterling, *Sexing the Body: Gender Politics and the Construction of Sexuality* (New York: Basic, 2000).

16. Ann Jones, *Women Who Kill,* 2d ed. (Boston: Beacon, 1996), 5. Jones investigates the fear surrounding the figure of the "monster woman," a violent figure that lashes out at men without motive.

17. "Charity," Feb. 3, 1997, and "Choice," Apr. 7, 1997.

18. "Half Life," Mar. 22, 1998.

19. "Nikita," Jan. 13, 1997.

20. Grindstaff, "A Pygmalion Tale Retold."

21. "Four Light Years Farther," Aug. 27, 2000.

22. "A Time for Every Purpose," Mar. 4, 2001.

23. "Nikita," Jan. 13, 1997. This line is also found in the original French movie.

24. "There Are No More Missions," Jan. 9, 2000.

25. Laura Mulvey, "Visual Pleasures and Narrative Cinema," in *Feminisms,* edited by Robyn R. Warhol and Diane Price Herndl, 438–48 (New Brunswick, N.J.: Rutgers Univ. Press, 1997). Although an older piece (originally published in 1975), Mulvey's work was one of the most influential of its critical time. For further discussion of performance and identity, please see notes 12 and 14.

10. We Who Are Borg, Are We Borg?

1. Hélène Cixous, "We Who Are Free, Are We Free?" *Critical Inquiry* 19, no. 2 (winter 1993): 201–19.

2. Donna J. Haraway, "Cyborgs and Symbionts: Living Together in the New World Order," in *The Cyborg Handbook,* edited by Chris Hables Gray (New York: Routledge, 1995), xvi.

3. Donna J. Haraway, "A Manifesto for Cyborgs: Science, Technology, and Socialist Feminism in the 1980s," in *Feminism/Postmodernism,* edited by L. J. Nicholson (New York: Routledge, 1990), 196.

4. Haraway, "Manifesto," 196. Haraway recently expressed reservations about the continued utility of the cyborg to accomplish the goals she set for it and has turned instead to an examination of companionate animals, specifically dogs. See "From Cyborgs to Companion Species: Kinship in Technoscience," keynote conference address, "Taking Nature Seriously: Citizens, Science, and Environment," Univ. of Oregon, Eugene, Feb. 27, 2001.

5. Cixous, "We Who Are Free," 201.

6. Ibid., 202.

7. Katrina G. Boyd, "Cyborgs in Utopia: The Problem of Radical Difference in *Star Trek: The Next Generation,*" in *Enterprise Zones: Critical Positions on* Star Trek, edited by Taylor Harrison, Sarah Projansky, Kent A. Ono, and Elyce Rae Helford (Boulder, Colo.: Westview, 1996), 95.

8. Thomas Richards, *The Meaning of* Star Trek (New York: Doubleday, 1997), 50.

9. Boyd, "Cyborgs in Utopia," 105.

10. Richards, *The Meaning of* Star Trek, 192.

11. Anne Cranny-Francis, "The Erotics of the (Cy)Borg: Authority and Gender in the Sociocultural Imaginary," in *Future Females, the Next Generation: New Voices and Velocities in Feminist Science Fiction Criticism,* edited by Marleen S. Barr (New York: Rowman and Littlefield, 2000), 158.

12. Richards, *The Meaning of* Star Trek, 74–77.

13. "Drive," episode no. 249, Oct. 18, 2000. All references to *Star Trek* episodes cite original U.S. airdates.

14. Cixous, "We Who Are Free," 204.

15. "I, Borg," episode no. 223, May 11, 1992.

16. Cynthia J. Fuchs, " 'Death Is Irrelevant': Cyborgs, Reproduction, and the Future of Male Hysteria," in *The Cyborg Handbook,* edited by Chris Hables Gray (New York: Routledge, 1995), 282, emphasis in the original.

17. "The Gift," episode no. 170, Sept. 10, 1997.

18. Susan Sontag, "The Imagination of Disaster," in *Against Interpretation* (1965; reprint, London: Vintage, 1994), 221.

19. Cranny-Francis, "The Erotics of the (Cy)Borg," 156.

20. For example, Zillah Eisenstein's *The Radical Future of Liberal Feminism* (Boston: Northeastern Univ. Press, 1981).

21. Cranny-Francis, "The Erotics of the (Cy)Borg," 161.

22. "Collective," episode no. 235, Feb. 16, 2000.

23. Robin Roberts, "Science, Race, and Gender in *Star Trek: Voyager,*" in *Fantasy Girls: Gen-*

der in the New Universe of Science Fiction and Fantasy Television, edited by Elyce Rae Helford (Lanham, Md.: Rowman and Littlefield, 2000), 204.

24. Ibid., 207.

25. Ibid., 204.

26. "One," episode no. 193, May 13, 1998.

27. "Infinite Regress," episode no. 203, Nov. 25, 1998.

28. "Survival Instinct," episode no. 222, Sept. 29, 1999.

29. "Human Error," episode no. 264, Mar. 7, 2001.

30. "Endgame," episode nos. 271–72, May 23, 2001.

31. "Nothing Human," episode no. 200, Dec. 2, 1998.

32. "The Gift," episode no. 170, Sept. 10, 1997.

33. "Child's Play," episode no. 239, Feb. 16, 2000.

34. "Imperfection," episode no. 248, Oct. 4, 2000.

35. Haraway, "Cyborgs and Symbionts," xix.

36. Richard E. Sclove, *Democracy and Technology* (New York: Guilford, 1995), 23–24.

37. Gary Westfahl, "Opposing War, Exploiting War: The Troubled Pacifism of *Star Trek,*" in *Science Fiction, Children's Literature, and Popular Culture* (Westport, Conn.: Greenwood, 2000), 74.

38. Ibid., 75.

39. Zillah Eisenstein, *Global Obscenities: Patriarchy, Capitalism, and the Lure of Cyberfantasy* (New York: New York Univ. Press, 1998), 141.

40. Ibid., 130.

41. Bill Joy, "Why the Future Doesn't Need Us," *WIRED* 8.04 (Apr. 2000), 240.

42. Ibid., 241.

43. Sontag, "Imagination of Disaster," 215.

44. Kevin Robins and Les Levidow, "Soldier, Cyborg, Citizen," in *Resisting the Virtual Life: The Culture and Politics of Information,* edited by James Brook and Iain A. Boal (San Francisco: City Lights, 1995), 106.

Bibliography

Books, Articles, and Unpublished Papers

Aeschylus. *Works.* Translated by Herbert Weir Smyth. Cambridge, Mass.: Harvard Univ. Press, 1963.

Ali, Asim. "Community, Language, and Postmodernism at the Mouth of Hell." Available on-line at: www.wam.umd.edu/~asimali/buffnog.html. Accessed Mar. 13, 2001.

Anzaldúa, Gloria. *Borderlands = La Frontera.* 2d ed. San Francisco: Aunt Lute, 1999.

Bacon-Smith, Camille. *Enterprising Women.* Philadelphia: Univ. of Pennsylvania Press, 1992.

Baker, Houston. *Modernism and the Harlem Renaissance.* Chicago: Univ. of Chicago Press, 1987.

Baym, Nancy K. *Tune In, Log On: Soaps, Fandom, and Online Community.* Thousand Oaks, Calif.: Sage, 2000.

Beard, Mary R. *Woman as Force in History.* 1946. Reprint. New York: Collier, 1971.

Bellafante, Ginia. "Bewitching Teen Heroines." *Time* 149, no. 18 (May 5, 1997): 82–84.

Bernardi, Daniel Leonard. Star Trek *and History: Race-ing Toward a White Future.* New Brunswick, N.J.: Rutgers Univ. Press, 1998.

Bordo, Susan. "Feminism, Postmodernism, and Gender-scepticism." In *Feminism/Postmodernism,* edited by L. J. Nicholson, 133–56. New York: Routledge, 1990.

Boulding, Elise. *The Underside of History: A View of Women Through Time.* Boulder, Colo.: Westview, 1976.

Bowers, Sharon. *Lucifer Rising.* Tacoma, Wash.: Justice House, 1999.

Boyd, Katrina G. "Cyborgs in Utopia: The Problem of Radical Difference in *Star Trek: The Next Generation.*" In *Enterprise Zones: Critical Positions on* Star Trek, edited by Taylor Harrison, Sarah Projansky, Kent A. Ono, and Elyce Rae Helford, 95–113. Boulder, Colo.: Westview, 1996.

"Buffy the Patriarchy Slayer." Available on-line at: http://daringivens.home.mindspring.com/btps.html. Accessed June 20, 2001.

"Buffy the Vampire Slayer." *The Nation* (Apr. 6, 1998): 35–36.

Burchill, Julie. *Girls on Film.* New York: Pantheon, 1986.

Butler, Judith. *Bodies That Matter.* New York: Routledge, 1993.

———. *Excitable Speech.* New York: Routledge, 1997.

———. *Gender Trouble: Feminism and the Subversion of Identity.* New York: Routledge, 1990.

"Calling All Buffy Boys." Available on-line at: http://board.buffy.com/bronze/mboard/thread. Accessed June 13–14, 2001.

Campbell, Joseph. *The Hero with a Thousand Faces.* Princeton, N.J.: Princeton Univ. Press, 1972.

Caudill, Helen. "Appropriation of a Hero: The World of *Xena, Warrior Princess* Alternative Fan Fiction Online." Paper presented at the Popular Culture Association Conference, San Diego, Calif., Apr. 1, 1999.

Cixous, Hélène. "We Who Are Free, Are We Free?" *Critical Inquiry* 19, no. 2 (winter 1993): 201–19.

Cleto, Fabio, ed. *Camp: Queer Aesthetics and the Performing Subject: A Reader.* Ann Arbor: Univ. of Michigan Press, 1999.

Clover, Carol J. *Men, Women, and Chainsaws: Gender in the Modern Horror Film.* Princeton, N.J.: Princeton Univ. Press, 1992.

Cranny-Francis, Anne. "The Erotics of the (Cy)Borg: Authority and Gender in the Sociocultural Imaginary." In *Future Females, the Next Generation: New Voices and Velocities in Feminist Science Fiction Criticism,* edited by Marleen S. Barr, 145–63. New York: Rowman and Littlefield, 2000.

Creswell, John W. *Qualitative Inquiry and Research Design.* Thousand Oaks, Calif.: Sage, 1997.

Curry, Renée R., and Terry L. Allison, eds. *States of Rage: Emotional Eruption, Violence, and Social Change/(Rage).* New York: New York Univ. Press, 1996.

Davis, Natalie Zemon. "Women on Top." In *Society and Culture in Early Modern France,* 124–51. Stanford, Calif.: Stanford Univ. Press, 1975.

Dean-Jones, Lesley. "The Cultural Construct of the Female Body in Classical Greek Science." In *Women's History and Ancient History,* edited by Sarah Pomeroy, 111–37. Chapel Hill: Univ. of North Carolina Press, 1991.

de Lauretis, Teresa. "Queer Theory: Lesbian and Gay Sexualities: An Introduction." *differences: A Journal of Feminist and Cultural Studies* 3, no. 2 (1991): iii–xviii.

———. *Technologies of Gender: Essays on Theory, Film, and Fiction.* Bloomington: Univ. of Indiana Press, 1987.

De Pauw, Linda Grant. *Battle Cries and Lullabies: Women in War from Prehistory to the Present.* Norman: Univ. of Oklahoma Press, 1998.

di Stefano, Christine. "Dilemmas of Difference: Feminism, Modernity, and Postmodernism." In *Feminism/Postmodernism,* edited by L. J. Nicholson, 63–82. New York: Routledge, 1990.

Doane, Mary Ann. "Film and the Masquerade: Theorising the Female Spectator." *Screen* 23, nos. 3–4 (Sept.-Oct. 1982): 74–87.

Dugaw, Diane. *Warrior Women and Popular Balladry, 1650–1850.* Cambridge, Eng.: Cambridge Univ. Press, 1989.

Dyer, Richard. "White." *Screen* 29, no. 4 (1989): 44–64.

Edwards, Lynne. "Slaying in Black and White: Kendra as Tragic Mulatta in *Buffy.*" In *Fighting the Forces: What's at Stake in* Buffy the Vampire Slayer? edited by Rhonda V. Wilcox and David Lavery, 85–97. New York: Rowman and Littlefield, 2002.

Eisenstein, Zillah. *Global Obscenities: Patriarchy, Capitalism, and the Lure of Cyberfantasy.* New York: New York Univ. Press, 1998.

———. *The Radical Future of Liberal Feminism.* Boston: Northeastern Univ. Press, 1981.

Elshtain, Jean Bethke. *Women and War.* New York: Basic, 1987.

Espiritu, Yen Le. *Asian American Women and Men: Labor, Laws, and Love.* Thousand Oaks, Calif.: Sage, 1997.

Faludi, Susan. *Backlash: The Undeclared War Against American Women.* New York: Crown, 1991.

Farwell, Marilyn R. *Heterosexual Plots and Lesbian Narratives.* New York: Columbia Univ. Press, 1996.

Fausto-Sterling, Anne. *Sexing the Body: Gender Politics and the Construction of Sexuality.* New York: Basic, 2000.

Feschuk, Scott. "It's Awesome . . . There Is a God.'" *National Post,* June 13, 2001, B1-B2.

Fiske, John. *Television Culture.* London: Methuen, 1987.

Flaherty, Mike. "Xenaphilia." *Entertainment Weekly* (Mar. 7, 1997): 39–42.

Foucault, Michel. *The History of Sexuality.* Vol. 1. New York: Vintage, 1980.

Frazier, Sir James. *The Golden Bough.* New York: Macmillan, 1922.

Friedman, Susan Stafford. *Mappings: Feminism and the Cultural Geographies of Encounter.* Princeton, N.J.: Princeton Univ. Press, 1998.

Fuchs, Cynthia J. " 'Death Is Irrelevant': Cyborgs, Reproduction, and the Future of Male Hysteria." In *The Cyborg Handbook,* edited by Chris Hables Gray, 281–300. New York: Routledge, 1995.

Fudge, Rachel. "The Buffy Effect or, a Tale of Cleavage and Marketing." *Bitch: Feminist Response to Popular Culture* 10 (1999): 18–21 and 58.

Fuss, Diana. *Essentially Speaking: Feminism, Nature, and Difference.* New York: Routledge, 1989.

Gagarin, Michael. *Aeschylean Drama.* Berkeley and Los Angeles: Univ. of California Press, 1976.

Gandhi, Leela. *Postcolonial Theory: A Critical Introduction.* New York: Columbia Univ. Press, 1998.

Gauntlett, David, and Annette Hill. *TV Living: Television, Culture, and Everyday Life.* New York: Routledge, 1999.

Gelder, Ken. *Reading the Vampire.* New York: Routledge, 1994.

Gibson, James William. *Warrior Dreams: Paramilitary Culture in Post-Vietnam America.* New York: Hill and Wang, 1994.

Gimbutas, Marija. *The Language of the Goddess.* New York: Harper and Row, 1989.

Gleason, Maud. "The Semiotics of Gender." In *Before Sexuality,* edited by David Halperin, John Winkler, and Froma Zeitlin, 389–415. Princeton, N.J.: Princeton Univ. Press, 1990.

Grindstaff, Laura. "A Pygmalion Tale Retold: Remaking *La Femme Nikita.*" *Camera Obscura* 47 (Dec. 2001): 133–43.

Grosz, Elizabeth. *Space, Time, and Perversion: Essays on the Politics of Bodies.* New York: Routledge, 1995.

———. *Volatile Bodies: Toward a Corporeal Feminism.* Bloomington: Indiana Univ. Press, 1994.

Hamer, Mary. *Signs of Cleopatra.* New York: Routledge, 1993.

Haraway, Donna J. "Cyborgs and Symbionts: Living Together in the New World Order." In *The Cyborg Handbook,* edited by Chris Hables Gray, xi-xx. New York: Routledge, 1995.

———. "From Cyborgs to Companion Species: Kinship in Technoscience." Keynote address in the conference "Taking Nature Seriously: Citizens, Science, and Environment," Univ. of Oregon, Eugene, Feb. 27, 2001.

———. "A Manifesto for Cyborgs: Science, Technology, and Socialist Feminism in the 1980s." In *Feminism/Postmodernism,* edited by L. J. Nicholson, 190–233. New York: Routledge, 1990.

———. *Modest_Witness@Second_Millennium. FemaleMan©Meets_OncoMouse™: Feminism and Technoscience.* New York: Routledge, 1996.

Hart, Lynda. *Between the Body and the Flesh: Performing Sadomasochism.* New York: Columbia Univ. Press, 1998.

Hartman, Saidiya V. *Scenes of Subjection.* New York: Oxford Univ. Press, 1997.

Helford, Elyce Rae. "Feminism, Queer Studies, and the Sexual Politics of *Xena, Warrior Princess.*" In *Fantasy Girls: Gender in the New Universe of Science Fiction and Fantasy Television,* edited by Elyce Rae Helford, 135–69. Lanham, Md.: Rowman and Littlefield, 2000.

———. "Introduction." In *Fantasy Girls: Gender in the New Universe of Science Fiction and Fantasy Television,* edited by Elyce Rae Helford, 1–43. Lanham, Md.: Rowman and Littlefield, 2000.

———. " 'My Emotions Give Me Power': The Containment of Girls' Anger in *Buffy.*" In *Fighting the Forces: What's at Stake in* Buffy the Vampire Slayer? edited by Rhonda V. Wilcox and David Lavery, 18–34. New York: Rowman and Littlefield, 2002.

————, ed. *Fantasy Girls: Gender in the New Universe of Science Fiction and Fantasy Television.* Lanham, Md.: Rowman and Littlefield, 2000.

Holder, Nancy. *The Watcher's Guide.* Vol. 2. New York: Simon and Schuster, 2000.

hooks, bell. "The Oppositional Gaze." In *Black Looks,* 115–32. Boston: South End, 1992.

Hughes-Hallett, Lucy. *Cleopatra: Histories, Dreams, and Distortions.* London: Bloomsbury, 1990.

Inness, Sherrie A. *Tough Girls: Women Warriors and Wonder Women in Popular Culture.* Philadelphia: Univ. of Pennsylvania Press, 1999.

Isaacs, Susan. *Brave Dames and Wimpettes.* New York: Ballantine, 1999.

Jacobs, Susie M., Ruth Jacobson, and Jen Marchback, eds. *States of Conflict: Gender, Violence, and Resistance.* New York: Zed, 2000.

Jenkins, Henry. *Textual Poachers: Television Fans and Participatory Culture.* New York: Routledge, 1992.

Jewett, Robert, and John S. Lawrence. *The American Monomyth.* New York: Doubleday, 1977.

Jones, Ann. *Women Who Kill.* 2d ed. Boston: Beacon, 1996.

Joshel, Sandra R., Martha Malamud, and Don McGuire, eds. *Imperial Projections: Ancient Rome in Modern Popular Culture.* Baltimore, Md.: Johns Hopkins Univ. Press, 2001.

Joy, Bill. "Why the Future Doesn't Need Us." *WIRED* 8.04 (Apr. 2000): 238–62.

Kaveney, Roz, ed. *Reading the Vampire Slayer: An Unofficial Critical Companion to* Buffy *and* Angel. London: Tauris Parke, 2002.

Keller, Donald. "Spirit Guides and Shadow Selvers: From the Dream Life of Buffy (and Faith)." In *Fighting the Forces: What's at Stake in* Buffy the Vampire Slayer? edited by Rhonda V. Wilcox and David Lavery, 165–77 (New York: Rowman and Littlefield, 2002).

Kennedy, Kathleen. "Writing Trash: Truth and the Sexual Outlaw's Reinvention of Lesbian Identity." *Feminist Theory* 1, no. 2 (Aug. 2000): 151–72.

King, Katie. "The Situation of Lesbianism as Feminism's Magical Sign: Contest for Meaning and the U.S. Women's Movement, 1968–1972." *Communications* 9 (1986): 65–91.

Kutzer, M. Daphne. *Empire's Children: Empire and Imperialism in Classic British Children's Books.* New York: Garland, 2000.

Lee, Robert G. *Orientals: Asian Americans in Popular Culture.* Philadelphia: Temple Univ. Press, 1999.

Leeming, David Adams. *Mythology: The Voyage of the Hero.* New York: Harper and Row, 1981.

Lewis, Regina. *Gendering Orientalism: Race, Femininity, and Representation.* New York: Routledge, 1996.

Liddle, Joanna, and Shirin Rai. "Feminism, Imperialism, and Orientalism: The Challenge of the 'Indian Woman.' " *Women's History Review* 7, no. 4 (1998): 495–520.

Lippert, Barbara. "Hey There, Warrior Grrrl [*sic*]." *New York* (Dec. 15, 1997): 24–25.

Lyons, Deborah. *Gender and Immortality.* Princeton, N.J.: Princeton Univ. Press, 1996.

MacDonald, Sharon. "Drawing the Lines—Gender, Peace, and War: An Introduction." In *Images of Women in Peace and War: Cross-cultural and Historical Perspectives,* edited by Sharon MacDonald, Pat Holden, and Shirley Ardener, 1–26. Madison: Univ. of Wisconsin Press, 1987.

McCaughey, Martha. *Real Knockouts: The Physical Feminism of Women's Self-Defense.* New York: New York Univ. Press, 1997.

McConnell, Kathleen. "Chaos at the Mouth of Hell: Why the Columbine High School Massacre Had Repercussions for *Buffy the Vampire Slayer.*" *Gothic Studies* 2, no. 1 (2000): 119–35.

McLaughlin, Megan. "The Woman Warrior: Gender, Warfare, and Society in Medieval Europe." *Women's Studies* 17, nos. 3–4 (1990): 193–209.

McNay, Lois. *Foucault and Feminism: Power, Gender, and the Self.* Cambridge, Eng.: Polity, 1992.

Minkowitz, Donna. "Xena: She's Big, Tall, Strong—and Popular." *MS.* (July-Aug. 1996): 74–77.

Mitchell, Esther. "Xena: Warrior Goddess." *SageWoman* 45 (1999): 28–32.

Morreale, Joanne. "*Xena, Warrior Princess* as Feminist Camp." *Journal of Popular Culture* 32, no. 2 (fall 1998): 79–86.

Mulvey, Laura. "Visual Pleasures and Narrative Cinema." In *Feminisms: An Anthology of Literary Theory and Criticism,* edited by Robyn R. Warhol and Diane Price Herndl, 438–48. New Brunswick, N.J.: Rutgers Univ. Press, 1997.

Neilen, Deirdre. "Review: *Xena, Warrior Princess.*" *Hera* 17 (1997): 1–3.

Nietzsche, Friedrich. *The Birth of Tragedy.* New York: Doubleday Anchor, 1956.

Ono, Kent A. "To Be a Vampire on *Buffy the Vampire Slayer:* Race and ('Other') Socially Marginalizing Positions on Horror TV." In *Fantasy Girls: Gender in the New Universe of Science Fiction and Fantasy Television,* edited by Elyce Rae Helford, 163–86. Lanham, Md.: Rowman and Littlefield, 2000.

Owen, A. Susan. "*Buffy the Vampire Slayer:* Vampires, Postmodernity, and Postfeminism." *Journal of Popular Film and Television* 27, no. 2 (summer 1999): 24–31.

Palmer, Paulina. *Lesbian Gothic.* London: Cassell, 1999.

Persons, Mitch. "Eliza Dushku, Vampire Slayer." *Femmes Fatales* 9, no. 1 (June 30, 2000): 24–27.

———. "Marti Noxon—Supervising Producer—on Teen Angst, the Dark Side, Sex, Censors." *Femmes Fatales* 9, no. 1 (June 30, 2000): 12–16.

Pink Rabbit Productions. "Blood for Blood." In *Pink Rabbit Consortium.* N.d. Available on-line at: www.altfic.com. Accessed Apr. 14, 2000.

Plutarch. *Parallel Lives.* Translated by B. Perrin. New York: Macmillan, 1914.

Pozner, Jennifer. "THWACK! POW! YIKES! Not Your Mother's Heroines." *Sojourner: The Women's Forum* 23 (Oct. 1997): 12–13.

Pratt, Annis. *Archetypal Patterns in Women's Fiction.* Bloomington: Univ. of Indiana Press, 1981.

Quince, Ella. "Well of Sighs." In *The Australian Xena Information Page.* N.d. Available on-line at: www.ausxip.com/fanfic2/sighs.html. Accessed Apr. 14, 2000.

Richards, Thomas. *The Meaning of Star Trek.* New York: Doubleday, 1997.

Roberts, Robin. "Science, Race, and Gender in *Star Trek: Voyager.*" In *Fantasy Girls: Gender in the New Universe of Science Fiction and Fantasy Television,* edited by Elyce Rae Helford, 203–21. Lanham, Md.: Rowman and Littlefield, 2000.

Robins, Kevin, and Les Levidow. "Soldier, Cyborg, Citizen." In *Resisting the Virtual Life: The Culture and Politics of Information,* edited by James Brook and Iain A. Boal, 105–13. San Francisco: City Lights, 1995.

Said, Edward W. *Culture and Imperialism.* New York: Vintage, 1993.

———. *Orientalism.* New York: Vintage, 1978.

Sallust. *Works.* Translated by John C. Rolfe. New York: J. P. Putnam's Sons, 1931.

Saxey, Esther. "Staking a Claim: The Series and Its Slash Fan-Fiction." In *Reading the Vampire Slayer: An Unofficial Critical Companion to Buffy and Angel,* edited by Roz Kaveney, 187–210. London: Tauris Parke, 2002.

Sclove, Richard E. *Democracy and Technology.* New York: Guilford, 1995.

Slotkin, Richard. *Gunfighter Nation.* New York: Atheneum, 1992.

Smith, Dorothy E. "Femininity as Discourse." In *Becoming Feminine: The Politics of Popular Culture,* edited by Leslie G. Roman and Linda K. Christian-Smith, with Elizabeth Ellsworth, 37–59. London: Falmer, 1988.

Sontag, Susan. "The Imagination of Disaster." In *Against Interpretation,* 209–25. 1965. Reprint. London: Vintage, 1994.

Spicuzza, Mary. "Bad Heroines." *Metro, Silicon Valley's Weekly Newspaper,* Mar. 15–21, 2001.

Stacey, Jackie. "How Do I Look?" In *Star Gazing: Hollywood Cinema and Female Spectatorship,* 1–18. New York: Routledge, 1994.

Stocker, Margarita. *Judith: Sexual Warrior.* New Haven, Conn.: Yale Univ. Press, 1998.

Stoller, Debbie. "Brave New Girls: These T.V. Heroines Know What Girl Power Really Is." *On the Issues* (fall 1998): 42–45.

———. "The Twenty Most Fascinating Women in Politics." *George* 8 (Sept. 1998): 110–13.

Suetonius. *Lives of the Caesars.* Translated by John C. Rolfe. New York: Macmillan, 1914.

Thornham, Sue. *Passionate Detachments: An Introduction to Feminist Film Theory.* London: Arnold, 1997.

Topping, Keith. *Slayer: The Totally Cool Unofficial Guide to Buffy.* London: Virgin, 2000.

Tracy, Kathleen. *The Girl's Got Bite: The Unofficial Guide to Buffy's World*. Los Angeles: Renaissance, 1998.

Trinh T. Minh-ha. "Not You/Like You: Post-Colonial Women and the Interlocking Questions of Identity and Difference." In *Making Face, Making Soul*, edited by Gloria Anzaldúa, 371–75. San Francisco: Aunt Lute, 1990.

Tulloch, John, and Henry Jenkins. *Science Fiction Audiences: Watching* Doctor Who *and* Star Trek. New York: Routledge, 1995.

Ventura, Michael. "Warrior Women: Why Are TV Shows Like *Buffy the Vampire Slayer, La Femme Nikita,* and *Xena, Warrior Princess* So Popular, Especially among Teens?" *Psychology Today* 31, no. 6 (Nov.-Dec. 1998): 58–63.

Wall, Brian, and Michael Zryd. "Vampire Dialectics: Knowledge, Institutions, and Labour in *Buffy the Vampire Slayer* and *Angel*." In *Reading the Vampire Slayer: An Unofficial Critical Companion to* Buffy *and* Angel, edited by Roz Kaveney, 53–77. London: Tauris Parke, 2002.

Warner, Marina. *Joan of Arc: The Image of Female Heroism*. 1981. Reprint. New York: Penguin, 1987.

———. *Monuments and Maidens: The Allegory of the Female Form*. New York: Atheneum, 1985.

West, Dave. "Concentrate on the Kicking Movie: Buffy and East Asian Cinema." In *Reading the Vampire Slayer: An Unofficial Critical Companion to* Buffy *and* Angel, edited by Roz Kaveney, 166–86. London and New York: Tauris Parke, 2002.

Westfahl, Gary. "Opposing War, Exploiting War: The Troubled Pacifism of *Star Trek*." In *Science Fiction, Children's Literature, and Popular Culture*, 69–78. Westport, Conn.: Greenwood, 2000.

Weston, Jesse. *From Ritual to Romance*. Garden City, N.Y.: Doubleday, 1957.

White, Rosie. "Feminist Icon? *Buffy the Vampire Slayer* and Postfeminist Television." In *Millennial Visions: Feminisms into the 21st Century*, edited by Carolyn Brina, Carolyn Britton, and Allison Assiter, 145–58. Cardiff, Eng.: Cardiff Academic, 2001.

Wilcox, Rhonda V. "Buffy and the Monsters of Teen Life: 'There Will Never Be a Very Special Buffy.' " *Journal of Popular Film and Television* 27, no. 2 (summer 1999): 16–23.

———. " 'Every Night I Save You:' Buffy, Spike, Sex, and Redemption." In *Slayage: The Online International Journal of Buffy Studies* 5 (2002). Available at: www.slayage.tv.

———. " 'Who Died and Made Her the Boss?' Patterns of Mortality in *Buffy*." In *Fighting the Forces: What's at Stake in* Buffy the Vampire Slayer? edited by Rhonda V. Wilcox and David Lavery, 3–17. New York: Rowman and Littlefield, 2002.

Wilcox, Rhonda V., and David Lavery, eds. *Fighting the Forces: What's at Stake in* Buffy the Vampire Slayer? New York: Rowman and Littlefield, 2002.

Wilson, Catherine M. "The Wedding Night." In *Catherine M. Wilson's Xena Fan Fiction*.

Nov. 12, 1996. Available on-line at: www.tsoft.com/~cmwilson/Stories/Wedding-Night.html. Accessed Apr. 18, 2000.

Winkler, John J., and Froma Zeitlin, eds. *Nothing to Do with Dionysus?* Princeton, N.J.: Princeton Univ. Press, 1990.

Wyke, Maria. *Projecting the Past: Ancient Rome, Cinema, and History.* New York: Routledge, 1997.

Yegenoglu, Meyda. *Colonial Fantasies: Towards a Feminist Reading of Orientalism.* Cambridge, Eng.: Cambridge Univ. Press, 1998.

Young, Robert J. C. *Colonial Desire: Hybridity in Theory, Culture, and Race.* New York: Routledge, 1995.

Zalewski, Marysia. *Feminism after Postmodernism: Theorising Through Practice.* New York: Routledge, 2000.

Zeitlin, Froma. *Playing the Other.* Chicago: Univ. of Chicago Press, 1996.

Zweerink, Amanda, and Sarah N. Gaston. "www.buffy.com: Cliques, Boundaries, and Hierarchies in an Internet Community." In *Fighting the Forces: What's at Stake in Buffy the Vampire Slayer?* edited by Rhonda V. Wilcox and David Lavery, 239–50. New York: Rowman and Littlefield, 2002.

Films and Videocassettes

Blade. Directed by Stephen Norrington. New Line Studios, 1998.

Bring It On. Directed by Peyton Reed. Universal, 2000.

Buffy the Vampire Slayer: The Buffy and Angel Chronicles. Vol. 3, *Becoming, Parts 1 and 2.* Twentieth Century Fox Home Entertainment, 1999.

Buffy the Vampire Slayer: The Slayer Chronicles. Vol. 1, *Bad Girls/Consequences.* Twentieth Century Fox Home Entertainment, 2000.

Buffy the Vampire Slayer: The Slayer Chronicles. Vol. 3, *Graduation Day, Parts 1 and 2.* Twentieth Century Fox Home Entertainment, 2000.

Buffy the Vampire Slayer: Welcome to the Hellmouth/The Harvest. Twentieth Century Fox Home Entertainment, 1998.

Evolution. Directed by Ivan Reitman. Umvd/Dreamworks, 2001.

Rosemary's Baby. Directed by Roman Polanski. Paramount, 1968.

Scary Movie 2. Directed by Keenan Ivory Wayans. Dimension Films, 2001.

Television Episodes (with original U.S. airdates)

Xena, Warrior Princess

"Destiny." Jan. 27, 1997.
"The Price." Apr. 28, 1997.

"The Furies." Sept. 29, 1997.

"Deliverer." Oct. 20, 1997.

"The Debt, Part I." Nov. 3, 1997.

"The Debt, Part II." Nov. 10, 1997.

"The Bitter Suite." Feb. 2, 1998.

"One Against the Army." Feb. 9, 1998.

"Forgiven." Feb. 16, 1998.

"Forget Me Not." Mar. 9, 1998.

"When in Rome." May 2, 1998.

"A Good Day." Oct. 26, 1998.

"The Crusader." Nov. 16, 1998.

"Endgame." May 3, 1999.

"Past Imperfect." Nov. 4, 1999.

"Seeds of Faith." Jan. 10, 2000.

"Antony and Cleopatra." Apr. 17, 2000.

"Looking Death in the Eye." Apr. 24, 2000.

"Legacy." Oct. 30, 2000.

"The Return of the Valkarie." Nov. 27, 2000.

"The God You Know." Jan. 29, 2001.

"Friends in Need, Part II." June 18, 2001.

Hercules: The Legendary Journeys

"Unchained Heart." May 5, 1995.

Buffy the Vampire Slayer

"Welcome to the Hellmouth/The Harvest." Mar. 10, 1997.

"Angel" and "Interview with Joss Whedon" (preceding "Angel" episode). Apr. 14, 1997.

"The Puppet Show." May 5, 1997.

"When She Was Bad." Sept. 15, 1997.

"Lie to Me." Nov. 3, 1997.

"Ted." Dec. 8, 1997.

"Faith, Hope, and Trick." Oct. 13, 1998.

"Helpless." Jan. 19, 1999.

"The Zeppo." Jan. 26, 1999.

"Bad Girls." Feb. 9, 1999.

"Consequences." Feb. 16, 1999.

"Doppelgangland." Feb. 23, 1999.

"Enemies." Mar. 16, 1999.

"Choices." May 4, 1999.

"Graduation Day, Part 1." May 18, 1999.

"Earshot." Sept. 21, 1999.

"Goodbye Iowa." Feb. 15, 2000.

"This Year's Girl." Feb. 22, 2000.

"The Yoko Factor." May 9, 2000.

"Fool for Love." Nov. 14, 2000.

"Tabula Rasa." Nov. 13, 2001.

La Femme Nikita

"Nikita." Jan. 13, 1997.

"Charity." Feb. 3, 1997.

"Choice." Apr. 7, 1997.

"Half Life." Mar. 22, 1998.

"There Are No More Missions." Jan. 9, 2000.

"Into the Looking Glass." Jan. 23, 2000.

"Four Light Years Farther." Aug. 27, 2000.

"Up the Rabbit Hole." Aug. 27, 2000.

"The Man Behind the Curtain." Feb. 11, 2001.

"A Time for Every Purpose." Mar. 4, 2001.

Star Trek: The Next Generation

"I, Borg." Episode no. 223, May 11, 1992.

Star Trek: Voyager

"The Gift." Episode no. 170, Sept. 10, 1997.

"One." Episode no. 193, May 13, 1998.

"Infinite Regress." Episode no. 203, Nov. 25, 1998.

"Nothing Human." Episode no. 200, Dec. 2, 1998.

"Survival Instinct." Episode no. 222, Sept. 29, 1999.

"Collective." Episode no. 235, Feb. 16, 2000.

"Child's Play." Episode no. 239, Mar. 8, 2000.

"Imperfection." Episode no. 248, Oct. 11, 2000.

"Drive." Episode no. 249, Oct. 18, 2000.

"Human Error." Episode no. 264, Mar. 7, 2001.

"Endgame." Episode nos. 271 and 272, May 23, 2001.

E-mail Messages

Messages to Helen Caudill (chap. 3)

Quince, Ella, to Helen Caudill, Jan. 15, 1999, and Mar. 19, 2001.
Wilson, Catherine, to Helen Caudill, Apr. 12, 2000, and Mar. 25, 2001.

Messages to Lee Parpart (chap. 7)

Amy to Lee Parpart, June 28, 2001.
Brennan, Marc, to Lee Parpart, June 26, 2001.
Clayton S. to Lee Parpart, June 28, 2001.
Daniel to Lee Parpart, June 27, 2001.
Darian to Lee Parpart, June 26, 2001.
David Eckelman to Lee Parpart, June 27, 2001.
eyeofnewt to Lee Parpart, June 13, 2001.
Hugh to Lee Parpart, June 28, 2001.
Idiot Savant to Lee Parpart, June 13, 2001.
James to Lee Parpart, July 6, 2001.
Kim and Megan to Lee Parpart, July 10, 2001.
Mathue Roth to Lee Parpart, June 24, 2001.
Michael and Doug to Lee Parpart, June 25, 2001, and June 26, 2001.
Mike and Nick to Lee Parpart, June 15, 2001, and June 18, 2001.
Mike H. to Lee Parpart, June 24, 2001.
MZ to Lee Parpart, July 7, 2001.
Neil W. to Lee Parpart, June 27, 2001.
Sasha to Lee Parpart, June 13, 2001.
Steve Sposato to Lee Parpart, July 11, 2001.
Ted to Lee Parpart, June 29, 2001.
Wendell to Lee Parpart, July 4, 2001.
xander79 to Lee Parpart, June 13, 2001.

Index

feminism (*cont.*)
  vs. third wave, 3–4; *Star Trek: Voyager*
    and, 125; variant definitions of, 80; view
    of *Buffy,* 56–58; view of just warrior
    narratives, 2; Whedon's approach to, 55,
    79, 91, 94, 144n. 21; women's rights and,
    131; *XWP* and, 40
Fiske, John, 67
Foucault, Michel, 57
Frazer, Sir James, 27
Friedman, Liz, 42
Fuchs, Cynthia, 122
Furies (fict.), 18–20
Fuss, Diana, 110
Futrell, Alison, 6, 7, 13–26

Gabrielle (fict.): in "Antony and Cleopatra,"
    25; Aphrodite and, 46; approach of,
    32–33; attraction to Xena, 28;
    development of character, 41–42; in
    "The Furies" episode, 20; purity of,
    43–44; redemptive love of, 42;
    relationship with Xena, 29–35, 38–39;
    role of, 11; in Über Xena stories, 35;
    Xena's treatment of, x, 28, 29–30, 32–33,
    34–35, 43, 141n. 16
Gaius Julius Caesar (fict.), 14–15, 16, 23–24,
    137n. 4
Gandhi, Leela, 50
gay viewers, 89
Gelder, Ken, 99
Gellar, Sarah Michele, 55
gender relations: *Buffy*'s representation of,
    55, 57–58, 64–65; essentialist view of,
    110; *La Femme Nikita*'s approach to, 113;
    politics of, 78–91; *Star Trek: Voyager* and,
    132
George, 66
Get Smart, 4
Gibson, James William, 5
girl power, 5–6, 8, 66. *See also* female just
    warriors

Gnaeus Pompeius Strabo, 23
god of love, 45–47
Graeco-Roman mythology, 6, 7, 13–14, 38, 40
Greek drama, 17, 137n. 9
Grindstaff, Laura, 105, 112
Grinhilda (fict.), 142n. 36
Grosz, Elizabeth, 56, 58, 59

Haraway, Donna, 1, 10, 119
Hart, Lynda, 44
Helford, Elyce Rae, 5, 30, 32–33, 37, 43
Hercules: the Legendary Journeys, 41
heroism, 13–14, 44, 48–49
heterosexuals: *Buffy*'s appeal to, 8, 85, 90–91;
    women on TV as, 4–5
high-school-is-hell motif, 61, 66
historiography, 25
homosexuality/homosexuals: *Buffy*'s appeal
    to, 8, 84, 89; on-line fan fiction and, 28,
    37; as subtext of *XWP,* 28; of viewers,
    147n. 11
hooks, bell, 95, 97, 102
Hope (fict.), 29–30, 43
horror films, 96
House of Atreid, 17–19
House of Xena, 17–22
Hugh (fict.), 85, 122, 123
human freedom, 120
human relationships, 18–21, 25–26
human rights, 120, 130–31
hybridity, 40, 41, 43, 44–45, 49

Icheb (fict.), 128–29
Idiot Savant (on-line identity), 82
imperialism: brutality of, 14–15; definition
    of, 140–41n. 4; opportunity to critique,
    40–41; self-reflective examination of,
    49–52; of Xena in "Furies," 20; Xena's
    atonement for, 47; *XWP*'s portrayal of,
    22
individuality, 120–22